Native Americans in Children's Literature

Native Americans in Children's Literature

by Jon C. Stott

▼ ▼ ▼

foreword by Joseph Bruchac

Oryx Press
1995

The rare Arabian Oryx is believed to have inspired the myth of the unicorn. This desert antelope became virtually extinct in the early 1960s. At that time several groups of international conservationists arranged to have 9 animals sent to the Phoenix Zoo to be the nucleus of a captive breeding herd. Today the Oryx population is over 1000 and over 500 have been returned to the Middle East.

© 1995 by The Oryx Press
4041 North Central at Indian School Road
Phoenix, Arizona 85012-3397

Cover Photos: Navajo Girl, c. 1955; Navajo Medicine Man, c. 1955. Photographs by Barry Goldwater. © by The Heard Museum (Phoenix, AZ). Elderly Woman. Photograph by Laura Gilpin. Courtesy of Alan and Christine Benoit.

Published simultaneously in Canada
Printed and Bound in the United States of America

The paper used in this publication meets the minimum requirements of American National Standard for Information Science—Permanence of Paper for Printed Library Materials, ANSI Z39.48, 1984.

Library of Congress Cataloging-in-Publication Data

Stott, Jon C.
    Native Americans in children's literature / by Jon C. Stott.
        p.   cm.
    Includes bibliographical references and index.
    ISBN 0-89774-782-8 (alk. paper)
        1. Children's literature, American—History and criticism.
    2. Indians in literature.   3. Children's literature, American—Study
    and teaching.   4. Children—Books and reading.   I. Title.
    PS173.I6S76   1995
    810.9'3520397'083—dc20   95-6547
                                                                    CIP

To Glenn Burne and Raymond E. Jones,
friends and colleagues—with affection and respect.

CONTENTS

FOREWORD

For the Seventh Generation

by Joseph Bruchac

N othing is so familiar and yet so invisible as the presence of the Indian
in North American culture. Whether we are in Canada or the United
States, we find ourselves surrounded by indigenous names on the living
land; we eat indigenous foods; the symbols of North American Native peoples
appear in our commerce and our clothing; our most popular sports have
Native roots; even the representative forms of government we enjoy and our
economic systems are based to some degree on Native models and Native
wealth.

Yet the vast majority of North Americans know little about the past or the
continuing presents of the original Americans. For most people, the hundreds
of different still-existing Native cultures are lumped under one inaccurate
heading: Indian. Although, as the Acoma Pueblo poet Simon Oritz once put
it, "Indians are everywhere," most non-Natives have either never knowingly
met a Native person or are unaware of the presence of contemporary Native
communities. They do not know Native American history and they assume
Native Americans are only to be found in history. As more than one child has
said to me when I've visited schools, "What was it like when Indians were
alive?"

For more than a quarter century, I've gone to schools as a writer and
storyteller, sharing my own limited knowledge of the Native peoples of this
continent—some of whom were my ancestors. Although I began my literary
career as a "serious" poet and I continue to write for so-called grown-ups, I

Abenaki storyteller Joseph Bruchac is also a poet, publisher, and author of numerous books,
including *Keepers of the Earth: Native American Stories and Environmental Activities for Children* and
(with Jonathan London) *Thirteen Moons on Turtle's Back: A Native American Year of Moons.*

found myself concentrating more and more on storytelling and writing for children. In part, this was because my wife and I had children of our own and I could think of no better way to pass on those things I felt important than through stories. When I wrote some of those stories down—my own tellings of traditional tales I'd learned from Iroquois and Abenaki elders who trusted me with those old and powerful words—those writings were published as children's literature. This is probably because they were stories and because Western culture has relegated "myths and legends" to the realm of the nursery. Yet I've never tried to write differently for children than I do for adults and I continue to believe, as I was taught, that these stories are for all ages, for all parts of the circle of life.

In that 25 years since I first began visiting schools, I have seen some positive changes in the attitudes and the understanding of kids and their teachers about Native people. (Before I go further, let me state strongly that our elementary school teachers and the children they teach are the very heart of our cultures. When we neglect teachers and children, we neglect ourselves. Any culture that pours money into defense and starves education ends up truly defenseless and at war with itself.) However, those changes have often been small and I still visit classrooms where kids—at the sight of an "Indian"— make warwhoops, where Native women are referred to as "squaws" and Native men as "braves," and where children ask, with the heartrending honesty of childhood, "Aren't the Indians all dead?"

I know that the stereotypes Native peoples suffer are partially a result of a United States entertainment industry built on the dual images of the Indian as Murdering Savage and Noble Vanishing Redman. Despite a more sympathetic attitude toward Native characters, we still find those two polar stereotypes at the center of such popular movies of recent years as *Dances with Wolves* and *The Last of the Mohicans.* (Both are also films in which the equally interesting image of the white man more Indian than the Indians themselves is central.)

But we cannot blame it all on Hollywood. We also need to take a close and honest look at the ways in which Native stories, Native life, and Native people are presented to our children in the classrooms. We need to examine and understand how important children's literature can be. It can reinforce the worst in us and in our children or it can encourage true intellectual growth.

"A little knowledge is a dangerous thing," in one of the truest and most often misconstrued quotes from British literature. Few know that Alexander Pope goes on to say we should "drink deep" or not at all from that spring of knowledge. The great preponderance of books written for children that deal with "Indians" suffer from having only a little knowledge. Often, as with Susan Jeffers' bestselling picture book, *Brother Eagle, Sister Sky,* those books are written with the best and noblest intentions but deeply flawed from a lack of real understanding about the Native cultures they portray. Far too many well-known children's books "about Indians" have been written entirely from library research and are finally based upon nineteenth-century texts of stories collected by European-American men who spoke only English and saw Indians as savage, ignorant, but interesting inferiors.

My point is *not* that only Native people can write about Native Americans, but that deep knowledge is necessary for anyone (Native or non-Native) to write well about those essential building blocks of Native American cultures—the words of their elders, the traditional stories told to their children. I am also not downgrading the importance of libraries. I am only pointing out that a library is a reflection of life. Without directly experiencing that life itself, we are looking into a surface that may be no deeper than a mirror—showing us our own faces more clearly than the vision of others.

With all of this in mind, I began to read Jon C. Stott's manuscript. The more I read, the more excited I became. I love to learn and, though there was much in his book that I found familiar and agreed with wholeheartedly, there was also much that was new to me and absolutely welcome. Stott proceeds with admirable patience and careful scholarship—scholarship based not only on research but in listening to living Native voices. The result is a book that can be described as essential. His discussion, for example, of the variety and the complexity of Native Tricksters, in which he beautifully describes the poetics and the problems of transmitting and adapting Native stories, should be read not only by every teacher, but also by every children's writer and every storyteller who has chosen to tell traditional Native stories.

More than purely didactic, *Native Americans in Children's Literature* is enjoyable to read. It is so well written that the sub-text is as interesting as the surface—as you will see when you read his precisely nonjudgmental descriptions of the novels of Scott O'Dell. I have long held that censorship, and the removal of books from libraries, solves nothing. Understanding how a well-loved book, such as Lynne Banks' *The Indian in the Cupboard*, makes mistakes about Native people and reinforces stereotypes will give teachers the tools to discuss that book and others like it in a more useful, informed way.

Stott's thoroughness is also a delight. He covers as much ground in some 200 pages as one might expect in an encyclopedia. His summaries of books, his extensive bibliographies, and his Appendix in which he sets forth a practical approach for "Incorporating Native Stories in the Language Arts Program" are only part of the mix that makes this book an absolute treasure. Along with Beverly Slapin and Doris Seale's *Through Indian Eyes*, it should be in every school library.

One of the prophecies I have heard spoken among my Abenaki people is that of the Seven Generations. Perhaps we learned it from our neighbors, the Mohawk. Perhaps—since I have heard it many places across this land among many Native nations—it is one of those things that the many Native peoples were given in common. The prophecy says that there will be seven generations after the coming of the new people to this continent we call Turtle Island. In the first generation, we will welcome them with respect and sharing. In the second generation, they will break that circle and begin to try to kill us. In the third generation, we will resist. In the fourth generation, we will lose most of our land. In the fifth generation, they will try to force us to be like them. In the sixth generation, many of us will no longer remember who we are and a great darkness will surround us. But, in the seventh generation, the children of the Native people and of the many other races who have come to live on this Turtle Island will join hands together and work to restore that circle of respect and sharing. I feel, deep in my heart, that *Native Americans in Children's Literature* is part of that Seventh Generation and so I reach out my hand.

INTRODUCTION

▼▼▼

Learning about Native Realities—A Personal Journey

During the late 1940s, Mondays and Wednesdays at 7:00 P.M. and Saturdays at 8:00 P.M. were very important to me. A small boy with a vivid imagination, I eagerly anticipated the beginning of *The Lone Ranger* radio program. During the introduction, the announcer, explaining the background of the hero, intoned, "With his faithful Indian companion Tonto, the daring and resourceful masked rider of the plains led the fight for law and order in the early western United States." Tonto had the first mention in this sentence, but the words applied to him, when contrasted with those describing the Lone Ranger, gave him a decidedly secondary status. He was honest and loyal and did what he was told; he spoke a pidgin English probably never spoken by any real Native American; he went to town to fetch supplies and gather information while his white friend stayed in camp and rested. He was certainly better than the bloodthirsty savages who occasionally attacked the wagon trains filled with good and simple people seeking new lives for themselves. But he certainly never called forth my admiration in the way the Lone Ranger did.

Near the end of the decade, Tonto was replaced as the best Indian I "knew" by another radio character, Straight Arrow. He was a Comanche who lived most of his life disguised as a white rancher named Steve Adams; his English was correct, even stentorian. He was almost as wonderful as the Lone Ranger and head and shoulders above Tonto. Only many decades later did I realize how subtly I had been manipulated to perceive Indians in the way that the white creators and sponsors of these series wished me to. Tonto's language and subservience made him safe, but unadmirable. Straight Arrow spoke like a white person and, although I did not perceive this in the 1940s, lived as one, following the profession of ranching, which whites considered more admirable than a life of nomadic hunting and raiding.

Growing up on the West Coast of Canada, I had no other contacts with Native peoples. I never met a member of the local Songhees band of the Salish Nation. However, my family frequently drove past the reservation on the way to our lake cabin. Living in a city that prided itself on its Englishness, especially its neat, well-kept houses and bright, carefully weeded gardens, we would comment negatively on the Songhees' houses. The cedar boards of their places were unpainted and weathered; their front yards were masses of weeds. "Why can't they paint their houses and tidy their yards?" we frequently asked each other. Only recently have I perceived how European our point of view was. Native peoples of the area had traditionally constructed their great lodges out of huge cedar planks that weathered to a silvery-gray. Painting was only for house poles and usually had ceremonial significance. As fishers, hunters, and gatherers, these people had never developed a tradition of gardening. To ask them, only four or five decades after they had left their traditional ways of living, to paint and plant would have been to impose standards totally foreign to them.

My response to the two radio programs and my attitude toward the Songhees' homes basically summarize my thinking about Native peoples for the first 30 years of my life. I uncritically accepted the stereotyped notions about Native Americans generally held by white people before the middle of this century; being widely held, those notions had conditioned me to such acceptance. As an English major at high school and university and later as a graduate student in English, I encountered no literature that changed these stereotypes. I learned about the great English literary tradition and the cultural values it embodied. The few Native peoples who appeared in the novels, plays, and poems that I read were minor characters.

As a teacher of American literature at Western Michigan University during the late 1960s and early 1970s, I became sensitive to minority literature and, hence, to minority cultural values and world views and included the newly discovered African-American authors in my courses. In presenting them, I had to become aware of a different historical and literary tradition, as well as a cultural past, that in no way resembled the past I had been taught to respect and admire.

When children's literature was added to my teaching schedule, I adopted an anthology that contained children's versions of folktales from a variety of cultures. However, I taught these simply as stories, without making reference to the cultural values they explicitly or implicitly embodied. This was easy to do, both because I had no knowledge of these cultural values and because the adaptations had been transformed so that they would be easily accessible to children of the majority (that is, white) culture. Two of the novels I regularly included in the course were Scott O'Dell's *Island of the Blue Dolphins* and Jean Craighead George's *Julie of the Wolves*. However, except for the fact that the heroine of the former lived on an off-shore California island at the time of white invasions and that the heroine of the latter lived in a modern-day Alaskan Eskimo community, it would have been difficult to tell from my lectures and the class discussions that they were Native. They were simply strong female characters in coming-of-age novels. Around that time, I published articles in which I related O'Dell's novel to the English tradition of the survival story and George's to the classical tradition of pastoralism. In other words, I was more interested in how these books related to patterns of English and European literature than in how well or poorly they reflected their central characters as members of Native cultures.

A major breakthrough in my approach occurred in 1976. I had returned to Canada to teach children's literature at the University of Alberta and had been asked to develop a course in Canadian children's literature. I included two survival stories on the reading list: James Houston's *Tikta'Liktak* and Markoosie's *Harpoon of the Hunter*. The former, written by a man who was for 12 years a territorial administrator in Canada's Arctic Islands, is a fairly conventional survival story. A boy who finds himself trapped on broken spring ice survives on a desert island and constructs a makeshift boat on which he returns to the mainland and eventual reunion with his family. The latter, the first novel ever written by an Inuit (the term by which Canadian Eskimos refer to themselves), appears to follow the same pattern. Hunting a rabid bear, Kamik, a young Inuit man, finds himself alone and must struggle for survival. Although on the final page of my edition of the novel he is not reunited with the members of his village, it is implied that he soon will be.

I began a lecture in which I compared the two works and related them to the genre of the survival story. The main point of my lecture was that, in order to survive, the individual in each story must fall back on the cultural and physical practices of his group. Just as Robinson Crusoe acted like a good eighteenth-century Englishman on his island, so Tikta'Liktak and Kamik drew on the physical and spiritual resources of their culture. But, argued my students, puzzled over my lecture, that just wasn't right. Kamik doesn't survive; in the end he commits suicide. And to prove the point, one of them asked me what I made of the final paragraph of the book:

> He was carried out to sea and soon disappeared from the rest. He had waited until he was out of sight to do what he had to do. "Before my father died, he said only dead people find everlasting peace. He said he was going where there was peace. And he said he would wait for me." Kamik looked at the harpoon in his hands. Now the time had come. Now was the time to find peace, and to find the family and people he loved. He kneeled and put

> the tip of the harpoon to his throat. Suddenly he pushed it in. And, for the
> last time, the harpoon of the hunter made its kill. (Markoosie 1970, 81)

It was then that I realized the problem: my copy of *Harpoon of the Hunter* ended
on page 68; it had been bound without the last gathering of pages!

After we had all enjoyed a chuckle at my expense, we considered the
serious implications of my mistaken interpretation. I had been able to develop
a consistent and complete—although erroneous—analysis by applying to the
incomplete text literary assumptions of the Western world. I saw little difference between *Harpoon of the Hunter* and Armstrong Sperry's *Call It Courage*
(which, although about a Pacific Islands culture, is by an American). Markoosie's
complete story simply did not fit that interpretation: Inuit stories do not follow
Western cultural patterns. This point was further emphasized by the horror
the violent ending of the novel elicited from many of my students. When I
asked one of them about his reaction, he replied, "Stories shouldn't end that
way." It turned out that all of us had been searching for a non-Inuit story about
Inuit culture. However, one of my students who had lived in Canada's
Northwest Territories reported having seen Inuit reviews of the book and
having talked to some Inuit about it. The reviews and the conversations
praised the book. It had a well-told story. No negative comments were made
about the violence that had upset members of my class.

The experience of that one class had a great influence on me. I realized how
wrong I had been in my approach to the Native Indian and Inuit materials I
had discussed in children's literature classes in Michigan and Alberta. I simply
could no longer include them in the mainstream of children's literature as I
had been doing. Moreover, I would have to go back and reevaluate *Julie of the
Wolves* and other stories about Native and Inuit people that had been told or
retold by non-Native authors. To do this, it would be necessary to study
traditional and contemporary Native cultures, to read fiction and nonfiction
by Native authors, to talk with both Native and non-Native authors about
their approaches to retelling traditional stories and writing original fiction
about Native peoples, and then to reread and carefully analyze and evaluate
picture books, folktale adaptations, and novels to see how fully and accurately
they reflected the cultural values and beliefs of the Native peoples the books
presented.

This book embodies many of the discoveries I have made about traditional
and contemporary Native cultures and the books about them. During the last
two decades, I have travelled far from my childhood home in Victoria, British
Columbia, where I liked Tonto, admired Straight Arrow, worshipped The
Lone Ranger, and wished that the Songhees people would make their houses
and front yards more like those of the English settlers of the area.

Chapter 1 of this study analyzes five books in detail to see how they
misrepresent Native peoples, misinterpreting some facts, ignoring others, and

subtly choosing language to construct an image—sometimes positive, some-times negative—rather than a reality of Native life. Chapters 2, 3, and 4 focus on detailed analyses of picture books, adapted folktales, and novels, respec-tively. Each chapter studies either a few major works by specific authors or books about a specific character, examining the cultural realities that should be embodied in the stories or events and considering how well the children's books have retained these realities. Following Chapters 2, 3, and 4 are detailed annotated reading lists of other picture books, collections of folktales, and novels. A brief outline of the contents of each book is followed by an evaluation and analysis and suggestions for presenting it in elementary or junior high classrooms. The epilogue focuses on the writing of Canadian Inuit (Eskimo) author Michael Kusugak, whose work is in many ways representative of an increasingly frequent phenomenon in children's literature: the writing and/or illustrating of books about Native Americans by Native Americans. An appendix presents brief outlines for thematic, culture-specific, or author units suitable for elementary and junior high classrooms and libraries. These units were created by working with schools in Edmonton, Alberta, and Munising, Michigan. There are two indexes: an author, illustrator, title index and a subject index. The subject index includes the names of specific Native nations mentioned in the text (with an indication of the locations in the text of traditional stories of and picture books and novels about each), characters and character types found in more than one work, and theses and topics discussed in the various chapters.

The journey I have taken in the writing of this book has not been a solitary one. I have received direct and indirect guidance from many people. My debt to generations of scholars and children's writers will be evident to those people who glance over the list of references following each chapter. I particularly wish to thank non-Native children's authors James Houston, Paul Goble, Gerald McDermott, and Jean Craighead George for their patience in answer-ing the dozens of questions I asked them over many years. They have given me a much clearer understanding of how the best non-Native writers have approached their subject. Maria Campbell, a Canadian Métis, and Michael Kusugak have generously explained to me elements of their creative processes. Glenn Burne, professor emeritus at the University of North Carolina, Char-lotte, and Paul Lumsden, lecturer at the University of Alberta, have spent long hours discussing aspects of the subject with me and have read over the manuscript in its early drafts, offering valuable suggestions. Julie Urion of the University of Alberta exhibited great patience and accuracy while compiling the indexes and proofreading the text. Sean Tape and John Wagner of Oryx Press have offered excellent advice in their roles of editors. Sandy Basket, Sharon Johnson, Gladys Macoway, Laurie Dunnigan, Maureen MacDonald, and Joanne Sakowsky generously invited me into their classrooms so that I could present stories about Native children to their students. Most important, they offered helpful, insightful criticism about my goals, organization, and methods. As always, Lynda Schultz has showed great patience in word-processing draft after draft of the manuscript. I thank the University of Alberta for a year's sabbatical leave that enabled me to complete this project. Finally, my children, Andrew and Clare, and my friend, Dr. P.E. Lamb, have been constant in their encouragement. Because of the input of all these people, this is a better book. Its limitations remain my own.

REFERENCES

George, Jean Craighead. 1972. *Julie of the Wolves*. New York: Harper and Row.

Houston, James. *Tikta' Liktak*. 1965. New York: Harcourt, Brace and World.

Markoosie. 1970. *Harpoon of the Hunter*. Montreal: McGill-Queen's University Press.

O'Dell, Scott. 1960. *Island of the Blue Dolphins*. Boston: Houghton, Mifflin.

Sperry, Armstrong. 1940. *Call It Courage*. New York: Macmillan.

Native Americans in Children's Literature

CHAPTER 1

▼▼▼

The Way It Wasn't:
Stereotypes and
Misrepresentations

EUROPEAN RESPONSES TO THE NEW WORLD

From 1492 onward, the European "discoverers" and explorers of North America arrived at and travelled through a continent filled with an incredible variety of cultures and languages and encountered peoples who had developed innumerable complex systems for responding to the physical, social, and spiritual dimensions of their lives. To the Europeans, the continent was, to adapt a line from William Shakespeare's *The Tempest*, a strange new world filled with wondrous creatures. It was completely different from the countries they had left. Compared to Europe, North America was relatively unpopulated; it was filled with undeveloped spaces of forests, plains, and mountains, and with heretofore unknown animal species; and its human inhabitants dressed and acted very differently from Europeans. As agents of political and religious powers from their homelands, or as settlers seeking new, permanent homes, the Europeans responded in ways typical of human beings encountering something new, unfamiliar, and alien. They defined what they were confronting with the religious, moral, cultural, and political concepts they had brought with them, and these concepts guided their responses to the unfamiliar human and natural environments they confronted. They imposed these concepts on the land and its human and animal inhabitants, making the New World more like their Old World and, thus, bringing it under their power and control. In many ways, they behaved like Professor Higgins, the male lead in the Broadway musical *My Fair Lady*, who, confronting Eliza Doolittle, the first woman he'd ever really gotten to know, woefully complained, "Why can't a woman be more like a man!"

Until the development of modern methods of anthropological study at the beginning of the twentieth century, philosophers, politicians, and literary artists, among others, did not usually consider the differences between the various Native cultures. Instead, they described generic Indians whose characteristics were not based on actual circumstances of their lives but on the ways in which they differed—usually for the worse—from what Europeans felt human beings are or should be, both collectively and individually. As indicated by the phrase *The White Man's Indian*, the title of Robert F. Berkhofer, Jr.'s study, Europeans could not see beyond their own preconceived notions about the nature of humanity. The elements they attributed to Native peoples were many and complex and have been examined in detail by such historians as Berkhofer; Roy Harvey Pearce, in *Savagism and Civilization*; and Olive Dickason, in *The Myth of the Savage*. Moreover, the elements were modified and adapted as the political structure and geography of the North American continent changed. However, certain general attitudes have remained fairly constant since Columbus arrived in the New World in 1492. Because these attitudes not only provided a theoretical basis for European conduct toward Native peoples but also fostered the development of stereotypes about them found in dime novels, movies, comic books, television programs, and, until recently, text books and literature for children, they need to be considered briefly.

Foremost among these attitudes is the belief that the religious and sociopolitical theories on which life in European countries was based represented the norm for all human beings on this earth. Orientals, Africans, and Native Americans were explained and judged according to the degree to which they achieved—but usually failed to achieve—these norms. Individuals, using their innate powers of reason, should strive, as Europeans did, to embrace Christian piety and to contribute to the well-being of an ordered and orderly state. Farms and, later, organized urban and industrialized centers provided evidence of civilized human existence. Europeans enjoyed a settled life governed by institutionalized political and religious organizations; they also possessed writing and created useful objects and machines from metals.

To the discoverers, explorers, colonizers, pioneers, and settlers, the North American continent and its indigenous peoples were the exact opposites of European countries and peoples. To use the title of a book by Henry Nash Smith, North America was a "virgin land" (Smith 1950), to be transformed, with its inhabitants, along European lines. The people, according to a seventeenth-century French view, were "sans roy, sans loy, sans foi," (Dickason 1984, 273)—without king, laws, or faith. They wore no clothes, ate outlandish foods, displayed no table manners, and hunted, an inferior occupation less civilized than farming. They were nomads, lacking the settlements that would exert humanizing influences on them. At best, they were possessed of only rudimentary powers of reasoning. Some of them were cannibals, and some of them made sacrifices; if they had any religion, it likely involved the worship of idols. They were superstitious and most likely served Satan, the Christian devil. Often they were referred to as brutes, sub-human beings who were not far removed from animals. They seemed to have no notion of private property, the basis of European social organization. Words such as "savage," "barbarian," and "depraved" were frequently applied to them.

Not all attitudes toward these indigenous peoples were completely negative. Sometimes they were seen as nature's children, existing in a state of purity and innocence, or as noble savages, relics from an earlier, more heroic age. However, as the terms indicate, even these attitudes made Native peoples inferior to the new, more advanced arrivals. While some aspects of their lives might be emulated by the colonists, the Native peoples would have to give way to the inevitable and ultimately beneficial and ennobling march of civilized progress. They either stood in its way or were incapable of attaining its fullest benefits.

Of course, such views ignored the facts of Native life. There were many different cultures, all of them in possession of sophisticated ways of dealing with the physical, social, and spiritual dimensions of their lives. Most Native peoples were extremely spiritual and reverential, but in ways vastly different from Christian spirituality. Unlike Europeans, who believed that animals did not possess souls and were inferior to human beings, most Native cultures believed that animals did have souls and that they were equal to and sometimes better than their human brethren. Not all groups were hunters; the peoples of the eastern woodlands and the southwest depended on farming for much of their food. Nor were they all nomadic. Those from the southwest, for example, developed large and relatively permanent urban centers. Some peoples, such as those of the northwest coast, had very complex social structures. Like the Europeans, peoples from across the continent had developed far-ranging trading networks. They did possess concepts of private property, although these concepts were different from those held by Europeans. Pueblo apartments, sections of Iroquois longhouses, and plains tipis belonged to specific families, as did certain hunting, fishing, and berry-picking areas. Stories, visual designs, medicine bundles, titles, and visions were often possessed by individuals who had the sole right to transfer ownership of them to other people. While active, aggressive warfare played a large role in some cultures, other cultures were relatively peaceful, even, according to some anthropologists, docile. Scalping, a symbol to many whites of the savagery of all Native peoples, was probably introduced by the French and British as a kind of bounty hunting. Finally, the various Native cultures were not static, existing for centuries in an unchanging sub-human or Golden Age era. Contacts with neighboring cultures and later with Europeans constantly modified the practices and customs of the various groups.

Europeans debated two ways to deal with these Native peoples. They could be converted to Christianity and assimilated into European ways, or they could be annihilated. They could not remain themselves or retain their cultures. Roy Harvey Pearce quotes a toast given by an American soldier during a 1799 Fourth of July celebration: "Civilization or death to all American Savages" (Pearce 1965, 55).

How Natives were treated depended on whether they were perceived as "good Indians" or "bad Indians." "Good Indians" were friendly and helpful to the settlers and appeared to accept the paternalistic religious, educational, and social ministrations of the colonizers. "Bad Indians," who were perceived as depraved sub-humans or Satan's minions, should be killed in self-defense or to clear away obstacles in the march of civilization. In essence, however, both "good" and "bad Indians" were, at least figuratively, annihilated. Their religions were taken from them; they were removed from homelands that provided spiritual, cultural, and physical sustenance; they were denied the use of their own languages when taken to distant residential schools; they were killed by warfare, European diseases, alcohol, the privations of long marches to new reservations, or prison life. Because of the whites' view of what they were and what their presence meant to European agendas, the Native peoples had very little chance of maintaining themselves within their cultures.

Not surprisingly, imaginative literature since the seventeenth century reproduced the various images of the "white man's Indian." Not only did this literature reflect these images, it also reinforced and perpetuated them, helping to make European domination of the continent possible. As the contemporary critic Ward Churchill, a man of of Creek, Cherokee, and Métis heritage, has said of modern movies and novels, colonialism "requires an extensive literature and film industry to win the hearts and minds of non-Indians" (Churchill 1992, 11). During the eighteenth century, narratives about white people, frequently women and children, captured by Natives emphasized the savagery of the captors and the Christian faith that sustained the captives. In the later eighteenth and early nineteenth centuries, novels modelled on gothic horror stories popular in England cast the Indian as the evil, demonic villain. Nineteenth-century Romantics, lamenting the negative elements of urbanization and industrialization and espousing the restorative powers of nature, celebrated the life of the noble savage and mourned his tragic passing. If civilized people could only emulate these noble savages' better traits, they would become more fully civilized themselves.

In the later nineteenth century, drawing on, but grossly distorting and exaggerating certain facts of the Indian wars in the western states, dime novelists and proprietors of Wild West shows revived the notion of savages standing in the way of progress. Creators of boys' adventure novels and comic strips, radio and television programs, and motion pictures continued this legacy. The good Indians were individuals like the Lone Ranger's faithful Indian companion Tonto, who did what he was told; Cochise, who befriended and assisted Indian agent Tom Jeffords; and Straight Arrow, who spent most of his time disguised as Steve Adams, the white owner of a prosperous ranch. Berkhofer has suggested that since the 1960s, the "good Indian" has been seen as a kind of hippie on the margins of the dominant, consumer-obsessed white society, as the first ecologist lamenting the rape of Mother Earth, or as the quintessential New Ager, whose music, diet, religion, and vision quests enabled him or her to lead a purer, holistic life.

Even the most casual reader or viewer of twentieth-century children's novels, comic books, and radio and television programs can easily spot the stereotypes and inaccuracies with which they are filled and can readily discern examples in them of the "white man's Indian." However, it is worthwhile to examine in detail five representative texts—a social studies book, a biography, a fantasy novel, and two picture books—to see more fully how authors and illustrators select, alter, and arrange details and manipulate language and pictures to create their desired and generally inaccurate and biased portraits of traditional Native Americans. The first of these texts appeared in 1901; the most recent, in 1991.

OUR LITTLE INDIAN COUSIN: A "GOOD" INDIAN BOY

Our Little Indian Cousin is one of a series of books written by Mary Hazelton Wade at the beginning of the twentieth century. Designed to introduce young, white readers to other, "lesser" cultures and races (there are no books about the English or French), this volume confirms the idea of the generic Indian, the "red" man as he is frequently called in the book. With the exception of a brief reference to the dugout canoes of the northwest coast, the traditional life described is that of the peoples of the eastern woodlands (although one illustration depicts a plains tipi). Such distinctive and vastly different cultures as the Pueblo, Cherokee, and Navajo are not mentioned. Moreover, although the book purports to show the way these people were living at the time of publication, most Native peoples of the late nineteenth century were Christianized, wore European clothes, and lived in European-style houses. As a recent history of the Ojibway people notes: "In the late 19th Century, many Ojibwa continued to gather wild rice and fish. However, because reservation lands lacked the natural resources necessary to support their population, the Ojibwa people began to adapt to a new way of life" (Tanner 1992, 81).

Even given the general geographical area depicted, there are many inaccuracies and odd mixings of cultures in the book. There is reference to Henry Rowe Schoolcraft, who lived among and described the Lake Superior Ojibway; but another to Heno, an Iroquois spirit being said to live behind Niagara Falls.

Yellow Thunder constructs a birch-bark canoe, as did the Ojibway, while his father uses elm bark, as did the Iroquois, who lived in what is now upstate New York, where birch is scarce. Describing the European conquest of the Native peoples, Wade states: "If the Indians had not been at war so much among themselves, it would have been far harder for the white people to conquer them" (Wade 1901, 19). "But they have not understood that they should work together. So the white man came and was able to conquer them" (Wade 1901, 20-21). The narrator either ignores or is ignorant of the Iroquois League of the eighteenth century, a confederacy that, among other things, attempted to resist European advances. Certainly the devious dealings of the French and English colonial administrations, the Europeans' possession of superior weapons, and the ravages caused among Native peoples by whiskey and smallpox, both imported from across the Atlantic, were more responsible for the conquest than intertribal warfare. For Native retaliations against Europeans, Wade offers a very qualified forgiveness: "They have been very cruel in warfare with us, but they felt they were treated unjustly" (Wade 1901, 34). And, if she is dealing with the Iroquois, among whom the women exercised great political power, why is Yellow Thunder's mother presented as being inferior and subservient to his father?

The narrator frequently denigrates everyday aspects of these peoples' lives, judging such things as a cradle board, sassafras tea, and facial makeup with the adjective "queer." More significant, she ridicules and incorrectly interprets many of the spiritual beliefs that were the foundation of all phases of the traditional lives of most Native peoples. The first paragraph of the book seriously misrepresents the ceremonies and significance of naming among the northern woodlands people, who are presumably the subjects of this book, and among Native peoples generally:

> They call him Yellow Thunder. Do not be afraid of your little cousin because he bears such a terrible name. It is not his fault, I assure you. His grandmother had a dream the night he was born. She believed the Great Spirit, as the Indians call our Heavenly Father, sent this to her. In the dream she saw the heavens in a great storm. Lightning flashed and she constantly heard the roar of thunder. When she awoke in the morning she said, "My first grandson must be called 'Yellow Thunder.' " And Yellow Thunder became his name. (Wade 1901, 9)

Thunder and lightning were powerful forces that signified the presence of supernatural beings. On a natural level, the eagle, who flew highest into the skies, and, on a supernatural level, the thunderbird, who brought thunder and hurled lightning, were closest to these powers. The boy's name would have been awesome rather than terrible; no suggestion of fault or blame would have accrued either to the giver or the receiver. Such a name would embody within it special powers, particularly because it came from a supernatural vision the grandmother had in her dream. Unless she had been converted by missionaries, she would not have "believed" (the word suggests a mistaken assumption) that the vision was from the Great Spirit, or whatever name her people gave to the Christian deity. She would have known with certainty that it came from a specific spiritual source important to her people. And the wisdom of her age and her ability to experience such a vision would have made her the best person to bestow the name.

True names are not bestowed lightly; nor are they used carelessly, for they have great power. To know and to use a person's name indiscriminately is to risk the diminishment of its power or the danger of another person using the name to gain power over its bearer. The author is ignorant of this for, in the third paragraph, she notes: "For some reason I don't understand myself, she rarely speaks his real name. Perhaps it is sacred to her, since she believes it was directed by the Great Spirit" (Wade 1901, 10).

Wade strongly ridicules several beliefs that Native peoples hold about animals: that animals, like people, have souls; that all people and animals are related, an idea embodied in the Lakota Sioux term, *mitakuye oyasin;* and that animals gave themselves up to hunters and should, therefore, be treated with reverence and respect. Wade incorrectly reports Yellow Thunder's idea "that all animals have souls, only they are not as wise as men" (Wade 1901, 36-37). She recounts a hunter's paying homage to a slain bear as "the amusing part of the story" (Wade 1901, 37). A shaman who cured the boy of a serious illness is treated as a near-fraud. He is "thought to have wonderful dreams. . . . No doubt you would laugh at the collection in the [medicine] bag" (Wade 1901, 59). She concludes: "Whether the treatment he got was any help, or whether Mother Nature did all the work, I leave for you to decide for yourselves. I have my own opinion in the matter" (Wade 1901, 61). The one saving grace for the mother is that, although she did not use Christian terms, she "taught him that there is one loving Heavenly Father for all" (Wade 1901, 32-33).

Although much of his daily life and his spiritual belief—whether correctly or erroneously reported—is termed "queer," Yellow Thunder's life can still be instructive to the book's young readers. "We call them savages, but there are many things we could copy with profit from them" (Wade 1901, 32). The boy is healthy because he spends a great deal of time outdoors, winter and summer; he eats good food and "does not miss the dainties of which you are so fond" (Wade 1901, 27). He heeds the lessons of his parents and the tribal elders and is observant in the wilderness. He is a good athlete and a proficient musician, making simple instruments from materials found in nature. In these ways, he is like the "manly boys" so popular in adventure and school novels of that era, and in this respect, is a model to be emulated.

Although the author's explicit purpose is to provide information about a different minority and, as she frequently notes, a conquered and now nearly vanished culture, she has an implicit purpose as well. She wishes to distance her readers from her Native subject and to make them feel superior to it. The book's opening paragraph, quoted above, sets both the tone and the point of view of the "biography" that follows. The first word of the first paragraph of the book, "they," referring to the unnamed tribe of Native Americans to which the boy belongs, distances that group from the reader, for the pronoun, lacking an antecedent, points toward a separate, indefinite group. In the second sentence, the possessive "your" introduces the child reader, who is permitted to feel some, but not too much closeness, to a cousin whose status is diminished through the adjective "little." In the third sentence, the first person "I" introduces and defines the role of the author/narrator in relation to both the reader and the cousin. Having controlled both by the use of the imperative voice in the second sentence, the author/narrator becomes protective, telling the reader, "I assure you" (Wade 1901, 9). She both knows the truth about her subject and will not allow her reader to be upset. Somewhere in the center is Yellow Thunder, referred to five times with variations of the third person singular pronoun. Controlled in his life by his grandmother, who decides his name, he will be controlled in his story by the narrator, who understands more fully than his people do that his name is terrible and who introduces him to the young readers in ways that make him seem both unthreatening and inferior.

Our Little Indian Cousin is a kind, often sympathetic, although usually erroneous and condescending treatment of its subject. Well-intentioned, it is a classic example of a "good-bad" book about Native peoples, one of a genre popular during the first half of the twentieth century. Read by children nearly 100 years ago, it established stereotypes and fostered incorrect notions that these readers, as parents, teachers, and librarians, would pass on to later generations. Only in the last two decades have these effects begun to be combated.

GERONIMO, WOLF OF THE WARPATH: FREEDOM FIGHTER AS "BAD" INDIAN

Before the last decade, many juvenile biographies of Geronimo, the nineteenth-century Apache warrior, neither knew nor considered significant such vital aspects of his life as who he was, what he was fighting about and where, and the dates of his dreadful deeds. He was the worst of all the "bad Indians," and that was thought enough to know. In reality, Geronimo, whose famous name was applied after a daring raid on a Mexican settlement on St. Jerome's Day, was an extremely complex individual, the nature of whose personality and motives are still debated by Native and non-Native historians and biographers. He has been termed a war shaman, possessor of spirit powers that made him very successful in battle; one of the first anti-colonialist guerrilla freedom fighters; a misguided visionary seeking a better future for his endangered peoples; a clear thinker who perceived the ruses and ambitions of the

white people invading Apache lands; and a supreme egotist, like such notorious nineteenth-century white leaders as Napoleon, Andrew Jackson, and
George Custer, who sought, above all else, to fulfill personal ambition.
Whatever elements of Geronimo's character were most important in deter-
mining the actions of his life, the dominant image the white world held of him
until well beyond the middle of this century was a construct designed to make
him embody all that the non-Native world wanted to hate and fear about the
people it was destroying and had destroyed in the name of expansion,
progress, and civilization.

From its title, *Geronimo: Wolf of the Warpath*, to its concluding statement
that "Geronimo cannot be honored as a hero" (Moody 1958, 183), Ralph
Moody's biography for older children reinforces, for readers of the late 1950s,
stereotypes of the title character and "bad Indians" generally. The alliterative
title, by linking wolves and war, draws on the European symbol of that animal
as an evil, malicious creature intent on cruelly destroying innocent, helpless
creatures, especially (in folktales) children and sheep. This symbol is an
inaccurate depiction of actual wolves and their behavior, for they are highly
communal creatures whose hunting is important in weeding out weak, dis-
eased, or aging members of prey species. Moreover, as a European symbol that
represents these animals differently from the way most Native cultures would,
it immediately predisposes its readers to approach the biography's Native
subject from a European and negative point of view.

At the end of the book, the reader is explicitly presented with a moral
judgment implicitly prepared for in the title. Not only is Geronimo not heroic,
but now, long since dead, he cannot even be posthumously "honored." Unlike
many other dead heroes who have finally received the accolades due them,
this war wolf will be denied them. Between the beginning and the end of the
biography, through emphatic statement, careful selection of incidents, and
deliberate choice of words and phrases with negative connotations, Moody
demonstrates the unheroic quality of his subject. This historical biography,
which, surprisingly, dates fewer than 10 significant events, offers not a
convincing explanation of how and why Geronimo thought and acted as he
did, but a portrait of everything a leader and an American hero should not be.

Geronimo: Wolf of the Warpath follows a pattern frequently found in
biographies written for younger readers. In these biographies, considerable
attention is given to the famous subject's childhood as a prefiguration of and
preparation for the deeds and character of the grown person. The child, as
Wordsworth would have said, is father to the man. And, for child readers, this
is important. Not only can they easily identify with the famous person
presented as someone their own age, but also they can seek to emulate that
child's good points so that they too will grow up to be famous, or at least, good
people. Over one-third of Moody's book has passed before the Apache has
achieved manhood and his famous, terror-inducing name.

However, the portrait of this boy as an apprentice brave does not emphasize the seeds of greatness and goodness to come, but the seeds of character
defects that will, in the author's view, make him so reprehensible a person.
His Apache background, presented in the opening chapter, is described in
language that renders his people inferior to the ancestors of the book's white
readers. The Apaches, called "naked Indians," (Moody 1958, 4), a term
designed to distinguish them from the civilized European, Christian settlers
who wore clothing, possessed "the endurance of the wolf . . . the cunning of
the fox, the courage of the panther and the fierceness of the wildcat" (Moody
1958, 4), qualities of animals, not humans. Seeking revenge against Mexi-
cans, the Apaches decided "to show them the true meaning of the words
[torture and cruelty]" (Moody 1958, 9). "Plunder . . . whooping . . . howling
. . . [and] massacre" (Moody 1958, 6), terms reminiscent of dime novel and
western movie vocabulary, are applied to their activities. Out of such an
environment, Geronimo emerged.

According to Moody, the young Geronimo, in spite of superior physical
strength and endurance, an incredible memory for landscape, and great
bravery and extreme cleverness, had serious flaws. A skilled tracker, a fine
strategist, and, when attacked by a panther, a courageous and fierce fighter,
he was, as is noted several times, cruel, ruthless, contemptuous of his peers, a
strutter, a liar, and a braggart. More significant, he is possessed by an
overwhelming personal pride and ambition. While many children's biographies display ambition as a positive character trait, one that enables the hero
to overcome the many obstacles standing between him and worthy fame, in
Moody's book Geronimo's ambition is a negative quality, one that, in the
ensuing chapters, will time and time again prevent him from achieving his
goals. In fact, before detailing the Apache's adult life, Moody states that he
might have been a hero

> if he had kept his bragging tongue still and had not been so insolent when
> he returned [from a horse raid]. But Geronimo had to be the center of
> attention at any cost. Glory meant more to him than love, honor, food or
> drink. . . . When his tribesmen failed to give him the glory he wanted, he
> tried to take it with his great skill as an actor and orator—strutting,
> boasting, and shouting his own praises. Failing all this, he determined to
> become the greatest of all raid leaders. (Moody 1958, 82)

Geronimo appears more like the fictional bad boys of nineteenth-century
children's morality stories than an actual Apache youth of the same era.

In the discussions of the raids and battles Geronimo led as an adult, there
is no mention of what must have been his most important motivation, the
murder of his wife and children by white men. Instead, discussion focuses on
his reported abandonment of his fellow raiders in order to save his own life
and the contempt he earned from his own people for his treachery. In a book

that states, "Among all races and people there are good men and bad ones" (Moody 1958, 29), it quickly becomes clear that Geronimo is being portrayed as a bad one and an Indian to boot, even worse than those few treacherous whites who provided whiskey to the Indians, cheated them of their government rations, and deceptively slaughtered some of them.

In describing the raids that made Geronimo the most famous, feared, and wanted man in the United States in the decades after the Civil War, Moody often uses the following terms: *cruelty, lust for blood, torturing, plundering, looting, burning, ran wild, atrocity, crimes, pack of rabid wolves, massacres*. No freedom fighter, Geronimo will strike at helpless victims, including women and children, aided by his assistant Hoo, a renegade chief described as "a cruel and treacherous drunkard" (Moody 1958, 118). In fact, Hoo, whose name is usually spelled Juh, had a speech impediment that people mistook for an alcoholic slur. With even his own people against him, Geronimo is finally defeated, becomes an alcoholic, and, following a drunken binge, dies of pneumonia. In defeat, "the wolf of the warpath sneaked back like a frightened coyote" (Moody 1958, 182). Not only is this picture of a man with great potential who deliberately went wrong and destroyed himself because of overwhelming pride and alcohol totally negative, it is also culturally inaccurate. The coyote, for example, is presented as a totally negative animal, as it was seen by white ranches, sheepherders, and farmers, not as the mythic folk hero, sometimes good and sometimes bad, but always a survivor, found in Native legends across the Great Plains.

Finally, it should be noted that the negative portrait of Geronimo is partially developed through a series of contrasts with good leaders, both white and Native. Juan José preached equal justice against whites: not massacre, but a white death for an Indian one, a cow for a slain deer. Magnas Coloradas advocated learning from whites: "We cannot hate all the white men because some of them are treacherous. . . . We will learn from them" (Moody 1958, 48-49). However, if these Apache leaders are so many good things that Geronimo is not, they are less than perfect and certainly not as good as strong white leaders. Juan José authorized a raid in which a white camp was surrounded by Apaches performing "a screeching, writhing dance of death" (Moody 1958, 32). Coloradas, at one point, joined Geronimo, and Cochise directed one of the greatest wars against white settlers.

Although the author states that some treacherous whites sought personal wealth dishonestly and cruelly and always at the expense of the Apaches, the admirable soldiers and civilians seemed beyond reproach, as even the best Apaches were not. Commissioner John R. Bartlett was "a kind and gentle man" (Moody 1958, 93); Tom Jeffords was justly admired and trusted by Cochise; General George Crook exhibited "courage, honesty, and fairness" (Moody 1958, 131); John P. Allen was "absolutely fearless, honest, farsighted, and had a keen understanding of human nature" (Moody 1958, 136-37);

Clay Beauford "inspired Indians and was a natural leader" (Moody 1958, 138). Even when such terms are applied to Native leaders, and this is seldom, they must be qualified in light of subsequent deeds and events.

Geronimo: Wolf of the Warpath would no doubt not be accepted for publication today. However, it still remains on the shelves in children's rooms of some public libraries. And so it should, not as a source book for understanding Geronimo and his people—a more detailed and complex volume is necessary for that, even for young readers—but as a classic example of how language, point of view, and details can be employed to reinforce and perpetuate a stereotype, a simplistic construct of a Native person as many white readers wished to believe he was.

IN SEARCH OF SEDNA: A CHILDREN'S VERSION OF A MAJOR ESKIMO MYTH

Found across the Canadian and Greenland Arctic, the myth of Sedna is a reflection of the Eskimo belief in a world filled with powerful and often terrifying and malicious spirit beings. It is extremely different from those traditional European tales that form the basis of much Western children's literature. Violent to the point of gruesomeness, the Sedna myth reflects cultural beliefs that are not only foreign, but also repugnant to the vast majority of adults who are the creators and custodians of children's literature. A study of a children's version of the Sedna story against the cultural backgrounds of the traditional Eskimo people reveals both the tremendous challenges faced by modern adaptors and the mistakes that can be made when they approach it without the necessary knowledge and sympathy.

The traditional Eskimo lived in a physically and spiritually dangerous and violent world. Both the weather and the animals they hunted could quickly bring death. Moreover, the spiritual beings who peopled the lands and seas could angrily turn on them for violating taboos. The most significant of these beings was Sedna, "the Old Woman of the Sea" or "the Food Basket," who lived on the ocean floor, controlling the lives of the sea mammals that provided the basic food supply of the people. Anthropologist Franz Boas wrote: "She has supreme sway over the destinies of mankind, and almost all of the observances of these tribes are for the purpose of retaining her good will or of propitiating her if she has been offended" (Boas 1888, 199).

Although the myth has many variants, all contain a basic plot line. A proud woman who has refused all suitors is enticed from her home by an unknown, handsome man who professes to be a great hunter. When she discovers that he is, in fact, a supernatural petrel and that she is living among seabirds on a rocky, windswept cliff, she calls through her spirit to her father for rescue. However, the supernatural husband follows the fleeing pair, creating a fearsome storm. In terror, the father throws her out of his boat, cutting off her fingers when she clings to the side. As she sinks to the bottom of the sea, the amputated digits are transformed into the various sea mammals, her children, whom she fiercely protects against irreverent hunters.

Hers is a lonely and bitter life. As one Eskimo song relates:

> "Nuliajuk [one of the names by which she is known] gave seals to mankind, it is true, but she is not friendly to people, for they had no pity on her when she lived on earth, throwing her into the sea like that to drown. So naturally she would like mankind to perish too. That is why we do our best to be as good as we can and make Nuliajuk think kindly of us" (Field 1973, 48).

In times of her greatest displeasure, Sedna can only be appeased by a visit from the angakok, the shaman. Casting himself into a trance, he travels to her abode where he asks forgiveness on behalf of the tribe and seeks to appease her by combing her hair and removing lice, actions she cannot perform because of her mutilated hands.

The non-Eskimo writer adapting this story is faced with many difficulties. Most important, the elements it contains—the necessity of marriage for continuation of the species and the wrongness of Sedna's willful, almost prideful rejection of suitors; the danger of hunting and the ever-present possibility of starvation; the terror of betrayal by a family member and the vindictiveness of Sedna; and the spiritual power of the angakok—although totally understandable within traditional Eskimo culture, are very unlike Western values embodied in most children's literature. Because what would be easily understood by an audience of Eskimo children might be meaningless to a Western audience, adaptors may be tempted into either rejecting the beliefs as foolish superstition or reinterpreting them to make them more consistent with their own and their readers' values. Robert and Daniel San Souci's *Song of Sedna* is so altered as to be virtually worthless as a reflection of Eskimo culture. While the first half of the San Soucis's adaptation, up to the point that Sedna is thrown from the boat, is fairly close to traditional versions, the second part adds incidents and changes the character of the heroine. Throughout, the illustrations are inaccurate and the visual depictions of the setting inappropriate.

As noted, traditional versions explained the origins of the sea mammals and the reasons for poor hunting. In *Song of Sedna*, the seals already exist. Not surprisingly, Sedna is not portrayed as an angry and vindictive protectress of her children; they are not hers. Instead, after engaging in a quest during which she is tested, she becomes a beneficent helper to the Eskimo. As she sinks beneath the waters, "A powerful blessing was on her" (San Souci 1981, n.p.), and two banded seals tell her, "Approach that mountain and you will find your destiny" (San Souci 1981, n.p.). They are, in a sense, like the guardian figures of European folklore, helping the quester to help herself.

When they urge her to avoid the temptations of the spirits of the dead who call on her "to forsake her journey and rest with them . . . [she] drew upon her inner strength and ignored the ghost-voices" (San Souci 1981, n.p.). The seals instruct her to use her courage to climb on the back of a ferocious looking killer whale. Finally, she crosses a knife-edged bridge of ice and, encouraged by the seals, swims to her throne.

Having achieved power, Sedna now faces a new conflict: how to use it. In the originals, she sits vengefully at the bottom of the sea. In *Song of Sedna*, however, she listens to the warning of seal spirits: "'use your power wisely . . . for a god uses power tempered by wisdom and mercy.' Sedna realized that she was being tested. She sensed that her powers might be taken from her if she misused them. So she followed the best instincts of her heart" (San Souci 1981, n.p.). She forgives her father and, sitting on her throne, helps the Eskimo: "The Eskimos seek her good will whenever they need protection on the open sea or help with harvesting the sea's bounty" (San Souci 1981, n.p.). Clearly, the conclusion of *Song of Sedna* subverts the tone and message of the traditional myth. The warnings against refusing marriage and violating the goddess's taboos do not appear. Instead of awe, fear, and reverence, this version communicates joy and a sense of fulfillment.

The text is profusely, lavishly, and inaccurately illustrated. The pictures counteract the traditional values the story ought to have embodied. This process begins on the half-title page, which contains a stylized killer whale. While this mammal plays a role in the story, the illustration is in the style of the Tlingit and Tsimshian people of southern Alaska and the northern British Columbia coasts. The title page compounds the cultural errors. Although the story is explicitly set "beside the Arctic Ocean" (San Souci 1981, n.p.), an Indian totem pole is visible. Such poles were found in groups in villages of the northwest coast; a single pole would not be located far from a village. In the foreground is a deciduous tree at least two feet in diameter, in the distance a large stand of evergreens. These, of course, are never found in the high Arctic. Further inaccuracies are seen in the portrayal of the characters and their artifacts. Sedna, her father, and her mate are tall, willowy figures with long, lean faces and slender, delicate hands. They bear greater resemblance to the figures depicted in the San Soucis's *The Legend of Scarface* (1978), a plains myth, than they do to Arctic Eskimo. The embroidery on the parkas resembles the beadwork of the northern Cree and Ojibway, and the woven grass sails of the umiak are of a type that was found on the boats of the Bering Sea Eskimo of western Alaska, a place where this legend is not told. The serpent the enraged husband rides while pursuing his fleeing wife has scales like those of rattlesnakes. In form, color, and size, such a serpent would probably not have been imagined by traditional Arctic Inuit.

The effect of these inaccuracies is to rob the accompanying story of its cultural background. More important, it implicitly reflects an attitude that cultural accuracy in portraying a story of these people is unimportant. Approximation is sufficient. These visual inaccuracies, along with the alteration of the character of Sedna and the meaning of her story, totally invalidate *Song of Sedna* as an acceptable presentation of this story for children. The authors appear to have respected neither the culture and the story it created, nor the child audience for whom they have adapted it. In addition to containing cultural inaccuracies, the San Souci version fails to embody the major cultural fact underlying stories of Sedna and the angakok's attempt to placate her. As religious scholar Mercea Eliade has noted, the shaman/angakok "in a manner reestablishes the situation that existed *in illo tempore*, in mythical times, when the divorce between man and the animal world had not yet occurred" (Eliade 1964, 94). In the story of Sedna, the girl's double betrayal is a kind of fall that results in the Mother of the Seals maintaining a very tenuous relationship with human beings, a relationship that, when broken, can only be re-established by the angakok. In essence, the story embodies dualities: land and sea, spirit and human, human and animal, faith and betrayal, love and anger, breach and reconciliation—that is, physical, spiritual, and psychic life and death. Only when opposing tensions are reconciled is a unified, whole life possible. The story of Sedna is a classic example of the dualities that Claude Lévi-Strauss (1958) has maintained provide the essential structure of mythology. These dualities are not embodied in *Song of Sedna*.

THE INDIAN IN THE CUPBOARD: MAKING PLASTIC INDIANS WOODEN

Although British author Lynne Banks' 1980 novel *The Indian in the Cupboard* contains two American characters, an eighteenth-century Iroquois and a nineteenth-century cowboy, it exists thoroughly within the tradition of twentieth-century English children's literature. In Banks' story, as in E. Nesbit's *Harding's Luck*, an ordinary child comes into possession of an object that allows him to bridge time and, in this case, to bring people from the past into the present. However, these characters arrive in the present in miniature form and, like the normal-sized human beings in Mary Norton's *The Borrowers* and T.H. White's *Mistress Masham's Repose*, the boy hero Omri must learn to treat the tiny people with respect, as human beings and not as curios to be used for his amusement.

The story begins when Omri places a miniature plastic Indian, a birthday present from his friend Patrick, into a cupboard, a birthday present from his brother, and locks the door with a very old key given him by his mother. During the night, the figure comes to life as Little Bear, an eighteenth-century Iroquois magically transported from the past and given the form of the now animated, tiny plastic model. In addition to keeping Little Bear's presence a secret from his family and protecting him from a pet cat and a rat,

Omri must provide food and shelter, as well as emotional support, for the three-inch-tall man. Later, when Patrick discovers his friend's secret and insists on having a model cowboy brought to life, Omri's difficulties and responsibilities increase. The cowboy and Indian have a natural antipathy for each other; Patrick's insistence that the two be taken to school has nearly disastrous consequences; and Little Bear wants a wife. At the story's conclusion, Omri realizes that he must put the tiny people back in the cupboard and send them back to their own times. However, in the tradition of English books that leave open the possibility of a sequel, the boy keeps the key, the cupboard, and the plastic figures.

In many ways, this is a very good book: the adventures are exciting and sometimes quite amusing, the moral dilemmas and various emotions Omri feels about the tiny people are convincingly portrayed, and the contrasts between the characters of Patrick and Omri are well delineated. However, because of its portrayal of Little Bear, the Indian in the Cupboard, and his adventures in the narrative, the novel has subtle, but serious limitations.

Banks is at pains to make clear that Little Bear is not a generic Indian, but an Iroquois, a member of the confederation of Native nations that sided with the British against the French during the eighteenth century. Where he lived—which would have been in what is now upstate New York—is not specified. She correctly explains that he would have lived in a longhouse, but then gives him a detailed knowledge of plains tipi decoration that he most certainly would not have possessed. She does make it clear that scalping was not an indigenous custom, but rather one introduced and encouraged by the Europeans, then later has Little Bear gleefully attempt to scalp the cowboy. Although he has never seen or ridden a horse, Little Bear quickly learns to ride bareback in plains fashion when Omri brings a toy horse to life. Strangely, he instinctively sees the nineteenth-century cowboy as an enemy, and, when he sees a Cowboy and Indian movie on television, he immediately responds in nineteenth-century terms: "White men move onto land! Use water! Kill animals!" (Banks 1982, 150), something surprising to hear from a member of a Native group allied to the English.

A study of Little Bear's character reveals greater problems. Although Omri realizes at one point that he is able to understand things from "the Indian's point of view" (Banks 1982, 39), he probably refers to the tiny size, not to specific cultural beliefs and behaviors. Little Bear acts more like the stereotyped brave of movies and dime novels than an individual raised as a member of a specific nation. Speaking what can best be described as generic pidgin English, he "barked" (Banks 1982, 20), "growled fiercely" (Banks 1982, 10), and made "a noise like a snarl" (Banks 1982, 10); he begins to "tear at" (Banks 1982, 19) his food, makes "ferocious and hideous faces" (Banks 1982, 22), and glares "blazing-eyed" (Banks 1982, 77) at the boy. When he is thwarted or ignored, as happens frequently, he folds his arms across his chest and stands in stony silence. These various responses would certainly reinforce any notions young readers might hold about Native peoples being savage, uncivilized, and rigidly stubborn. Indeed, in his folded-arm pose, Little Bear resembles the wooden cigar-store Indians still seen in some North American souvenir stores (including, unfortunately, one in the town of Cherokee, North Carolina).

The nature of another major problem in *The Indian in the Cupboard* is hinted at in the title character's name: Little Bear. The diminutive adjective reflects his tiny size, but also helps diminish his importance as a human being. Within his own culture, this name would most likely have been his childhood nickname, one that would have been replaced when he had achieved adult status. Although he is grown up and has lost a wife, he still retains the name and, by implication, his inferior role in the story. He may, to use a favorite cliché among many whites, be "nature's child." He is certainly a child in his relation to the huge, but much younger Omri. His petulance, stubbornness, and tantrums are those of a spoiled, self-centered child. And as the novel progresses, Omri, while stating that he likes and respects him as a real human being, treats him like a child. When Little Bear mounts his horse, the boy tells him not to go out of sight; Omri responds like his mother when the man wants to have his own way; he tells the Iroquois, as a mother would a child being taken on an outing, that at school, "you must do as I tell you and not make any noise" (Banks 1982, 95). He scolds Little Bear for not eating the food he has been "to a lot of trouble to cook" (Banks 1982, 98), breaks up Little Bear's fight with the cowboy by using "his father's firm end-of-the-fight voice" (Banks 1982, 103), and later uses a voice that "Mr. Johnson [the school principal] himself might have envied—it commanded obedience" (Banks 1982, 151). Omri may be learning to respect Little Bear as a human being; he himself is learning how to behave as adults do toward children. Unfortunately, his nascent paternalism is directed at an adult from another culture whom he perceives as parents often perceive their children.

Omri's behavior to the Indian subtly but definitely reflects the imperialistic attitudes exhibited by European people toward their colonial subjects in the New World and elsewhere. In a place where he has absolutely no power, where the physical diminishment caused by Omri's turning the magic key in the cupboard symbolizes the status of his people since shortly after contact with Europeans, Little Bear is completely dependent on Omri for his survival. Deprived of the products of his natural environment and the support of his culture, he must turn to the boy, whom he at one time believes to be the "Great White Spirit" (Banks 1982, 21). The term is reminiscent of the phrase "Great White Mother," used in nineteenth-century Canada to describe Queen Victoria, or "Great White Father," used for various American presidents. In times of petulant annoyance, Little Bear calls Omri a boy. However, this boy provides him with food, a horse, building materials, weapons, and European medical aid, just as colonial administrators, who deprived Natives of animals, hunting grounds, and villages, supplied the goods they thought appropriate for their new subjects. Omri even supplies a chief's headdress, in effect assuming power to make Little Bear a chief, an activity frequently undertaken by colonial leaders. He also finds Little Bear a wife. Benevolent though he is, and as some of the colonial administrators were, Omri is in control. At the end of the novel, Omri realizes that he must grant the Iroquois the right to live freely, if dangerously, in his own times with his own people. However, for Little Bear and readers, this realization comes only after much damage has been done. As the sequel, *The Return of the Indian*, reveals, the Indian is still dependent on the English boy. And for readers, a sense of Omri's benevolent colonial power has been firmly established.

The title of the chapter in which Little Bear assumes or is given his leadership, "The Chief is Dead, Long Live the Chief" (Banks 1982, 50), symbolizes the imperialist, British point of view that subtly pervades all of *The Indian in the Cupboard*. It is an echo of the ceremonial phrase used at the time of the death of a British monarch and emphasizes the continuity of the traditions of British rule. While Omri may develop admirable moral qualities in his new comprehension of the integrity of individual human beings, he also develops the qualities of imperialistic, although benevolent, control of a subject people. At a time when Native peoples are rediscovering their traditions, developing a pride in their cultural beliefs and achievements, and struggling to achieve the dignity of self-government and economic independence, *The Indian in the Cupboard* transmits unacceptable viewpoints and messages to young white and Native readers alike.

BROTHER EAGLE, SISTER SKY: DID CHIEF SEATTLE REALLY SAY THAT?

Among many adults, Susan Jeffers's *Brother Eagle, Sister Sky*, an illustrated adaptation of the 1974 Spokane Exposition adaptation of Chief Seattle's purported speech of 1853 or 1854, is an ideal picture book—gorgeously illustrated and topical in its sensitive ecological message. However, no matter how well-intentioned Susan Jeffers is, no matter how great her respect for traditional and contemporary Native Americans, her book is another example of the creation of a "white man's Indian," a construct which reflects not realities but a view of what a white author, painter, motion picture director, actor, politician, missionary, activist, or conservationist believes Native peoples to be, wants them to become, or wishes they already were.

Technically, *Brother Eagle, Sister Sky* is an excellent picture book. Individual illustrations, done with fine-line pen, ink, and dyes, not only reveal Jeffers's superb craftsmanship but also enhance and expand on the short, poetic text. Taken in sequence, they create a parallel between events of the mid-nineteenth century and the late twentieth century, events involving a conflict between white settlers and indigenous residents, and they offer a possible solution. The opening illustration, accompanying a brief account of the nineteenth-century displacement of many Native peoples from their traditional homelands, is a depiction of the famous 1838 "Trail of Tears" forced westward marches of the Cherokee people (unidentified in this book). Mounted on ponies and watched over by rifle-carrying soldiers, the exiles ride through the snow.

The illustrations accompanying Chief Seattle's accounts of the relationship between human beings, the land, the plants, and the animals also imply another western journey. By horse and canoe, men and women and boys and girls from the eastern woodlands and the northern and southwestern plains travel across the prairies toward and through the mountains, each of the areas profuse with the flora and fauna mentioned in the text. However, when they reach the northwest, they confront a scene of devastation: clear-cut logging has virtually denuded the landscape. But hope is not lost; a nuclear white family, descendants of the whites addressed by Chief Seattle nearly a century and a half earlier, are shown planting seedlings among the stumps. In the final illustration, the family leaves the reseeded area followed by the ghostly image of a horse-riding plains Indian and his wife, who walks beside him carrying a papoose. Past and present and the two races are united, and a long ago message about respecting the environment is finally observed.

Certainly few people would quarrel with the message of the words, the actions of the white family, or the respectful and accurate portrayals of the various traditional Native peoples. However, many questions can be raised about the text on which Jeffers based her adaptation and about the use of illustrations of a variety of Native peoples to accompany a speech that referred to a specific historical event related to one northwest coast nation. The first difficulty arises when one studies the dust jacket illustration and title. A plains chief bedecked with a buffalo horn and feathered headdress stands protectively behind a blue-eyed boy wearing a gaily striped tee-shirt. Above is the title *Brother Eagle, Sister Sky*. As is noted on the copyright page, the illustration is based on a photograph by Edward Curtis. As has been frequently noted, Curtis's photographs were often deliberately staged; he would require his Native subjects to remove their European clothing and don ceremonial regalia seldom used, thus making them more closely conform to the image already popular in the eastern United States and Europe of the "noble savage," a stereotyped individual usually represented as being from the northern plains. Moreover, Jeffers's painting is based on a photograph of a Cheyenne Chief, Two Moons, and was taken in 1910, several decades after Seattle's death. Even overlooking the problems of Curtis's photographs, one is led to ask why Jeffers would choose to depict a northwest chief as a plains leader? More important, perhaps, is the title phrase "Sister Sky." Virtually all Native peoples considered the earth to be the great mother and the sky, the father. In fact, even the text on which the Spokane Exposition text seems to have been based makes reference to "his mother, the earth, and his brother, the sky" (Kaiser 1987, 526).

Chief Seattle's speech, which first became widely popular during the later 1960s at about the same time that John Neihardt's *Black Elk Speaks* was rediscovered, was published in a Seattle newspaper in 1887, over 30 years after it was purportedly delivered. It was based on notes taken by Dr. Henry Smith, who reportedly listened to a translation of words being delivered in the Lushotseed language in 1853 or 1854 on the occasion of Governor Stevens's arrival in what is now Seattle. Although Chief Seathl (as his name is generally spelled), a Christian who ceded his people's lands, would probably not be viewed favorably by contemporary Native militants, Smith's version of the speech reveals an embittered and cynical individual, a person who recognized the unbridgeable gaps between the two cultures and despaired of the survival of his people.

The most popular version of the speech, written for and displayed at the Spokane World's Fair Exposition of 1974, omits all of the harsh, critical passages, and is, in the words of one commentator, "wholly ecological and nature-related in outlook" (Kaiser 1987, 511). It concludes with a sentiment totally absent in Smith's version: "There is only one God. We are all brothers" (Kaiser 1987, 532). Smith's Seattle had lamented, "Your God loves your people and hates mine" (Kaiser 1987, 519). The 1974 text, which was clearly designed to be "user friendly" for visitors to the World's Fair, is, with slight changes in order and with brief additions, used almost in its entirety by Jeffers. The Seattle who emerges is not an embattled and cynical chief hopelessly ceding his lands, but a wise Indian generously offering his advice to future whites who can benefit from it.

Jeffers's changes in the order of sentences and phrases are not significant; however, her alterations are. The 1887 text is specifically masculine, the words "man" and "brothers" are used 15 times, with the final word being "brothers." "Sisters" is used once; "mother," twice. Jeffers, who states in the afterword that "What matters is that Chief Seattle's words inspired a most compelling truth: In our zeal to build and possess, we may lose all we have" (Jeffers 1991, n.p.), has introduced into the speech two modern messages the earliest text does not contain: one ecological, the other gender related. Creating her book in 1991, when gender equality in children's books was emphasized, she casts Seattle's speech as a series of his remembrances of wisdom transmitted to him by both his parents and by ancestors of both sexes: "My mother told me. . . . My father said to me. . . . The voice of my grandfather said to me. . . . The voice of my grandmother said to me. . . . The water's murmur is the voice of your great-great grandmother" (Jeffers 1991, n.p.).

While she correctly writes, "The earth is our mother" (Jeffers 1991, n.p.), she incorrectly, as noted above, ascribes the same gender to the sky. Certainly there is no quarrel with Jeffers's modern belief in sexual equality, but it is wrong for her to attribute this view to Seattle. Similarly, her ecological message is appropriate and necessary, but there is no evidence that it was articulated by Chief Seattle in the 1850s.

Jeffers's illustrations, though technically excellent and related to her ecological theme, create serious difficulties. "My aim," she writes on the flyleaf of the dust jacket, "was to portray people and artifacts from a wide array of nations because the philosophy expressed in the text is one shared by most Native Americans." In its most general sense, this is no doubt correct. However, in using illustrations depicting a variety of geographically and culturally diverse Native nations, Jeffers is creating a Pan-Indianism that would not have existed at the time of Seattle's speech. Two early elements of Pan-Indianism, the Ghost Dance religion of the 1880s, on the positive side, and the residential Indian schools of the early twentieth century, on the negative, were at least two generations later than Seattle's speech. The American Indian Movement, the most politically well-known manifestation of modern Pan-Indianism, would certainly not have envisioned the kind of white-Native interrelationships depicted on the picture book's cover and concluding page. Moreover, Seattle, who in the 1853 version of the speech, spoke of "our ancient enemies far to the northward, the Simsians and Hydas" (Kaiser 1987, 519) (a passage omitted from both the Spokane Exposition and Jeffers texts), certainly did not envision any sense of widespread Native brotherhood.

The illustrations include three from the eastern woodlands, four from the plains, and three showing groups from these areas crossing the mountains to the clear-cut areas. There are horses in seven of the illustrations. Only on the title page are a west coast Native, the seashore, and a dugout canoe seen. These illustrations imply an erroneous notion of Pan-Indianism. The dominance of pictures of people riding horses perpetuates a long-held stereotype that people of the nineteenth-century plains horse culture represented the way all traditional Native peoples looked in the past and still look today. Virtually ignoring the landscape, artifacts, and regalia of the west coast peoples—notice that the westward trek stops before reaching the seashore where Seattle lived—Jeffers overlooks the distinct and different Native groups, the uniqueness of each Native nation, and the cultural and environmentally specific aspects of each group's response to its relationships with the animal and natural worlds around it.

Virtually all readers would agree with the ecological message of *Brother Eagle, Sister Sky*. However, as a visual and verbal representation of Native realities past and present, the book must be approached with extreme caution. It does not use the text most likely to represent what Chief Seattle actually said, and it presents the one it does use in a way that is more in accord with the author's own (worthwhile) views on gender equality and the environment. The depiction of Native peoples and their views reinforces stereotypes, albeit positive ones, for Susan Jeffers has created a portrait of a "good Indian," which she employs to reinforce her own agenda. Although viewed with sympathy and respect, her Chief Seattle becomes an "ecological visionary" created from her imagination. He is as much a "white man's Indian" as were the heathen savages, nature's children, noble savages, and vanishing Americans of earlier eras.

Teachers, parents, librarians, and university students frequently ask: "Should all these books be on the shelves, accessible to children?" The answer is a definite "Yes!" However, they should not be used as resource materials for discovering how things were; they should be used as examples of how and why non-Native peoples presented Native cultures, histories, and individuals the way they did. With adult guidance, children will be able to understand more fully the nature of stereotyping and the importance of creating more accurate portrayals. They will realize the problems involved in depicting "others" and recognize the kinds of stereotypes that were created and are still appearing. For those adults wishing to examine more fully the wide range of stereotypical representations of Native peoples, the following books are recommended: *American Indian Stereotypes in the World of Children*, edited by Arlene B. Hirschfelder; *Shadows of the Indian*, by Raymond William Stedman; and *Books without Bias: Through Indian Eyes*, edited by Beverly Slapin and Doris Seale.

Certainly, in the past two decades, creators of children's books have frequently succeeded in their attempts to present more accurate and sensitive books about Native peoples. In examining these books, several questions shall be asked: How accurate are their portrayals of Native cultures? What cultural realities do the books reveal? What visual and verbal methods are used in the presentation? And how do the authors' and illustrators' own non-Native backgrounds and their views about the nature and purpose of children's books and the nature of their intended audiences influence their portrayals?

REFERENCES

Banks, Lynne Reid. 1982. *The Indian in the Cupboard*. New York: Avon. (First published in 1980.)

Berkhofer, Robert F., Jr. 1978. *The White Man's Indian: Images of the American Indian from Columbus to the Present*. New York: Alfred A. Knopf.

Boas, Franz. 1888. *The Central Eskimo*. Washington, DC: Bureau of Ethnology.

Churchill, Ward. 1992. *Fantasies of the Master Race: Literature, Cinema and the Colonization of American Indians*. Monroe, ME: Common Courage Press.

Dickason, Olive Patricia. 1984. *The Noble Savage and the Beginnings of French Colonialism in the Americas*. Edmonton, Canada: University of Alberta Press.

Eliade, Mercea. 1964. *Shamanism: Archaic Techniques of Ecstasy*. Translated by William R. Trusk. New York: Pantheon.

Field, Eugene, translator. 1973. *Eskimo Songs and Stories*. New York: Delacorte Press.

Hirschfelder, Arlene B. 1982. *American Indian Stereotypes in the World of Children*. Metuchen, NJ: The Scarecrow Press.

Jeffers, Susan. 1991. *Brother Eagle, Sister Sky: A Message from Chief Seattle*. New York: Dial Books.

Kaiser, Rudolf. 1987. "Chief Seattle's Speech(es): American Origins and European Reception." In *Recovering the Word: Essays on Native American Literature*, edited by Brian Swann and Arnold Krupat. Berkeley: University of California Press.

Lévi-Strauss, Claude. 1958. "The Structural Study of Myth." In *Myth: A Symposium*, edited by Thomas A. Sebock. Bloomington: Indiana University Press.

Moody, Ralph; illustrated by Nicholas Eggenhofer. 1958. *Geronimo: Wolf of the Warpath*. New York: Random House.

Pearce, Roy Harvey. 1965. *Savagism and Civilization: A Study of the Indian and the American Mind*. Baltimore: The Johns Hopkins Press.

San Souci, Robert D., reteller; illustrated by Daniel San Souci. 1978. *The Legend of Scarface: A Blackfoot Indian Tale*. Garden City, NY: Doubleday.

San Souci, Robert D., reteller; illustrated by Daniel San Souci. 1981. *Song of Sedna*. Garden City, NY: Doubleday.

Doris Seale, editor. 1988. *Books without Bias: Through Indian Eyes*. 2nd ed. Introduction by Beverly Slapin. Berkeley, CA: Oyate.

Slapin, Beverly and Doris Seale. 1992. *Through Indian Eyes: The Native Experience in Books for Children*. New Society Publishers.

Smith, Henry Nash. 1950. *Virgin Land: The American West as Symbol and Myth*. Cambridge: Harvard University Press.

Stedman, Raymond William. 1982. *Shadows of the Indian: Stereotypes in American Culture*. Norman: University of Oklahoma Press.

Tanner, Helen Hornbeck. 1992. *The Ojibwa*. New York: Chelsea House.

Wade, Mary Hazelton. 1901. *Our Little Indian Cousin*. Boston: L.C. Page.

CHAPTER 2

▼▼▼

Imaging Native Worlds

PICTURE BOOKS AND TRADITIONAL STORIES

The picture book, the genre most closely identified with modern, printed children's literature, may be the best medium for introducing children to the traditional stories that were (and still are) told orally to young and old Native people for centuries. Original audiences would have watched the facial expressions and gestures of the tellers and would have been able to imagine the settings, animals, dwellings, costumes, and designs depicted in the stories. Most modern non-Native children, being unfamiliar with these Native elements, benefit from the pictures, which make important details visible, suggest tone, and replace the voice and gestures of the teller. It is not surprising, then, that the largest number of children's books about Native peoples are illustrated versions of traditional tales and that, with the increased interest in Native and other minority cultures, more picture books on the subject appear annually.

A major issue surrounding books about Native peoples written by non-Natives concerns the acceptability of treating the lives, cultures, and stories of people who are "other." Many traditional tales were, and in some cases still are, the property of Native families and individuals and cannot be used without permission. To do so is perceived by the owners as "illegal" cultural expropriation—in short, theft. Fortunately, such theft is now rare. However, many Natives and non-Natives alike view even the "legal" use of traditional stories as, at worst, continued exploitation for personal gain, and, at best, presumptuousness. How, they ask, can individuals from outside a culture possess the factual knowledge, imaginative insight, or spiritual wisdom to recreate stories in ways that embody the many meanings they had for the original tellers and listeners?

Conversely, many Natives and non-Natives argue that in an increasingly multicultural world all individuals and culture groups must make determined efforts to understand, appreciate, and sympathize with people who are different from themselves. Only then can world harmony and peace move closer to becoming a reality. As Abenaki author Joseph Bruchac has stated, referring to his retellings of stories from other Native cultures, "We learn about ourselves by understanding others. Our own traditions can be made stronger only when we pay attention to and respect the traditions of people who are different from ourselves" (Bruchac 1993, x-xi). Aware of their limitations and their differences from their subjects, many authors and illustrators have engaged in extensive research, have gotten to know members of different Native groups, and have attempted, as far as is possible, to get outside of themselves and into the spirit of the cultures they are depicting. Because most of the creators of children's picture books are from the dominant white society, it is not surprising that they have produced the most books about Native peoples. There is simply a greater population base from which to draw. Nevertheless, some white creators of children's picture books have expressed a willingness to turn over the responsibility of writing children's books that retell Native tales to those members of traditional cultures with the ability and means to tell their peoples' stories.

Adult evaluators and selectors of picture books about Native peoples must establish firm guidelines for judging the available materials and must be forceful in their application of these guidelines. No matter how well-intentioned an author or illustrator may be, a book must be rejected if it is inaccurate or otherwise disrespects the culture it attempts to depict.

Picture books must be culturally accurate. *The Rough-Face Girl*, a beautiful picture book written by Rafe Martin and illustrated by David Shannon, is, as the "Author's Note" states, about an Algonquin Indian Cinderella. Yet, the opening sentence sets the story "by the shores of Lake Ontario" (Martin 1992, n.p.), even though the shores of that lake were peopled by tribes speaking Iroquoian, not Algonquian, languages. In addition, the term "Cinderella" implicitly brings with it the European cultural values associated with French and German versions of a story familiar to most young readers.

The originating culture of a story should be identified as specifically as possible. Another fine recent picture book, Ed Young's *Moon Mother*, is subtitled *A Native American Creation Tale*. Although the author-illustrator may have followed his sources accurately, the subtitle gives the reader no clues about the myth's cultural origin. As a result, the story appears to be a "generic Indian" myth that could be easily (and sometimes inappropriately) applied to any part of the continent.

A picture book adaptation of a traditional tale should also list the specific sources—anthropological texts, legend collections, or personal contacts—on which the current retelling is based. Such a list serves several functions. First, it allows the reader to check the sources, if they have been printed, to see how closely these were followed. An awareness of differences between the retelling and its sources—additions, deletions, expansions, alterations—helps readers better understand the meanings and intentions of the adaptors. The alterations may indicate the author's motivations for retelling Native legends for modern, non-Native children. In addition, interested readers can examine the earlier versions, some of which may themselves distort Native originals for their own purposes. For example, Andy Gregg's *Great Rabbit and the Long-tailed Wildcat* was based on a story collected by a nineteenth-century American folklorist, Charles Godfrey Leland, whose style and interpretation were influenced by his Anglo-European training and cultural background. Finally, a list of sources enables interested readers to pinpoint more accurately the culture of origin and engage in background research that will further enable them to understand and to judge the accuracy of the visual and verbal details found in the picture book. Are the designs on tipis, masks, totem poles, and clothing, for example, appropriate to the group that originally told the story? The dwellings and clothing in *Baby Rattlesnake*, for instance, are unlikely to have been envisioned by Chickasaw listeners to Te Ata's oral narration.

Not only must illustrations be geographically and culturally accurate, they should be appropriate to the story. In all good picture books, illustrations amplify, enhance, and expand on the written text. Do the tipi designs in a story set on the northern plains communicate meanings about the occupants and their roles in the plot? Do the totem poles, which presented family emblems and traced genealogies for northwest coast Native peoples, add more than cultural atmosphere to a story? Good illustrators do not merely haul out sets, props, and costumes from some backstage storeroom; they create them as their share in the partnership of telling the story in all its dimensions. Author-illustrators Gerald McDermott and Paul Goble are masters of this dual art of visual and verbal storytelling.

Finally, it should be emphasized that no matter how accurate, sympathetic, and respectful the creators of picture books about Native people may be, unless they tell good stories—visually and verbally—their works will not be successful. A true picture book is a marriage between words and pictures, a partnership that is incomplete when one of the elements does not communicate to its fullest power. Each picture book contains three stories: one the words communicate, one the pictures communicate, and one the interaction of words and pictures communicates. Within individual pictures, successful use of three visual elements is essential: design, details, and color. The relationships between these three elements across a series of pictures or in contrasting pictures is also vital. Just how successfully these visual elements can be used is seen in a careful examination of the works of McDermott and Goble, whose books have received acclaim in their own country and abroad, among adults and children, and from Native and non-Native readers.

Both winners of the Caldecott Medal awarded for the best American picture book of the year, Goble and McDermott are interesting studies in contrast. British-born Goble has written and illustrated tales exclusively from the hunting cultures of the northern plains, whose mythology, history, art, and sociology he has studied deeply. American-born Gerald McDermott, a student of mythographer Joseph Campbell, began writing and illustrating picture books as an offshoot of his creation of short animated films. He has adapted hero and trickster tales, many of them from agricultural societies around the world. These works, three of which are based on Native myths and legends, contain McDermott's distinctive style and thematic concerns, which are designed to reveal underlying similarities among culturally diverse stories.

TRADITIONAL PLAINS CULTURES AND STORIES IN THE PICTURE BOOKS OF PAUL GOBLE

Like many authors who both write and illustrate their own books, Paul Goble begins by creating the written text and then painting the illustrations—a long and arduous process. He noted of *The Great Race* that "to come up with the final draft of three typed sheets, double spaced, I had to work through 170 pages of typed and hand-written drafts" (Stott 1984b, 872). With the exception of his first three books, *Red Hawk's Account of Custer's Last Battle*, *Brave Eagle's Account of The Fetterman Fight*, and *Lone Bull's Horse Raid*, which are fictional accounts of old men remembering important deeds of their youth, each of Goble's texts is short. In many ways, this brevity makes the books like the oral sources on which they are based. Traditional storytellers, who depended on their audience's familiarity with factual and mythological details, used voice intonations, facial expressions, and body language, and frequently encouraged their audiences to respond to elements in the stories, becoming, in effect, cocreators. Thus, the original storytellers did not need to elaborate in great verbal detail. Lacking the performance setting of the original tellers, Goble uses his illustrations to expand and deepen his written texts. And, as they become more fully understood through careful and thoughtful viewing, the illustrations also make the readers/viewers of the books cocreators of meaning.

However short, closely related to, and, in part, dependent on the illustrations they may be, the verbal texts of Goble's books are carefully structured and written. The adaptations of traditional myths and legends display a general pattern. After an author's introduction and a bibliographical note, the legend is narrated. The conclusion relates the event to the audience, referred to as "we" or "you," and traditional poems about the legend's topic finish the book. Not every book contains every element, but the presence of many or all of them in a given book implicitly conveys Goble's attitudes as an adapter or reteller. The introductory materials clearly identify the sources of the stories and give them a firm cultural and historical context; these are the stories the people actually told, and these are some of the reasons they told them. The narratives, free of authorial comment, are then placed immediately before readers to be experienced directly. In two books, *Star Boy* and *The Lost Children*, Goble recreates the conditions under which the stories would originally have been told, thus, providing a bridge across which his audience can move, entering as much as possible into the oral experience of the storytelling. The conclusions emphasize the continuing relevance of the story. We are still able to see the goatee on the buffalo, the sheen on the magpie's wings, the constellations. Looking at the stars of the Big Dipper, "It is good to know that they once lived here on earth. . . . We are never alone at night" (Goble 1988a, n.p.). "*Mitakuye oyasin*," Goble writes at the conclusion of *Buffalo Woman*—"We are all related" (Goble 1984, n.p.). What the hero learned through his adventures and long-ago audiences learned through listening, we can still learn through the reading—and should! The traditional poems—about crows, horses, buffaloes, wolves, the sun, and death—bring the written texts full circle, back to the Native traditions on which they are based—but with a difference. Instead of facts and sources, the poems present those words of the traditional peoples that embody their beliefs about the relatedness of the spiritual, natural, and human worlds. Because of the words and particularly the illustrations of the narratives, the implicit, complex meanings of these apparently simple poems are more fully appreciated by readers.

The four books presenting the misadventures of Iktomi, a trickster and a fool, use the written text in a different manner. As before, Goble includes bibliographies and written notes that provide source information and cultural contexts. However, there are no concluding poems because the central character's actions are not sacred; in fact, in each of the stories, Iktomi violates an important social or religious custom. The second and subsequent books in the series include a second introduction. On their title pages, the central character speaks deprecatingly of the white author's attempts to tell his story. In addition to indicating Goble's awareness of the sensitive issue of retelling a story from someone else's culture, Iktomi introduces an important aspect of the written text to follow. There will be at least two voices presenting the story: the narrator, who is here named Paul Goble, and Iktomi, who suggests that he will correct the distortions and lies of the white narrator. Ironically, Iktomi's views will be more distorted and untrue than those of the foreign storyteller.

The use of three different typefaces for the written text in the Iktomi series indicates, in effect, the presence of three different narrations. Large, bold-faced roman type presents the direct narrative. Large, gray italic type presents the narrator's questions and observations, which are addressed to the audience. Small, bold-faced roman type is used to present Iktomi's own running commentary on the events in which he is involved. The effect of these three texts is to create a constantly shifting perspective for the readers. After being told what is happening, they are presented with questions or observations in which the narrator intrudes on his narrative and unsettles the readers by not allowing them to accept unquestioningly the apparently factual statements he has made. The readers are also allowed to listen to Iktomi, who may either be talking to himself or aware of their presence. In either case, he seems anxious to appear in a better light than he thinks the narrator, Paul Goble, will present him. Shifting back and forth between the three texts of voices, the readers become actively involved in the story, responding to material coming at them in rapid fashion, trying to create a unified response, a fourth voice, their own. Writing for a young audience, Goble comes very close to recreating on the printed page the dynamic interplay of the oral situations in which the stories were originally told. Of course, there is another text in the story, the visual one that relates to the written ones and to which the reader must react while at the same time responding to the interplay between it and the three written texts.

This discussion of the written texts of Goble's adaptations of Native tales may seem extremely complex and intricate. However, it is important to realize that the texts play a crucial role in communicating the meanings and tones of the stories, bringing them as close as possible to the original oral tellings. But Goble is also a picture book creator, and his second task, after carefully shaping the words of the story, is to complement them with illustrations that both expand on and amplify the meanings and tones conveyed by the words.

Paul Goble's illustrations are the products of an exquisite artistic talent, extensive research into the art and culture of the traditional peoples of the northern plains, and accurate observations of the land and skyscapes in the midst of which these people lived. These qualities are employed in creating single pictures and groups of illustrations that precisely communicate the factual, social, and spiritual elements of each story. The illustrations employ one or more artistic styles to achieve the desired effects. These styles not only depict the geographical and cultural settings of each story but also advance conflict, theme, characterization, and tone.

With the exception of the Iktomi stories, where the egotistical character's focus is totally on himself, each of Goble's stories precisely represents the landscape: animals, birds, flowers and trees, ridges and hills, towering mountains in the distance, daytime skies dappled with white wind clouds or covered with towering thunderheads, and night skies whose indigo darkness is dotted with stars of differing intensities. Initially sketched in pencil and then outlined in pen and ink, each illustration is painted with watercolors so meticulously applied that the artist frequently holds a magnifying glass in one hand to carefully guide the strokes of a tiny brush held in his other hand. In many cases, as Goble has stated in the Author Note to *Beyond the Ridge*, the watercolor is "applied almost up to the pen outline; this has the effect of leaving thin 'white lines' which give brightness and clarity to the painting" (Goble 1989a, n.p.). Such a technique recreates the quality of the light found on the prairies; it also suggests a spiritual presence that traditional tellers of the legends would have believed was all around them, as well as in the stories.

The landscapes also indicate stages in the movement toward narrative and thematic resolution of conflicts. In *Beyond the Ridge*, the spirit of a dying woman walks up a slope to the crest, the point of transition from life to death, where she looks down upon a valley similar to the place she left, but "more beautiful, and with a greater abundance of birds and animals" (Goble 1989a, n.p.). The pictures of the ascent depict a rugged, rock-strewn landscape; there are no animals and only a few scrubby bushes; gray clouds fill the skies. In the valley beyond the ridge, birds and butterflies abound in the now blue skies; antelope and buffalo graze on lush green grass, filling a plain that stretches out to a distant stand of trees. In the foreground, early summer flowers bloom in profusion. The contrasts of the landscapes parallel the situations of the woman who was old, sick, and dying, but who now lives "without fatigue or sorrow or illness" (Goble 1989a, n.p.), reunited with loved ones who have preceded her.

At the beginning of *The Gift of the Sacred Dog*, the starving people, searching vainly for the buffalo herds, walk across a rocky landscape devoid of green vegetation, while vultures look on. But the landscape is dramatically altered when a boy who has successfully completed a vision quest returns to his village with a gift from the spirit beings, the horses that will help his people survive. Beneath the brilliant green leaves of the cottonwoods hang seed pods, the promise of new life. There are saskatoon berries, one of the first harvests of the summer season; blue lupine and wild roses are in bloom; butterflies seem to cavort above the flowers.

The illustration of the landscape at the conclusion of *Death of the Iron Horse* produces an ironic effect. As young braves ride their horses away from the train they have wrecked and burned because it was invading their land, clouds of dark smoke billow into the air. However, the young men have achieved a pyrrhic victory. The smoke obscures the sun, symbol for the plains people of the revitalizing forces of life. Their raid will no doubt bring retaliation; more trains and white people will invade their land, destroying their centuries-old ways of life. The total absence of background landscape in the illustrations depicting the attack on the train may well symbolize the power of the new technology to destroy the natural world in which the plains Indians lived and on which their spiritual and physical lives depended.

In his fictionalized recreations of historical events and traditional customs in *Custer's Last Battle*, *The Fetterman Fight*, and *Lone Bull's Horse Raid*, Goble adapted the tradition of ledger-book art. This style, drawing on the older male tradition of depicting historical events on buffalo hides, was developed in the 1870s. Imprisoned in Fort Marion, Florida, Native men used pencils, pen and ink, crayons, and watercolors to depict nostalgically scenes from their traditional lives and homelands in ledger-books given them by their white captors. The drawings that filled the lined pages of the ledger-books presented animals and human beings in two-dimensional profile form. Given the retrospective nature of his books—old men's proud reminiscences of their youthful exploits—Goble's use of the ledger-book style is most appropriate.

In the mythical stories, Goble adapts elements of tipi decoration and vision painting. The former celebrated the familial, communal, and social significance of the tipi for its occupants. This dwelling faced east, toward the rising sun, the source of life. Regarding the decorations painted on the outside of the hide coverings, Reginald and Gladys Laubin have written: "Most of the painted tipis had a darkened area at the top to represent the night sky, with white discs for constellations. . . . [There was] a similar border at the bottom with one or two rows of star-signs (fallen stars), and a row of projections for hills or mountains. At the rear and at the top was a cross, said by some to represent a moth, or the sleep-bringer, by others the morning star" (Stott 1984a, 122). Between these bands were depicted animals on which the people depended, with arrows from their mouths to their stomachs representing their life-lines; events from the lives of the occupants or their ancestors; or designs based on personal visions.

In many stories, Goble uses tipi designs to enhance the meanings of the narratives. *Her Seven Brothers* features tipis with buffaloes on them, prefiguring the animals who attack the girl and her adopted family, and stars, embodiments of the celestial beings the girl and her family later become. In *Buffalo Woman*, the absence or presence of buffalo designs on tipis symbolizes the absence or presence of harmony between the human and animal people. *Star Boy* makes the most significant use of tipi patterns. Bands resembling those on tipis run across the tops, the bottoms, or both tops and bottoms of the pages, indicating the extent of the relationships between the earth and sky people. On one of the tipis is a human figure holding a pipe in one of its raised arms, a fan-shaped object in the other. When the title hero meets his father, the Sun, the sky being stands in the same pose and holds the same objects. Interestingly, there are only two tipis in the Iktomi books. In the front of one, seen on the copyright page of *Iktomi and the Boulder*, is the sign "Back Tomorrow" (Goble 1988b, n.p.). The other, in *Iktomi and the Buffalo Skull*, is represented in silhouette in the background of a picture. Iktomi, his head trapped in a skull, struggling in the water, seems as oblivious to the tipi as the people who are setting it up are to him. Perhaps this use of tipis in the Iktomi stories suggests that the buffoon in his egotism is separated from and uncaring of the cultural values tipis embody.

While female characters play important roles in several of Goble's works, the importance of girls and women is celebrated most fully in *Her Seven Brothers*. Significantly, in his illustrations, Goble makes extensive use of the design patterns from the most distinctive art-form of the women of the northern plains: quill-work. Using carefully prepared and dyed porcupine quills, they created exquisite designs, many of them containing symbolic meanings now unknown, to adorn clothing they made for the children of their families. Goble emphasizes the importance of this activity: "*Her Seven Brothers* showed that the art of the quill-workers . . . could take them out of this world into higher realms" (Goble 1992c, 5). Without brothers and uncourted by young men, the heroine, who feels a closeness to the animals and spirit beings, decorates clothing using quill-working secrets said to have been communicated to her by Porcupine "who climbs trees closest to Sun himself" (Goble 1988a, n.p.). She leaves the village carrying seven sets of clothing that she gives to a group of boys to whom she becomes mother and sister, the central figure in a new family unit. Attacked by buffaloes intent on capturing the heroine, the group ascends to the skies where they become the stars of the Big Dipper. The heroine's quill work, seen in several of the illustrations, symbolizes her link to the animal and spiritual worlds and her sense of family unity. The characters' continued existence in the sky is an ongoing reminder of her work and the values it mirrors.

Vision paintings, most frequently placed on warriors' shields, represented the incursion of spirit beings and powers into the lives of human beings. Waving lines, stylized representations of lightning, a potent spiritual force, frequently emphasized the sacred content of these paintings. Goble uses such shields in the battle scenes of *Custer's Last Stand*, *The Fetterman Fight*, and *Lone Bull's Horse Raid*. Not surprisingly, Iktomi, who is overdressed in traditional regalia at the beginning of each of his misadventures, never carries such a shield. He is oblivious to all powers but those of his own ego.

Similar supernatural designs appear in Goble's retellings of the myths, all of which feature interactions between the human and supernatural worlds. When the neglected brothers in *The Lost Children* are translated into the sky, or when, in *Crow Chief*, the savior Falling Star descends to the earth, their areas of passage are marked by luminescently colored columns bordered by waving bands. Searching for the home of his father, the hero of *Star Boy* follows a glowing trail of waving lines created by guiding loons. In *Love Flute*, elk men communicate the secrets of the flute and, in *Her Seven Brothers*, porcupines disclose the secrets of quill working through similar flowing lines. In the climactic scene of *The Gift of the Sacred Dog*, when the boy on his vision quest learns of the horses that will save his people, stylized thunderbirds, flowing ribbon patterns adorning their wings, swoop toward the earth, while blue lines of color curl upward. The two worlds are joined. It is apt that in *Death of the Iron Horse* vision lines are found only at the beginning of the story, before the arrival of the white people who will seek to destroy the spiritual basis of traditional Native life.

Closely linked to the supernatural lines of power found in the vision paintings is the radiating sun circle design. The sun was seen as the life source of the plains people, who celebrated its influence in the annual Sun Dance ceremonies of spiritual and physical renewal and rejuvenation. Concentric circles of rays, often painted with the different colors of the spectrum, symbolized not only the sun's power, but also the circles of harmony that unified all living beings and dimensions of life. That the porcupine who gives the girl the secret of quill working in *Her Seven Brothers* is an intermediary between the sun and human beings is indicated by the fact that his body is surrounded by radiating circles. The flute with which the young lover courts his lady on the half-title page of *Love Flute* is a sacred gift of the spirits and animals, and the couple are united with the sun circle behind them. When the Great Spirit appears to the human beings in *The Great Race*, when the Sun Man greets the lost children in the sky world, or when the Sun awaits Star Boy at the end of the latter's quest, radiating circles emphasize the spirit power of these celestial beings. As a clue to its sacred nature, the horse on the cover of *The Gift of the Sacred Dog* is embraced by an arch from one of the sun circles. Such sun designs appear above Iktomi in only two of his escapades, and his response is only to complain about the excessive heat. In its encircling, embracing quality, the sun circle design is an appropriate visual metaphor for the major theme in Goble's works: the need of human beings to achieve harmony with all creatures that exist under the powerful, life-giving sun.

This analysis of Paul Goble's picture books has focused on aspects of language and elements of landscape and traditional plains' iconography as they are characteristically employed throughout his works. These elements serve to embody and communicate as fully as is possible in picture book form the meanings the stories may have had for tellers of or listeners to the oral versions. A more detailed examination of one of the adaptations of a myth, *The Girl Who Loved Wild Horses*, and one of the trickster stories, *Iktomi and the Berries*, will show more fully how, in each book, Goble combines the visual and verbal texts to achieve a unified, artistic entity that is greater than the sum of its component parts.

The Girl Who Loved Wild Horses emphasizes the importance of horses to the physical and cultural lives of the plains peoples. Generally within a generation of the first appearance of the animals in a given territory, they had become basic elements of the people's lives. Relatively sedentary people became nomadic hunters and, as more than one historian has noted, members of one of the three or four greatest equestrian cultures of all times. Horse handling and breeding skills were quickly developed, and, with these big-dogs, great-dogs, red-dogs, magic-dogs, or elk-dogs, as horses were variously called, Native groups were able to move their camps easily, hunt buffalo, and raid enemy villages. The arrival of the horse considerably altered social structure: wealth was now measured by the number of horses owned, and generosity, by the number given away. Young men earned social prestige by going on horse raids, often venturing into the midst of hostile villages to steal the mounts of prominent enemy warriors, a practice Goble described in *Lone Bull's Horse Raid*.

However, as Frank Gilbert Roe has noted, "the most profound influences exerted by the coming of the horse into Indian life were in the spiritual realm" (Stott 1984a, 119). For example, young men were reported to have received spiritual visions of horses that were later to become their own, and a horse medicine cult developed in which shamans used the accepted supernatural powers of horses to influence the course of tribal events. Not surprisingly, the horse was important in the visual and verbal art of the traditional plains peoples. Horse figures believed to embody spiritual powers were important possessions, and images of horses adorned tipis and articles of clothing. Most important, the horse was a major subject of poetry and mythology. Origin accounts from across the plains explain the why and the how of the arrival of the first horses by emphasizing supernatural donors and worthy recipients. John Ewers wrote that "These myths constitute evidence that to the native mind the horse was a godsend of importance comparable to that of their most sacred ceremonies [these generally believed to have been given by a sacred White Buffalo Woman]" (Stott 1984a, 120).

The Girl Who Loved Wild Horses, winner of the 1979 Caldecott Medal, is based on traditional sources; however, Goble's retelling, as he has noted, is his own, a synthesis of many sources, the result of his extensive study of plains art and culture, and a response to his daughter's love of horses. The underlying theme of the book is the unity of all creatures. According to Goble, the book expresses "the Native American rapport with nature" (Stott 1984a 121). A young woman noted for her ability to tend horses and for her great rapport with them is carried away with the herd during a summer storm that flashes the supernatural lightning across the sky. When she is discovered a year later by the villagers, she is leading a young colt. Unhappy back at home, she rejoins the wild horses she has befriended, and, years later, she disappears.

Her people then see the chief of the wild stallions running with a magnificent mare who, it is implied, is the girl. She has found fulfillment in nature. "Today," the closing lines of the narrative state, "we are still glad to remember that we have relatives among the Horse People. And it gives us joy to see the wild horses running free" (Goble 1978, n.p.).

The presence in the story of what the Lakota would call *wakan*, or spirit power, and the movement toward a union between the girl and the horse are visually embodied in the illustration on the half-title page, and in the illustration for the final page of narrative. In the former, the girl is mounted on the back of the chief of the horses. Behind them are the radiating arcs of the sun circle; part of the innermost arc forms the white line marking the curve of the stallion's neck. No other animals are in the picture, nor are there any flowers. In the latter illustration, a doublespread, the girl, now transformed into a horse, stands on the hill with her mate, the line of her mane also part of the arc of the sun circle. The two are facing in opposite directions, creating a sense of balance. Pairs of birds and animals cavort with each other; flowers bloom among the sagebrush. The significant differences between the two very similar illustrations indicate the incompleteness of the girl's life at the beginning, or, in general terms, the lack of complete harmony between the human and animal worlds, and the fulfillment achieved at the conclusion with her transformation. Moreover, the use of the sun circles emphasizes the spiritual aspects of the story. What has occurred is truly marvellous, an indication of the presence of great powers operating in the lives of people and animals. Visually a part of the sacred circle, the two are part of a unified and harmonious universe, sharing their fulfillment with the birds, animals, and plants around them.

The illustrations placed between these two pictures depict the gradual movement toward the union of the central characters and their worlds. On the title and copyright pages, the girl's fascination with and desire to befriend horses is indicated. First, she lies on her blanket looking at five horses; then she stands before five others, her hands spread in a gesture of greeting. It is worth noticing that in each of these illustrations there are five horses, one of which stands apart from the others, alone, and that there are two groups of horses, the second group being part of the wild herd she joins. Clearly the girl is moving away from her human home toward a group in which one of the animals does not have a companion. The two doublespreads illustrating the storm are dominated by towering thunderclouds and forks of lightning. Her movement away from the secure world of her childhood is caused by more than natural events; the supernatural powers embodied in the thunder and lightning are involved. When the girl first sees the spotted stallion, she is reclining on her blanket as she was early in the story. However, there are no tipis around; her position seems to suggest dazed wonderment; and instead of watching placidly grazing ponies, she perceives a vital, active wild animal, "strong and proud and more handsome than any horse she had ever dreamed of" (Goble 1978, n.p.). A rainbow arcs over the horse's body.

Tensions, fear, and separation are emphasized in those illustrations in which the girl is discovered and returned to her village. First, the stallion stands between the human beings and the girl; then, he is seen in a series of aggressive positions, pawing the air and kicking his heels as she flees from her human pursuers. The separation is complete when the girl is back at her village. In the upper left-hand corner of the picture, in the background, is the silhouette of the horse, small on the horizon, his head in the air as he calls to the girl. She is seen in the foreground in the lower right-hand corner, separated from him by the intervening distance, a wall of tipis, and two human figures. Whereas, in the first picture of the village, one of the tipis had been decorated with a horse figure, in this one there are no horse designs. The gulf between the people and the horses is at its greatest.

The final three doublespread illustrations depict the stages in the resolution of the conflict and the establishment of a new relationship between people and animals. First, the human beings invite the wild horses into the village where they are seen in the foreground, the shadowy mesas and tipis behind them, the people in front, regarding them intently. The spotted stallion is the dominant member of the group, rearing joyously, not aggressively, as he had earlier. Then, when the girl is back in nature, she leads a colt and rides a black mare, a foreshadowing of her transformation into a black mare. Blue lupine are in bloom; adult buffaloes and a calf graze nearby; there is an abundance of butterflies, and a large sun is above. The girl wears different clothing: a red, rather than blue dress, adorned with elk teeth. This illustration marks the final stage before her complete transformation into a horse. Back in the natural world, she still retains her human form and each year she revisits her village. That her assimilation into the herd is as yet incomplete is further symbolized by the fact that the sun is a simple orange ball emitting no rays of power. On the next page, the union is completed, both the girl and the sun are transformed, and, as has been noted above, the design of the illustration includes the mare, the stallion, and the sun in one unifying circle.

Goble sets the myths in a time when animals, people, and spirits interrelated, and the historical stories occur during the last half of the nineteenth century, but Goble gives his adaptations of stories about the Lakota trickster Iktomi a contemporary, late twentieth-century setting. This is appropriate, for trickster stories have been constantly updated to reflect changed conditions, as well as changing relationships between Native and white people.

The trickster frequently ended up as the foolish victim of his own actions. Such is the case in *Iktomi and the Berries*. Denouncing white people, Iktomi sets out to hunt in the traditional way, nearly drowns himself, and returns home looking very much like the white people he rejected. The illustration accompanying the first page of narration shows him dressed for hunting "in the old traditional way" (Goble 1989b, n.p.). He arrives with a coil of rope, coyote-skin disguise, quiver of arrows, skinning knife, ashwood bow, and strike-a-light bag, and he wears a wig, traditional vest, leggings, and moccasins. The objects of his hunt are prairie dogs with which he hopes to make a feast designed to impress friends and relatives. However, his costume and accoutrements are unsuitable for his task, and his preparation for the hunt is inadequate. He has more implements than are necessary, and his coyote-skin disguise would not have worked against prairie dogs. Coyotes frequently lurked at the edge of buffalo herds, and hunters wore these hides in order to move closer to their prey without appearing unusual. Since coyotes often preyed on prairie dogs, Iktomi's garb would only have frightened them off. Finally, even if the hides did provide an effective disguise, Iktomi is wearing too many clothes (and highly ornamental ones at that) to be able to move near the animals quickly and unobtrusively. An illustration on the copyright page suggests that he has not performed the preparatory ceremonial rituals traditional hunters practised. A brass bed is positioned outside under an arbor. Next to it, an alarm clock shows the time: 10 o'clock in the morning. Did Iktomi lie comfortably in bed until a time too late to hunt effectively and then quickly overdress and depart?

Having failed to spot any of the prairie dogs, who are all around him, Iktomi blames their apparent scarcity on white people, who earlier killed the buffalo and who, he says on the title page, are guilty, in the person of Paul Goble, of telling stories about him. Shifting his attention to ducks, he falls off a bank he cannot see because of his coyote-skin disguise, notices what he thinks are berries in the water, and tries unsuccessfully four times to gather them, nearly drowning himself in the process. His four attempts may be a parody of the sacredness of the number four among the plains people. Interestingly enough, he uses a European expression, "Third time lucky!" (Goble 1989b, n.p.) before a dive in which his head becomes stuck in the mud. This incident may also be a parody, this time of a creation myth widespread on the northern plains. In the "Earthdiver" type of creation story, the world is covered by water and a small animal dives to the bottom, coming up with a handful of mud from which new land is created. In each of his four dives, Iktomi comes up empty handed, and, in the final attempt, with a rock attached to a rope tied around his neck, he nearly drowns.

Goble's statement that "Tales about Iktomi remind us that unsociable and chaotic behavior is never far below the surface" (Goble 1988b, n.p.) is quite literally pictured in the illustrations depicting the "diving." In 10 of 12 pictures, the character does not stand steadily on his two feet. He is pictured lurching forward and falling backward, plunging downward, diving sideways in one direction and then being pulled sideways in another. In two pictures, his head is not seen as his body is being pulled off the page. He has, as it were, lost his head. What is interesting is that the angle of his body is never the same in successive illustrations. Accordingly, readers/viewers are being constantly unsettled as they must change their angle of viewing the character. Goble has made his audience participate in the chaos Iktomi's foolish actions have caused.

In this group of illustrations, as well as in those that precede and follow, Iktomi successively loses the items of traditional clothing and the implements with which he had set out. In the final picture of the book, only the moccasins are left. Iktomi now wears a T-shirt, green boxer shorts, gym socks, and a wrist watch. The derider of white people, a person whose actions, despite his avowals of traditional ways, are a parody of tradition (much of it sacred), seems like a white man himself. Even his hair, which he had covered in a wig made up to resemble traditional braids, is close-cropped. Goble has noted that many Cheyenne apply the word *Veho* to both white people and the trickster, and quotes a Native woman who remarked, "He is like some tourists who come into an Indian village not knowing how to behave or what to do" (Goble 1989b, n.p.). As Goble's account of the trickster's actions and the style of his undergarments strongly imply, there is more white man than traditional Native in Iktomi. He is not even a successful trickster!

In a recent interview, Paul Goble commented on the fact that he only adapts stories from the northern plains: "I was once with the Zunis at the invitation of their schools; they wanted me to write stories of their mythology. But how can I? I know almost nothing about them, and would make major and minor mistakes all the time" (Goble 1992c, 6). Using his long familiarity with the history and traditions of the plains peoples, drawing on his close friendship with many of them, and engaging in extensive research before creating each book, he has justly earned the high praise his work has received. The approach of Gerald McDermott, who has retold myths and trickster stories from around the world and who has also received great praise, is much different and provides both a contrast and a complement to Goble's methods.

NATIVE FACES OF THE UNIVERSAL HERO IN THE PICTURE BOOKS OF GERALD MCDERMOTT

Like Paul Goble, Gerald McDermott has retold legends of hero quests and folktales about tricksters. However, *Arrow to the Sun: A Pueblo Indian Tale*, *Raven: A Trickster Tale from the Pacific Northwest*, and *Coyote: A Trickster Tale from the American Southwest* are not part of a group of stories dealing with one specific Native culture area or group. They are titles in a collection of

McDermott's stories of hero quests and trickster tales from around the world. They reflect his training in modern graphic art, his own personal interests, and the influence of Joseph Campbell on his works.

In several essays and interviews, McDermott has spoken of the presence of these diverse elements in his books.

> The goal of my quest as an author and illustrator is to give contemporary voice and form to traditional tales; to release the spirit of the story through my own words and pictures, to infuse it with my own spirit, emotions, and energy. . . . Once these tales have passed out of their original community and context, those elements that transcend time and space, those essential ideas that are touchstones of wisdom and insight, become the basic material for the artist, the themes upon which new works will be composed. It becomes a form of literature, not archaeology or anthropology. At its core is tradition, but the finished form is unmistakably that of the individual artist. (McDermott 1988, 1-2)

His first animated motion picture, *The Stonecutter*, contains McDermott's basic theme: "the idea of the individual who goes out on a quest of self-fulfillment, the hero quest, in a phrase, and there was a really unconscious need to tell that story in many different ways. I was drawn again and again to the same story, even though I must have read a thousand tales just to choose the ones I was to use" (Stott 1979, 2). *Arrow to the Sun* has basic thematic similarities to *The Magic Tree*, a tale from the Congo; to *The Stonecutter*, from Japan; to *Sun Flight*, from Greece; and to *The Knight of the Lion*, from England. The film version of *Arrow to the Sun* lists Joseph Campbell, the mythographer and literary critic, as a consultant. McDermott, who had met him while working on an earlier film, commented about Campbell's influence on his adaptations of traditional stories: "Campbell has shown that the prime function of mythology is to supply the symbols that carry the human spirit forward, 'to waken and give guidance to the energies of life.' These ideas, illuminated in . . . *The Hero with a Thousand Faces*, became the basis for all my subsequent work" (McDermott 1975, 125).

McDermott has noted that the artwork for his books is a blend of his own graphic style and the traditional art styles of the culture from which a story originates.

> I have always admired and been fascinated by the art of the Pueblo cultures and my style, my graphic style, really grew out of a combination of the influence of folk art style, the simple bold approach to symbolism and color, as well as training and background in contemporary graphics, in twentieth-century design. And what I was trying for . . . was a fusion of these two very bold styles, trying to conjure up a feeling for a particular folk art while, at the same time, being true to my own age and putting it in a format, a form that was very contemporary. (Stott 1979, 3)

To depict the hero's failure to achieve a mature relationship with the princess in *The Magic Tree*, McDermott designed faces like those on masks used in traditional initiation rites in the Congo. The successful quest of the young Yvain in *The Knight of the Lion* is depicted in black-and-white ink and lithographic pen drawings that resemble brass rubbings taken from medieval churches.

Like Goble, McDermott precedes the actual work on a book with extensive research into the literature, customs, and art styles of the originating culture. The results of these studies are blended with his own artistic style and philosophy of life to create works that are simultaneously culture specific, universal, and distinctively personal. The characteristics found in all of the adaptations of hero quests are seen most fully and at their best in *Arrow to the Sun*.

In this work, which was awarded the Caldecott Medal as the best American picture book of 1974, McDermott adapts Pueblo iconography to invest his story with implicit meanings that specifically link it to the cultural and religious beliefs of these people. Pueblo religions reflect the basic relationship between the people and the environment. Agriculturalists whose primary crop was corn, the Pueblo peoples depended on the correct mixtures of sun and rain to grow plants in the arid landscape. However, they did not approach the physical environment only in an empirical, scientific manner. Living in a cosmos in which the human, non-human, and supernatural were closely interrelated, they believed that a successful harvest depended to a great extent on their achievement of a right relationship with those powers controlling the rains and the growth of the corn. The Kachina dances, which extended from winter to the time of harvest, were major ritual observances designed to assist in the development of the corn.

Arrow to the Sun reflects this spiritual orientation in many ways. Generally, the boy, whose logo is a stylized cross-section of an ear of corn, lives in an arid land to which he brings life by supplying the rainbow, symbol of sun and rain. On nearly every page, the visual elements reflect the cultural processes by which he succeeds. The designs on the endpapers approximate the stylized rain cloud designs found throughout Pueblo artwork; the orange colors parallel the dry land; both the logo and the boy's hair style (which develops in the story) emphasize the centrality of corn; and, finally, the rainbow on which he dances signals the arrival of rain and life for the people.

Moreover, the manner in which the boy proves himself worthy of bringing the power of the sun to the people is deeply rooted in elements of Pueblo belief. McDermott has done his research thoroughly and has implicitly embedded it within his presentation of the tests the hero undergoes on the sun. It is appropriate that the boy enter four kivas, for the kivas, chambers entered through a hole in the roof, were sacred places where, among other things,

Pueblo youths were initiated into the mysteries of the spiritual lives of the people. What happens in the story's kivas is at once important to the specific quest of the boy and generally to the religious life of the people. The boy must successively enter rooms containing lions (cougars), serpents (rattlesnakes), bees, and lightning. In terms of the culture, his four tests involve steps necessary to help the corn grow. Mountain lions symbolize war societies, and, in taming the lions of the first kiva, the boy is establishing the peace necessary for agriculture. Rattlesnakes were not only valuable pest controllers, attacking the rats who ate stored corn, they were also important in rain-making ceremonies. After being used in ritual dances, they were released at the edges of the villages so that they could return to the hills, there to report to the rain spirits the reverences accorded them by the people. In turning the snakes into a circle, symbol of unity and harmony, the boy is extending to them the necessary reverence. By forcing the bees to order themselves into a functioning hive, he is establishing the organization that is necessary if the processes of pollination are to occur. Finally, in submitting himself to the supernatural power of lightning, so frequently seen above the hills beyond the villages, he is able to achieve new power and bring sun and rain to the people.

Analyzing the story in the light of Pueblo culture, we see that the boy is much more than a rejected child who achieves peer group recognition. In his quest, he establishes his identity as the son of the Lord of the Sun, and, to do that, he undergoes tests that fulfill the prime responsibility of a god—social responsibility and leadership. In the case of Pueblo culture, displaying social responsibility and leadership involved engaging in those spiritual activities necessary for the creation of a bountiful harvest. The story is thus an accurate reflection of Pueblo culture, visually, physically, and spiritually. And it is accurate not just in its presentation of these different aspects, but in its presentation of these as integrally linked.

Although based on Pueblo culture, *Arrow to the Sun* cannot be traced to a specific source. Several collections of Pueblo mythology contain tales that include incidents and motifs which reappear in McDermott's story. However, just as he has drawn from various elements of the culture, he has also drawn from each of these stories to create his own unique work.

By reading *Arrow to the Sun* against this brief survey of Pueblo culture and mythology, it becomes apparent that the picture book is an eclectic mixture. But it is far more than a pastiche or kaleidoscope of fragments McDermott gleaned from his studies; *Arrow to the Sun* is, in both words and pictures, a tightly unified narrative. While a specific source cannot be found in the ethnological background, there is a structural principle underlying it. Joseph Campbell's ideas about the quest of the hero can be seen as the unifying force giving shape to and even dictating the ultimate meanings of the elements of Pueblo mythology found in *Arrow to the Sun*. The central thesis of *The Hero with a Thousand Faces* has been quoted by McDermott: "A hero ventures forth from the world of common day into a region of supernatural wonder: fabulous forces are there encountered and a decisive victory is won: the hero comes back from this mysterious adventure with the power to bestow boons on his fellow man" (Campbell 1949, 30). Reading Campbell's study explains the universal meanings of the elements of Pueblo culture that McDermott included in the book.

At the beginning of his life, the Campbell hero lives in obscurity, without a known father and often despised by the people around him. "He and/or the world in which he finds himself suffers from a symbolical deficiency" (Campbell 1949, 37). However, "The godly powers . . . are revealed [finally] to have been within the heart of the hero all the time" [Campbell 1949, 39]. In *Arrow to the Sun*, neither the boy, his mother, nor his peers recognize his paternity, the source of the latent powers within him. Not only the actions of the other children and the unhappiness of the mother and son, but also the dominant orange colors of the first half of the book, reflect the deficiency. There is no rain, the corn has not yet ripened; and the aridity of the land parallels the state of the people who jeer and reject the boy. All fail to see the potential of the boy, symbolized by the corn-sun logo that he has worn since his conception. But the visual depiction of the logo travelling from the sun to the maiden's home symbolizes, in Campbell's words, "the communication of divine energy to the womb of the world" (Campbell 1949, 42).

The boy's search for his father is an integral part of the quest as defined by Campbell. After living in obscurity, "[The hero] is thrown inward to his own depths or outward to the unknown; either way, what he touches is a darkness unexplored. And, this is a zone of unsuspected presences, benign as well as malignant. . . . alone in some little room . . . the young world-apprentice learns the lesson of the seed powers" (Campbell 1949, 326-27). The boy's journey is a lonely one, foiled twice by individuals who cannot give answers. Even Arrow Maker, the wise one, does not give him an answer, but, pointing him in the right direction, sends him outward into the darkness of space, again alone. Even when he meets the Lord of the Sun, his father, he must continue his solitary tests, entering the kivas to face animals that could kill, but that, when properly controlled, help him in bringing the boon back to the earth. Campbell has noted that "The realm of the gods is a forgotten dimension of the world we know" (Campbell 1949, 217). We have seen that the animals of the kivas represent those that are found in the southwestern landscape and that are related to the physical growth of the corn crops. The boy rediscovers their spiritual potentials; in controlling them, he makes it possible for these energies to revitalize the world to which he will return.

The test of the fourth kiva is the most important; in the other three the boy is an actor, but here he is acted upon. The potentially dangerous lightning does not destroy him; rather, it transforms him, bringing him to his full potential. Trailing a rainbow, wearing the multicolored vestments of his new status, the boy is prepared to return to his home. This relates to Campbell's argument that:

> The effect of the successful adventure of the hero is the unlocking and release again of the flow of life into the body of the world. The miracle of this flow may be represented in physical terms as the circulation of food substance, dynamically as the streaming of energy, or spiritually as the manifestation of grace. . . . An abundant harvest is a sign of God's grace; God's grace is the food of the soul; the lightning bolt is the harbinger of the fertilizing rain, and at the same time the manifestation of the released energy of God. (Campbell 1949, 40)

The illustrations of the concluding pages of *Arrow to the Sun* make it abundantly clear that McDermott is depicting this process. After being struck by the lightning, the boy trails the rainbow behind him, an emanation of his new power. On the final doublespread, he dances on a rainbow, surrounded by the figures representing the kiva powers on one side and figures representing the growing corn on the other. In the background, the sun and his mother, the sky father and earth mother, look on. The circular designs and the abundance of color indicate the unity and the new vitality he has given to a world that once rejected him.

McDermott's visuals, while reflecting the Pueblo culture, are influenced by Campbell's ideas. One final obervation will confirm this influence. McDermott has stated that he invented the boy's logo himself. "In searching for a graphic motif that would unite these two concepts [of sun and corn], I slowly turned an ear of corn in my hands, studying the color, texture, and form. Then I broke the ear in half. At that moment, the symbol hidden beneath the surface was revealed" (McDermott 1975a, 127). McDermott is here describing his movement from a Hopi symbol to a universal one. Although McDermott does not state it explicitly, it seems clear that the logo that emerged from the cross-section of corn is what Campbell has called "the World Navel." Campbell explained the significance of this mandala image in terms that cast light on *Arrow to the Sun*. "The hero as the incarnation of God is himself the navel of the world, the umbilical point through which the energies of eternity break into time. Thus the World Navel is the symbol of the continuous creation" (Campbell 1949, 4). This navel-like logo on the boy's torso reveals the spiritual power of the sun that, through the boy's energy, has become manifest on Earth in the growing corn.

Considered in the light of Joseph Campbell's ideas, *Arrow to the Sun* is not so much a specific treatment of a Native American culture—although it is this in part and an excellent treatment as well—but more a variant of a theme McDermott explored in all of his works of the 1970s. The boy shares kinship with Tasaku, Mavungo, Icarus, Osiris, and Yvain, heroes of other McDermott books. The setting is not only a Pueblo village and the mythic landscapes of Pueblo culture, but also a general landscape of world mythology.

Although not so important to the procuring of food as the Sun's child was to the Pueblo people or the mythic hunter was to the plains peoples, Raven is the central figure in the mythology of the Tsimshian, Tlingit, and Haida peoples of the northwest coast. He plays many roles—creator, culture-hero, transformer, and trickster. Like such similar characters as Coyote and Nanabozho, he is extremely clever and often possesses magical qualities. Sometimes his work is beneficial: creating the world, sometimes creating human beings, providing benefits for human beings, and giving the landscape, plants, and animals their present form. At other times, he uses his abilities to satisfy his voracious appetite and enormous lust. The stories, which are believed to have originated in Siberia, have travelled across the Arctic and down the west coast of North America to what is now Washington State. Some of them suggest the influence of shamanism; Raven, in Tlingit legend, is said to have been the first shaman. While some of the tales were intended to provide comic instruction and delight, especially those dealing with the bird's lust and greed, many were considered extremely serious, although elements of humor can occasionally be seen lingering at their edges. Raven is sometimes presented as a man who dons a raven cloak in order to fly and sometimes as a bird who can transform himself into a human being.

The best known of the Raven stories forms the basis of McDermott's picture book *Raven*. In traditional versions, the tale includes most or all of the following plot elements. Flying in a world of darkness, the bird decides, as much for his own good as for anyone else's, to fly to the sky world where an old man, often a chief, selfishly keeps daylight. There he sees the old man's daughter, whose beauty he is quick to notice; he transforms himself into an evergreen needle that falls into a spring and that she then inadvertently swallows, and he causes himself to be born as a baby boy, whose distinguishing features are a protuberant nose and round, bright eyes. Noticing a box or bag that contains the light, he begins to cry so loudly that his doting grandfather allows him to play with it. Releasing the sun, Raven resumes his bird form, grabs the sun in his beak, and flies away. Meeting some human beings who fear the light and refuse to give him some of their fish, he angrily tosses the sun into the sky. In some versions of the legend, Raven, flying out through the smokehole, becomes covered with soot, thus acquiring his present color.

The elements of this legend reveal the complexity of Raven. A shaman with spirit powers, he experiences a physical attraction to a young woman; bird-man-spirit, his actions appear to be selfishly motivated, but nonetheless benefit human beings. Egotistical, he loses his beautiful coat in escaping, assuming his dull black color. Jennifer Gould has stated that the story marks "a turning point in the history of the order of the universe" (Goodchild 1991, 110), with the transformation of a world of darkness into one of light. The new state symbolizes the end of formlessness, chaos, blindness, and self-centeredness and the beginning of social interaction and organization, as well as insight. Certainly the story represents a reconciliation between binary opposites—light and dark, male and female, human and animal, physical and spiritual, egocentric and sociocentric—that French anthropologist Claude Levi-Strauss considered the essential function of myths for the societies that created them. Finally, it is worth noting that the myth has been extensively examined by Joseph Campbell in several of his books, including his *Historical Atlas of World Mythology*.

McDermott's adaptation follows the basic outline of the legend. In a world of darkness, Raven sets out to find the light, causes himself to be born the grandson of the possessor of the light, and tricks the old man into letting him play with the light, which he then releases into the sky. Noticeably absent are Raven's initial desire to find light to make his own life easier, his physical attraction to the chief's daughter (although in one illustration his eyebrow is raised as part of what looks like an appreciative leer), and his release of the light because frightened human beings do not immediately give him some of their fish. McDermott has the hero begin his quest because "[m]en and women lived in the dark and cold. Raven was sad for them" (McDermott 1993, n.p.). At the conclusion, it is stated that he gave the sun "to all the people" (McDermott 1993, n.p.) and that the people to this day feed Raven in thanks for his gift. McDermott also omits the explanation of Raven's black color, an element peripheral to the story's main focus.

Both the choice of this story as one of a series of trickster tales McDermott published in the early 1990s and the nature of his adaptation are not surprising when *Raven* is considered in relation to his other picture books. McDermott has commented on the importance of myth in presenting a mediation between extremes, in presenting characters, and, by extension, readers with examples of ways of life that offer unity and completeness. Many of these trickster stories involve the interaction between the central figures and the sun or moon, with the central figures offering a potential middle way between the sky and earth worlds. In *Anansi*, *Daniel O'Rourke*, *Sun Flight*, *The Stonecutter*, and *Coyote*, wholeness of being, an integration of diverse elements, is not achieved. As its final illustration reveals, *Arrow to the Sun* presents the success of the boy's quest to achieve personal, social, and spiritual fulfillment in terms of a renewal of the relationships between the sun and the earth.

The trickster figure, with his many-sided nature of opposing forces leading him to perform both positive and negative actions, has interested McDermott from early in his career, perhaps because, as scholars have frequently noted, this character symbolizes the conflicting forces at war within the individual that often thwart the search for fulfillment as an individual and a social being. The Ashanti trickster Anansi, whose fragmented nature is illustrated by the distribution of his various attributes among his seven sons, whom he cannot keep from quarrelling, loses the boon, a luminous disc that the sky god removes into the night sky. However, two of the tricksters of McDermott's more recent books are able to integrate their various elements of character, and, in two cases, to work for the good of others. *Zomo the Rabbit* deals with the Nigerian folk hero's quest for wisdom. Having proved to the sky god that he is "clever enough to do the impossible" (McDermott 1992, n.p.), Zomo receives wisdom, which includes courage, common sense, and caution. In *Papagayo the Mischief Maker*, an original story by McDermott, a parrot whose greatest delight has been to annoy the other jungle creatures, uses his cleverness to devise a plan in which all the animals work cooperatively to prevent the moon from being devoured by "the ghost of an ancient monster dog" (McDermott 1980b, n.p.).

Like McDermott's other questers, Raven undergoes a transformation. However, whereas Tasaku's and Mavungu's transformations led to failure, his, like those of Yvain, Osiris, the boy, and Zomo, are positive. Like the Pueblo boy's, his is a miraculous birth; like the boy, Osiris, and Yvain, his transformation is beneficial to other people. However, there is a significant difference. Raven's birth and rebirth are self-induced; he is a fully realized, integrated individual at the beginning of the story and consciously wills his transformation so that he may help others. In some ways, Raven, although male, is the creator of new life. His actions in relation to the imprisoned sun parallel his own situations. He is "born" in the lodge and later emerges in another form into the larger world. He releases the sun from its confinement in the nested boxes and then takes it into the world where, flinging it into the sky, he gives it independent life.

The written text of *Raven* is short, just under 600 words; it contains mainly words of one or two syllables and is made up of simple, rhythmic sentences. The style is appropriate for the intended audience of young readers and listeners. It also approximates the style of an oral telling and, in its simplicity, allows the illustrations to amplify and expand on the stated meanings. These illustrations bear the hallmarks of McDermott's artistic style, adapted to meet the specific needs of this story and designed to reflect the art of the originating northwest coast culture.

Raven is depicted with bold designs and vivid colors characteristic of the modern graphic art style found in McDermott's works of the 1970s. He also resembles, although in simplified form, the representations of the bird found in traditional Tlingit, Tsimshian, and Haida art of the northwest coast. The picture of him flying into the sky, the sun in his beak, is similar to the most common depictions of him in Native art. It is significant that the color green dominates his wings in McDermott's illustrations, for this color was used by the Native artists of that area to symbolize the supernatural or sacred powers inherent in the being they were presenting. Like the boy in *Arrow to the Sun*, Raven wears a logo appropriate to his story, one which, like the boy's, relates him to the sun. The boy brings the life-giving power of the sun to earth to facilitate the growth of the corn; Raven liberates the sun from the boxes and then the lodge to give light to the literally benighted human beings. A red diamond set against a black background is surrounded by, but appears to be shining across, three concentric rectangles symbolizing the three boxes. Just as the boy's supernatural nature was unknown to the Pueblo villagers, even though it was symbolized by the design on his chest, so too, Raven-child is surrounded by adults who are unaware of the trickster who, even in his human form, wears his distinctive logo.

McDermott presents Raven in boldly stylized abstract illustrations, vividly depicted in primary and secondary colors rendered in gouache. The land-scape, lodge, and human figures are represented in pastels in a more realistic manner. This aspect of McDermott's artistic technique is unique to this book; it emphasizes Raven's centrality to the narrative, the difference between him and both the human figures and the landscape, and his influence on the world around him. The contrast in styles distinguishes Raven from his surroundings and foregrounds him. While much of the landscape is green with conifers, the color is muted, signifying the natural world, unlike the vivid green on Raven's body that is a presentation of the supernatural. Paradoxically, in order to relieve the landscape of its dull green, gray, and blue, caused by endless night, Raven magically turns himself into a pine needle, a bit of natural green, to gain access to the Sky Chief's house. Within the lodge, the only green other than Raven's in the eight doublespreads is a rattle the chief holds in one picture, and part of the designs on the box containing the sun. Again, Raven's centrality and power are emphasized.

As in *Arrow to the Sun*, the hero's beneficial transformation of the land-scape is revealed in part through the use of color. The first three pictures depict the darkness of the world over which Raven flies. Trees are shrouded, their greenness dulled by overlays of dark gray. Human figures and their dwellings can barely be seen. The only light comes from the Sky Chief's house, and it does little to dispel the gloom. In the lodge, yellows and oranges dominate and, as noted above, there are no natural greens. The Sky Chief keeps the light for himself; the natural and human worlds are kept apart from the sun they need so badly. The doublespread depicting Raven flying away from the lodge is in marked contrast to that in which he flew toward it. Now, no light radiates from the dwelling, which is on the extreme left edge of the page. The newly released sun reveals mountains, trees, and a lake in clear outline. The color of the evergreens now resembles that on Raven's wings, chest, and beak. His power is affecting the world. The final illustration, like that of *Arrow to the Sun*, embodies the resolution of the conflict, the achievement, through Raven's mediation, of a vital relationship between the sky and the earth. Raven dominates the picture: behind his head, the sun shines in a clear blue sky; a village, a totem pole, and people in canoes are clearly seen below him. In his beak, Raven holds a fish, a gift from the people who can now see to go about their work. The fish is colored with green and with an orange used for the first time in the portrayal of the stylized figures. The orange shade is a combination of the yellow from the sun and the red prominently featured on Raven's body; it may symbolize the union of the power of the sun and Raven that now allows human beings to acquire more easily the fish on which their life depends.

McDermott's most recent book, *Coyote: A Trickster Tale from the American Southwest*, appeared too late for detailed analysis. However, a brief examination of the process of its composition reveals a new stage in the author-illustrator's approach to traditional Native narratives. Based on a Zuni story collected by the nineteenth-century anthropologist Frank Cushing, *Coyote* tells of the disastrous results of Coyote's attempts to fly with a group of birds. Like two of McDermott's earlier works, *Sun Flight*, the legend of Icarus and Daedalus, and *Daniel O'Rourke*, an Irish folktale, *Coyote* is about an overreacher who falls from the sky because of character flaws. Headstrong and unheeding, Icarus had plunged into the ocean and drowned. Gluttonous and unheeding, Daniel had experienced a nightmare in which he fell from the moon into the water; awakening, he made an unconvincing vow to reform. Following Cushing's version of the tale, McDermott's Coyote plummets earthwards because his egotism annoys the birds who have given him "wings" made from their feathers.

In frequent trips to a Zuni Pueblo elementary school, McDermott had told the story as he was then developing it (Stott, 1994). From the children he learned that the suppliers of feathers were crows, that they had deliberately set out to cause Coyote's fall, and that, after landing in a pool of water, the animal had chased the birds. Tumbling down a mesa, he had rolled in dirt, acquiring the dirty gray-colored fur (he had originally been an almost electric blue) he still has. Whereas *Arrow to the Sun* had been written after extensive research but before McDermott visited the Southwest, *Coyote* emerged in its present form as a result of the author's visits and interaction with Native school children.

Like Paul Goble's picture books, these three by Gerald McDermott reveal the author-illustrator's careful study of and sympathy for traditional Native cultures and their stories. They also reveal contrasting, although equally valid, approaches to the presentation of the mythological stories of Native

Americans. Goble, embodying in his books universal themes of love, courage, cooperation, and respect, emphasizes the specific interpretation given these qualities by plains culture groups. McDermott proceeds in the opposite direction, showing how three of the most significant myths of the peoples of the southwest desert and northwest coast are variations of themes found around the world, different aspects of what his friend and mentor Joseph Campbell called "The Hero with a Thousand Faces."

LIVING BY OCEANS AND DESERTS: REALISTIC PORTRAYALS OF MODERN NATIVE LIFE

Library and bookstore shelves are filled with picture book adaptations of traditional Native tales; however, they contain considerably fewer picture books of realistic stories about historical and modern Native life. Perhaps this is because of the greater appeal that traditional stories from all cultures have had for illustrators and young readers alike. Perhaps it is because, with their ready-made plots, the old stories provide specific starting points and frameworks for elaborating character and conflict and for designing vivid, imaginative illustrations. And perhaps it is because, on the one hand, there is a danger of realistic stories becoming thinly disguised social studies texts showing the way little Native boys or girls from specific cultures do live or used to live, and, on the other, because there is a danger of the characters becoming generic children, just like the readers except for differences of clothing, houses, food, and facial features.

However, there are many fine realistic picture books, including those written by Ann Nolan Clark, an award-winning author of stories about Native children of the Southwest and a long-time educator for the Bureau of Indian Affairs. One of her best-known books, *In My Mother's House*, was illustrated by Velino Herrera. Clark designed the book to provide appropriate reading material for the Native children with whom she worked; the book's simple, rhythmic language evokes the parallel structures of much traditional Native poetry. An unnamed young narrator celebrates the Tewa world of eastern New Mexico, beginning with the warmth and security of her mother's house, built by her father, and extending to the distant mountains, the source of the people's water supply. The underlying theme is interrelationship—among members of the family, within the community, and between all human beings and the land, water, plants, and animals. Herrera's illustrations, in full-color and black-and-white, give a detailed picture of the human and natural environments and the activities that take place in them.

At the conclusion, the narrator lists the various aspects of her Tewa world and states, "I string them together/Like beads" (Clark 1941, 56). The metaphor is an apt one for the way the words and pictures join together to create a unified picture of a life that mixes both traditional and 1940s customs and activities.

Although this Caldecott Honor Book is sympathetic, accurate, and well executed, it has limitations that are linked to its worthwhile purpose. Relevant for reading and social studies instruction for Tewa children of 50 years ago, the book is now dated. Pickups have replaced wagons, and tractors have replaced horse-drawn ploughs, and Native children of the 1940s did not, as a tour guide recently remarked to a group of visitors to his pueblo, "spend all their time glued to the TV watching the Flintstones and the Simpsons." Rather than an imaginative recreation of their grandparents' childhood, the book would serve contemporary children as an example of something old-fashioned that their grandparents read when they went to school. Perhaps its secular, educational purpose also explains why there is virtually no treatment of the rich spirituality that underlays all areas of these people's lives, an expression of the reverence with which they regarded the natural and supernatural worlds around them.

Two recent books, both set on Canada's west coast, reflect elements in the lives of contemporary Nootka boys. *A Salmon for Simon*, written by Betty Waterton and illustrated by Ann Blades, and *Jason and the Sea Otter*, written by Joe Barber-Starkey and illustrated by Paul Montpellier, have many similarities. Both are created by non-Native Canadians; both portray the adventures of solitary young boys interacting with sea creatures they encounter; and both conclude with the boys' having achieved new relationships with these creatures and new awareness of the links between themselves and the natural environment. However, both books also contain differences that exemplify two major approaches to creating picture books about modern Native children.

In *A Salmon for Simon*, only one direct reference identifies the title hero as a Native. When Simon calls a salmon "Sukai," the author explains that "Sukai was an old Indian name for the salmon" (Waterton 1978, n.p.). Otherwise, Simon's story resembles many others written for younger children. Living in a village where fishing is a major occupation, Simon has spent all summer unsuccessfully attempting to catch a salmon, and, now that it is September and the spawning run has begun, time is running out for him. Discouraged, he sets off for home thinking that "I'm not good at catching salmon, but I am a good clam-digger" (Waterton 1978, n.p.). On the way, he discovers a salmon trapped in a water-filled hole he and his sisters had dug earlier. Although this is the fish he has been looking for, he decides he should allow it to live and sets about digging a channel through which it can swim back to the deep water and then to the spawning streams. As night falls, he returns to his home cold and sore, "but warm inside" (Waterton 1978, n.p.).

The plot of the story is a universal one: a solitary child is discouraged because he has failed at an activity that would make him a valuable, contributing member of his group. With fortitude and determination, he performs an act that allows him to rejoin his family with a sense of well-being and achievement. The plot is also implicitly culture-specific. For the Nootka people, salmon is the main foodstuff and the ability to fish successfully is vital. Moreover, it is essential that the salmon return to the streams of their birth to spawn and to ensure a supply of fish in later years. Although Simon does not bring home food for this evening's dinner, in helping the salmon to escape from the pool, he has, in a small way, made sure that there will be fish for future dinners.

In her watercolor paintings, Ann Blades, one of Canada's foremost children's book illustrators, has amplified the universal and culture-specific elements of Waterton's written text. Early in the story, Simon's disappointment is pictured as he slouches on a rock staring disconsolately into the water. The lines of his bangs, eyebrows, mouth, and shoulders slope downward as does the outline of the rock. Although the starfish and urchins are of different hues, the colors are muted. The rock is dull gray, the sand is a dingy brown, and the trees are dark green. No sunlight or sky is seen. However, when he begins his task of liberating the salmon, the background lightens considerably: the sand seems a golden brown, the sea sparkles, and the sky is blue. As the fish travels down the channel, a brilliant orange sun sinks into the sea. Simon travels home toward a house illuminated by cheerful light; he strides confidently, a smile on his face. There are no traditional Native artifacts in the pictures; but Simon's facial features and jet black hair indicate that he is Native, and the settings are those of the west coast area where the Nootka live. In both words and pictures, Waterton and Blades have presented the universal conflicts and emotions of the hero while, at the same time, firmly, but implicitly basing them on contemporary west coast Native life.

Nootka history and traditions play an explicit role in *Jason and the Sea Otter*. The title hero, who spends his summer days fishing in an old-style dugout canoe, enjoys watching and listening to the natural world that surrounds him. When he peers into the water, shutting out the sunlight by "pulling his jacket over his head, like an old-fashioned photographer" (Barber-Starkey 1989, n.p.), the boy is making contact with the past, for the kelp (seaweed) he sees was used for a variety of purposes by members of his tribe long before the Europeans arrived. The closeness he feels to his natural environment is something he learned from his grandfather, who had also told him of the traditional winter feasts with their songs and dances. When an animal he has never seen before swims up from the depths, Jason goes back to his village to relate his experience to his grandfather, who sits outside their home "dreaming of days gone by" (Barber-Starkey 1989, n.p.). The old man explains that the boy has seen a sea otter, a once-thriving animal that had been hunted to the verge of extinction by white people. Jason has encountered another link to his past. The boy spends days observing the animal, who now has a mate and who becomes accustomed to him. When Jason falls from his canoe into the freezing waters, the otter is instrumental in saving the boy. Paddling home, Jason imagines a future time in which, like his grandfather, he will be able to tell stories of his past to his grandchildren.

On one level, the tale belongs to a favorite type of children's story in which a young person befriends a wild animal. On another level, it is a story about a modern Native boy establishing links to his past. The grandfather is the facilitator, like the wise old man of many traditional stories. He maintains the continuity of a people's traditions by providing a boy with knowledge of the past necessary for the young person to have a mature and fulfilling future. The otter is a symbol of that past: like the traditions of Jason's culture, it had virtually disappeared with the arrival of European civilization. Emerging from the depths of the sea and soon joined by a mate, it will have a future, just as the cultural beliefs of the Nootka people will have a rebirth because of the responses of individuals like Jason. The otter, which is described as "looking like a friendly little old man" and "lying back like a whiskered old man" (Barber-Starkey 1989, n.p.), is symbolically associated with Jason's grandfather, both being survivors from times long gone. It is appropriate that Jason, who does not at first know what the animal is, must go to his grandfather to learn its identity and find out about its past.

Paul Montpellier's illustrations both depict the events of the narrative and reinforce the symbolic elements of the story. Like Ann Blades's pictures in *A Salmon for Simon*, his are realistic, portraying the west coast setting and the emotions the boy experiences. However, they also contain details that explicitly refer to Native traditions. Jason wears his hair long, as many Native boys and men now do. His canoe is of Nootka design, and an old totem pole, vegetation creeping over it, is in the woods. Near his village there are two other poles. Most significant are three illustrations depicting the old Nootka ways: men fishing from canoes, villagers celebrating the winter feasts, and the people welcoming a newly arrived sailing ship. The designs on the canoes, clothing, and ceremonial regalia are accurately reproduced. And each of the illustrations about the past is framed by a border adorned with stylized designs taken from totem poles and other decorated objects. At each of these points, Jason is remembering what his grandfather told him about the past. However, just as that past is distant from him, the illustrations are set off by the borders from those portraying the immediate present. However, past and present are united in the book's closing picture. As Jason paddles back to his village thinking of the stories he will some day be telling his grandchildren, ghostly images of people from the old times appear in the sky behind the boy. Because past and present are now united for him, Jason will have a rich and fulfilling future.

These picture books depicting old stories, past traditions, and contemporary life provide excellent introductions for children of all ages to various aspects of Native cultures. Through careful, thoughtful engagement with and response to such works, younger readers can develop fuller, more sympathetic and respectful understanding of the histories and present lives of Native peoples. The next step is to introduce them to more complex presentations of the traditional past: nonillustrated adaptations of myths, legends, and folktales.

PICTURE BOOK VERSIONS OF TRADITIONAL TALES

Bernhard, Emery, reteller; illustrated by Durga Bernhard. *Spotted Eagle and Black Crow: A Lakota Legend.* New York: Holiday House, 1993.
In adapting this traditional legend, the author notes that he has "magnified the conflict between Spotted Eagle and Black Crow by making them brothers" (n.p.). This alteration fits the story into the world-wide good/bad brother/sister story motif and emphasizes the positive and negative attitudes and values each embodies. Because they are suitors for the same woman, Black Crow betrays his brother, abandoning him on a cliff ledge next to an eagle's nest. After four days without food and water—an echo of a young man's traditional preparation for a sacred vision—Spotted Eagle is visited by a supernatural eagle, the possessor of what the Lakota would call *wakan*, or sacred power, who bequeaths it to him, stating that it must never be misused. With the aid of the eagles, from whom he receives a feather, he is able to return to his village, where he fights against attacking Pawnee, forgives his dying brother, and marries his beloved. True to his word, the hero offers thanks to his eagle brothers. The story honestly depicts the conflicting values and emphasizes the centrality of the eagles as intermediaries between the spirit and physical worlds. The visionary climax of the narrative is powerfully represented by a doublespread in which the young man is dwarfed by the supernatural eagle from whose claws flash lightning, emblem of spirit power. Upper elementary and junior high students can notice general similarities between the brothers in this story and those in the Iroquois story *The Woman Who Fell from the Sky* (Bierhorst 1993) and can then discuss the unique cultural aspects of the personalities of each set of brothers. Middle elementary students can see how the illustrations reinforce the differences between the brothers.

Bierhorst, John, reteller; illustrated by Leo and Diane Dillon. *The Ring in the Prairie: A Shawnee Legend.* New York: Dial Press, 1970.
Underlying virtually all Native star myths are beliefs about harmony and interrelationship between the celestial and terrestrial worlds. In this story, White Hawk, whose name suggests this interrelationship, is incomplete, for

even though he is an accomplished hunter, he is without a family. However, when he uses his spirit powers to capture a star maiden who becomes the mother of his son, he creates a disharmony, for she misses her sky family and home. Returning there with her son, she leaves White Hawk desolate. Only through the wisdom and spirit power of the woman's star father is a lasting harmony achieved: transformed into birds, the members of the family can travel between the two realms, linking them together. The continued existence of white hawks and mysterious rings on prairie grass are constant reminders of the original legend and its lessons about the importance of family relationships and the links between earth and sky. The young man's initial journey from his home at the western edge of the woodlands onto the unknown prairies testifies not only to his courage but also to the need to enter new areas if one is to encounter supernatural powers. While the Dillons' illustrations do not work so well as their pictures for retellings of African legends, they are culturally accurate and emphasize the supernatural forces pervading the narrative. Students in the upper elementary grades can notice techniques the Dillons use to emphasize the presence of these powers and can see how the illustration on page 2 foreshadows the conclusion. They can discuss the significance of the hero's name and the appropriateness of his final transformation, as opposed to his first one, and can trace the family separations and compare them to those in Paul Goble's *Buffalo Woman*.

Bierhorst, John, reteller; illustrated by Robert Andrew Parker. *The Woman Who Fell from the Sky: The Iroquois Story of Creation*. New York: William Morrow, 1993.

This famous Iroquois myth is one of the best examples of the "Earthdiver" category of creation legends. When an angry husband living in the sky hurls his wife toward the world, spirit people transform themselves into birds and water animals, guiding her down to the back of a turtle (hence the frequent reference among the eastern Native peoples to Earth as "Turtle Island"). A muskrat brings earth from beneath the water, and the woman spreads it on the turtle's back, making the land as it is today. Between them, Sapling and Flint, Sky Woman's twin sons, create the positive and negative elements of the world: the former, rivers, fish, and spring; the latter, dangerous rapids, fish bones, and winter. Their opposing natures are symbolized by the two roads of the Milky Way, which they travel on their return to the Sky World. The woman also ascends, leaving behind the song of prayer the people still use to praise the blessings received from her and Sapling. Parker's gouache and pen-and-ink illustrations are an appropriate complement to the text, particularly the early pages reflecting the original watery world. A group of facing illustrations emphasizes the positive and negative "gifts" of the sons. After noticing the two roads of the Milky Way, upper elementary and junior high readers can discuss the dual natures of the sons, beginning with their names. In addition to listing the opposites mentioned in the story, readers can consider other opposites still existing in the natural and human worlds. The creation of the world from a place of water, as well as the characters of the creators, can be compared to the California creation myth *And Me, Coyote!* (Baker).

Cleaver, Elizabeth, reteller and illustrator. *The Enchanted Caribou.* Toronto: Oxford University Press, 1985.

In this Caribou Inuit (Eskimo) legend, a young woman lost in the fog is rescued and befriended by a hunter and his brothers. When, in spite of their warnings, she allows an evil shaman to enter their tent, Tyya is transformed into a white caribou and joins the nearby herd. The brothers, informed of the situation by the spirit of their grandmother, restore her to her human form. She and the hunter live happily together, and, since that day, hunters do not kill white caribou that might also be enchanted. The story is rich in traditional belief: the importance of the family unit, the good and/or evil power of shamans, the close relationship between hunters and their game, and the need of the former to respect the latter. It is also a powerful female coming-of-age story, as Tyya, who once made dolls for little children, undergoes a kind of deep trance from which she emerges a mature woman. Cleaver's use of shadow puppets, in which silhouette cutouts are projected on a back-lit screen, is appropriate for this legend, giving a feeling for the rugged, foggy landscape and enhancing the aura of the supernatural present in the story. Students in upper elementary and junior high grades can discuss the psychological changes that the girl's physical journey symbolizes, comparing it to parallel situations in such European stories as "Snow White" and "Sleeping Beauty." They can also discuss how the brothers' ceremony and hunting activities relate to Caribou culture.

Cohen, Lee Caron, reteller; illustrated by Shonto Begay. *The Mud Pony: A Traditional Skidi Pawnee Tale.* New York: Scholastic, 1988.

For the plains people, ownership of horses was vital for success in hunting and warfare and for bolstering personal pride. Drawing on a legend collected at the beginning of this century, Cohen tells of a poor boy who, with the aid of a miraculous pony, becomes a great leader of his people. Not owning a horse, he fashions one out of clay, taking "care of it as if it were real" (n.p.). Lost after the tribe departs in search of buffalo, he dreams that his effigy has come to life and awakens to find the dream true. He obeys the animal when it informs him that it is created from Mother Earth and must be protected from rain, and he becomes instrumental in defeating an enemy who is keeping the people from their hunting grounds. When he becomes wealthy in horses and powerful, he grants the horse's request that it be permitted to return to the earth. This is not just another poor, rejected-boy-makes-good children's tale. While it contains universal story elements, it is firmly rooted in its culture, for the boy's early fate befell many orphans: without a horse he was virtually nothing; without proper care and respect for this almost supernatural gift, he would never have succeeded. Although depicting a legend from a culture other than his own, Navajo artist Shonto Begay recreates the supernatural power pervading the legend.

Students in the upper elementary grades can notice how the details of the first three illustrations, when compared to later ones, indicate the boy's separation from the tribe. After having read the narrative, they can discuss the importance of horses to these people. They might also ask why the boy is not given a name.

Cohlene, Terri, reteller; illustrated by Charles Reasoner. *Ka-ha-si and the Loon: An Eskimo Legend.* Mahwah, NJ: Watermill Press, 1990.
While other boys are learning the skills they will need as adults, Ka-ha-si spends his days sleeping. However, unknown to the mocking villagers, he is being prepared for important deeds by loons, emblems of supernatural power to the Eskimo. When his village suffers its greatest hardships—starvation, invasion by hostile people, and natural disaster—the boy uses his newly acquired powers to locate and kill several walruses, defeat a strange giant, and push back encroaching mountains. Having proved himself, he assumes his greatest role, replacing his deceased grandfather as the one who holds up the earth. The story accurately depicts the traditional Eskimo value of working for the well-being of everyone, the use of ridicule to change behavior, and the supernatural power of the loon (the shaman's bird). Ka-ha-si, whose name means The Strong One, is like misunderstood folk heroes from around the world but with specific Eskimo meanings. Reasoner's illustrations accurately reflect the story's events, and a 16-page documentary supplement places the story in historical and contemporary Eskimo contexts. This story can be compared with the Japanese tale of a lazy boy, *The Boy of the Three Year Nap* (Dianne Snyder). Students in the middle elementary grades can contrast the actions of the two boys and their relationships with their mothers and can discuss how the differences reveal different cultural attitudes. The role of loons in this story and in Elizabeth Cleaver's *The Loon's Necklace* can be examined.

Cohlene, Terri, reteller; illustrated by Charles Reasoner. *Turquoise Boy: A Navajo Legend.* Mahwah, NJ: Watermill Press, 1990.
To the people of the plains and southwest, the arrival of horses was considered a miraculous, sacred event. The animal that dramatically altered their lifestyles was seen as a god-send, a divine gift. Turquoise Boy, the son of Sun Bearer and Changing Woman, two of the supreme Navajo deities, wishes to alleviate the difficult living conditions of the people and is told by his mother that he must prove his worth. Like the heroes of many cultures, this involves a departure from home, a long journey, and the overcoming of physical and psychological obstacles. However, the details are specifically Navajo. First, the boy must travel to the four sacred directions where he receives shells and semi-precious gems important to his people. Next he must travel skyward to his father and then beneath the earth, where Mirage Man gives him a vision of horses and sacred pollen. The final direction is significant because for many southwestern peoples living beings emerged from worlds beneath the earth's surface. Several times during the tale the importance of song is mentioned, and, to the Navajo, chants or songs have great spirit power to heal the sick and call forth blessings from

sacred beings. The story invites comparison with Paul Goble's *The Gift of the Sacred Dog* and Gerald McDermott's *Arrow to the Sun*. Students in middle and upper elementary grades can make and illustrate a large map tracing the boy's journeys and can discuss how the events prove the boy's worthiness to bring help to the people.

DePaola, Tomie, reteller and illustrator. *The Legend of the Bluebonnet*. New York: G.P. Putnam's Sons, 1983.

_____. *The Legend of the Indian Paintbrush*. New York: G.P. Putnam's Sons, 1988.

These companion books about the origins of the bluebonnet and the Indian paintbrush, state flowers of Texas and Wyoming, respectively, are both about excluded children who act unselfishly for the good of their people and are given new names. In *The Legend of the Bluebonnet*, the shaman tells the Comanches that the spirits will not end the drought and famine caused by their selfishness until the people burn their most sacred possessions and offer the ashes to the four sacred directions. She-Who-Is-Alone, a poor orphan, willingly gives up her beloved doll and discovers the next day that its blue feathers have been transformed into flowers and that the drought is over. The people acknowledge her goodness by bestowing on her the name One-Who-Dearly-Loved-Her-People. Physically weaker than the other boys, Little Gopher, hero of *The Legend of the Indian Paintbrush*, a member of an unnamed plains tribe, is told by the shaman and by spirit beings that his role is to paint pictures of the hunts, great deeds, and sacred visions of his people. His reward is a batch of special paint brushes that, after he creates his vision of the setting sun, become the Indian paintbrush flowers. The flowers in both stories are reminders of the legends and the virtues of the heroic children. DePaola's illustrations, which accurately reproduce physical details of traditional life, are particularly good in their depictions of styles and purposes of plains art. Students in the early elementary grades can notice the changes in the heroes' names and discuss how their actions and characters prove them worthy of their new names.

Esbensen, Barbara Juster, reteller; illustrated by Helen K. Davie. *Ladder to the Sky: How the Gift of Healing Came to the Ojibway Nation*. Boston: Little, Brown, 1989.

Many Native cultures have legends about the world before it assumed its present form. In some cases, this is a kind of golden age analogous to the time Adam and Eve lived in Eden before the fall. For the Ojibway people of the upper Great Lakes region, this was an era when all people enjoyed great health, living harmoniously in nature and never dying. The very old were carried by spirit beings up a magic vine into the Gitchi Manitou's sky home, there to live happily forever. However, members of a village became jealous because they feared that one young man was favored by the spirits and made his life so miserable that he asked to be taken into the sky. When his grandmother, trying to follow him, broke the law that prohibited touching the magic vine, the people lost their connection with the above world and began experiencing illness and death. In recompense, the spirits gave a specific group—the Mi-di-wi-win, or Grand Medicine People, the secrets of the healing power of plants, secrets the society still uses to help sick Ojibway. In addition to containing the theme of prohibition found in myths around the world, this story emphasizes the close relationship between the Ojibway and the world of nature around them. Davie's watercolor illustrations admirably create the northern woodlands setting, reproduce Ojibway design patterns, and evoke the supernatural presence of the myth. Students in upper elementary and junior high grades can compare the prohibition against touching the vine with the prohibitions in the Book of Genesis and the Greek myth of Pandora. Why are these prohibitions given, and how does each reveal elements of the religious beliefs of each culture? The myth's concepts of death and the afterlife can be compared to those of the plains people depicted in Paul Goble's *Beyond the Ridge*.

Esbensen, Barbara Juster, reteller; illustrated by Helen K. Davie. *The Star Maiden: An Ojibway Tale*. Boston: Little, Brown, 1988.
Set in an era of peace and harmony, a time before the world took its present form, this legend describes the creation of the waterlilies that grow so plentifully in the small lakes of the northern woodlands. When the people, who are fond of watching the night skies, see a new star hovering close to the land, they send two young men to investigate. In a dream vision, one of them is visited by a star maiden who wishes to live close to the people, and he asks the advice of the wisemen in choosing a location. Significantly, they agree to "let her choose the form she will take," respecting her individuality. She and her sisters become the star-shaped flowers floating in the water near the village of her friends. The legend's closing words are directed to the audience: "Touch them gently and remember." Their presence is a reminder of the harmony that existed between human beings, plants, animals, celestial bodies, and spirit beings—a harmony the people should strive daily to maintain. Whereas modern children are frequently told of the incredible distances between the earth and even the moon and the extreme unlikelihood of finding in the stars either landscapes or beings resembling those they know, the Native cosmos emphasized the links between the world around, the world above, and the world beyond. Stars could be human beings or animals elevated to the skies or supernatural beings; a meteor shower could be a group of such beings coming to earth and transforming themselves into waterlilies. The landscape of the Minnesota Ojibway, with its abundance of animals and plants, is emphasized through the double panels and border patterns of each of Davie's pictures. Into this land of plenty, further beauty is added by the waterlilies that dominate the final picture—being represented both realistically and stylistically. Upper elementary and junior high students can examine other Native star and flower myths, seeing how, like this story, they emphasize the spiritual values associated with and linking together the earth and the heavens.

Greene, Ellin, reteller; illustrated by Brad Sneed. *The Legend of the Cranberry: A Paleo-Indian Tale.* New York: Simon and Schuster, 1993.

This tale of the Delaware people of New Jersey tells of the disappearance of the great mastodons whom the Great Spirit created to help human beings. When the huge animals rebelled, destroying and killing, the small animals sought the aid of the Great Spirit. Together the people and animals fought and killed many of the giant animals, but hundreds of people and animals were killed as well. Only the lightning bolts of the Spirit killed or drove away the remaining destructive creatures. In the bogs where many met their end, there appeared fields of pink blossoms of the bitter tasting berries used in making pemmican, poultices, and dyes. The berries were a divine gift, "a symbol of peace and of the Great Spirit's abiding love for the People" (n.p.). In addition to many traditional stories about the misfortunes that befall people who fail to respect the land and its creatures, there are several about what happens when certain animals misuse their size or cleverness to achieve unfair advantage over human beings. Because the mastodons have upset the divinely created harmony and balance, they are destroyed. However, good results from evil: from the place of the animals' death comes a treasured source of food and medicine. Sneed's illustrations, with one exception, are realistic depictions of the people, the animals, and their environment. When the Great Spirit intervenes, vivid, luminescent hues and zig zags of supernatural lightning dominate the page. This story, ideal as Thanksgiving reading for all ages, can form the basis of a discussion of Native belief in the necessity of harmony and respect between people and the rest of creation. Middle and upper elementary students can compare the dominance of the mastodons with that of the buffalo early in Paul Goble's *The Great Race.*

Larry, Charles, reteller and illustrator. *Peboan and Seegwun.* New York: Farrar, Straus and Giroux, 1993.

Based on a simple Ojibway legend collected in the nineteenth century by Henry Rowe Schoolcraft, this picture book describes the defeat of winter by spring. On a cold winter night, a lonely old man is visited by a young man, and each tells the other how his breath transforms the landscape. The rising sun reveals to Seegwun, the Spirit of Spring, that his host is Old Man Winter, and as the sun warms the lodge, Peboan melts, giving way to spring. Although the text makes no reference to human beings, three pictures reveal how the breaths of the two spirits influence human activities: winter is dominated by ice fishing, spring by hunting and birch bark canoe making, and fall by harvesting wild rice. The opening and closing doublespreads present the different appearances of the same landscape in midwinter and late spring. Early elementary students can compare these illustrations, noticing the details that mark the different seasons. They can reread the dialogues listing the effects of the two spirits' breaths and link these to the features of the landscape. They can also compare the story with William Toye's *How Summer Came to Canada.* Middle elementary students can discuss Ojibway activities depicted in the illustrations and notice how these are influenced by seasonal cycles.

Littlechild, George, illustrator; translated and edited by Freda Ahenakew. *How the Birch Tree Got Its Stripes.* Saskatoon, Canada: Fifth House, 1988.

_____. *How the Mouse Got Brown Teeth.* Saskatoon, Canada: Fifth House, 1988.

Based on assignments in an Intermediate Cree course at the Saskatchewan Indian Languages Institute, these simplified versions of two well-known Native tale types—the greedy hunter and the sun snarer—were written by students of Cree, translated into English, and illustrated by a Cree artist. In the former, Wisahkecahk, having caught a large number of ducks, instructs two birch trees to hold him fast, keeping him away from the cooking food so that he may discipline himself against hunger. However, when the birches refuse to release him while other animals devour his feast, he becomes so angry that, gaining his freedom, he lashes the trees with willow branches, giving them marks they bear to this day. As usual, the trickster acts foolishly, deciding to test himself unnecessarily and punishing the birches unjustly. Their stripes are an ongoing reminder of his folly. The latter story is another pourquoi legend explaining the origin of a distinctive animal or natural feature. When a boy ignores his grandmother's injunction against climbing and sets a snare on some branches, he traps the sun, creating continuous night. After several larger animals fail to liberate the sun, a little mouse chews through the snare, burning his teeth brown. In each of the books, Littlechild's illustrations add dimensions to the simple text, emphasizing the legendary elements of the tales. Students in the early elementary grades can discuss the moral lessons of the stories. Those in the middle grades can search for Native pourquoi legends explaining characteristics of plants and animals in their geographical area.

McDermott, Beverly Brodsky, reteller and illustrator. *Sedna: An Eskimo Myth.* New York: Viking Press, 1975.

In hunting cultures, successful acquisition of food involved spiritual power and goodness, as well as physical ability. Because animals possessed spirits, they had to be given respect. Sedna, the mother of the sea mammals on whom the Eskimo depended, kept her creatures from the hunters' harpoons when these men had violated taboos. When this occurred, only the angakok (shaman) could help his people by travelling to Sedna's home beneath the sea to seek her forgiveness. Although the story is a violent one, reflecting the harsh and precarious existence of the Eskimo people, it also expresses the sense of relationship with the spiritual and animal worlds that was at the center of their lives. McDermott's illustrations, which make use of traditional Eskimo design patterns, use the colors blue and purple to indicate the two worlds of the story, the land-human world of the people and the sea-spirit world of Sedna, respectively, and to indicate the conflicts and balances between them. Upper elementary and junior high students can study how the two colors reveal which of the two worlds is dominant at each stage of the story and can compare the first picture of the narrative with the second to last, noticing how, although they are similar, the changes in the use of color, the size of the characters, and the overall patterns suggest the differences in the relationships between the two worlds at the beginning and end of the story. The story can be compared to *Buffalo Woman* (Paul Goble) and *The Enchanted Caribou* (Elizabeth Cleaver) as an embodiment of the values of traditional hunting cultures.

Martin, Rafe, reteller; illustrated by David Shannon. *The Boy Who Lived with the Seals.* New York: G.P. Putnam's Sons, 1993.

This well-adapted version of a Chinook legend from the lower Columbia River combines two widespread mythic motifs, the coming-of-age of a young person whose parents must allow him to leave home and the transformation of a human being into an animal. A few years after he has mysteriously disappeared during the people's spring migration, a boy is discovered living with seals. Captured and returned to his family, he slowly regains his human ways and develops great abilities as a carver. However, after the seals have called to him several times, he escapes into the water to rejoin his other family. Each spring, he leaves his human family a magnificently carved and painted dugout canoe, a reminder of the link between himself and his family and, more generally, between the Chinook people and the seals that they hunt and that provide them with food and so many needed materials. Throughout North America, tales of animal-human transformation emphasize that human beings are a part of and not apart from the rest of the creation and that respect must be shown to our animal relatives. Shannon's illustrations accurately depict both the land and sea settings of the Chinook peoples and their stylized design patterns and carvings, works of art that were not merely decorations, but embodiments of spiritual powers. Students in the upper elementary grades can compare this transformation story with the Celtic legend *Selkie Girl*, by Susan Cooper. They can also notice the differences between the first and last illustrations, considering the implications of the absence of the boy and inclusion of the full-color of the canoe designs at the conclusion. How do the parents' attitudes toward the boy's leaving relate to readers' experiences of relationships between maturing children and their mothers and fathers?

Rodanas, Kristina, reteller and illustrator. *Dragonfly's Tale.* New York: Clarion Books, 1991.

For the Pueblo peoples of the southwest, who depended on the corn they grew in the desert, a reverential attitude toward the land and the spirit beings who watched over the crop and careful, respectful use of the gift of food provided by the land were essential. This Zuni legend, originally collected by late nineteenth-century anthropologist Frank Cushing, tells of "the days of the Ancient Ones," when the people enjoyed the bounty provided by the Maidens of the White and Yellow Corn. However, unwarranted pride in their plenty causes the people to lose everything. To impress their neighbors, they stage a huge food fight, wasting rather than sharing what they have. In fact, only two small children offer bread to two old woman beggars, really the Corn Maidens in disguise. When the crops fail and the village is abandoned, the boy and girl are left behind. Because of their kindness to the Maidens and later to a toy dragonfly the boy makes for his sister, they are given food, the fertility of the fields is renewed, and the humbled villagers return. Like the legends of so many agrarian peoples, this one emphasizes that correct spiritual values are as important as correct horticultural procedures. Rodanas's illustrations emphasize the significance of the landscape, with several pictures revealing the different conditions of the corn fields. However, school children at one Pueblo have objected to paintings of Kachinas, which, they report, should only be depicted by males who have gone through religious initiation ceremonies. Middle and upper elementary students can compare the illustrations of the fields before the food fight, after it, and after the children are rewarded, noticing how the changed appearance reflects the changed spiritual attitudes of the people. Upper elementary and junior high students can compare this version of the legend with Tony Hillerman's *The Boy Who Made Dragonfly*. This story can be contrasted with C.J. Taylor's retelling of a northeastern corn legend, *How Two-Feather Was Saved from Loneliness*.

Scribe, Murdo, reteller; illustrated by Terry Gallagher. *Murdo's Story: A Legend from Northern Manitoba*. Winnipeg: Pemmican Publications, 1985. One of the mythic tale types found around the world explains the origins of the seasonal cycles. For traditional hunting and agricultural peoples, the procurement of food was determined by the progress of the seasons, and, not surprisingly, many of them believed that supernatural beings or animals with spirit powers were responsible for the seasons. The Swampy Cree of northern Manitoba have a legend about the interrelationships between those animals on whom their survival depended. A Native elder and educator, Murdo Scribe explained that the adventures of these creatures were intended "to teach as well as to entertain" (p. 5) young audiences. The conflict outlined in the first two pages represents the first moral lesson: the animals who control summer are selfish and do not wish to share its bounty, causing hardship and creating the possibility of starvation for others. Through cooperation and creative problem-solving, the animals being denied summer are able to steal the medicine bag containing the season. Each animal is given a task suited to its special talents or physical characteristics, and each must work with the others for success. Finally, both groups must reach a compromise so that each can benefit from the warm weather. One of the animals has been trapped in the sky, where its body forms the outline of the Big Dipper, a directional guide to human beings and a constant reminder to them of the moral lessons of the story. Gallagher's bold pen-and-ink sketches realistically embody the main events of the story. Many of them contain groups of animals, underscoring the theme of cooperation. Students in the lower grades can discuss the moral lessons of the story; those in the middle grades can analyze the steps in the creative problem-solving used by the animals and can compare the story with William Toye's *How Summer Came to Canada*.

Seymour, Tryntje Van Ness, reteller; illustrated by Apache Artists. *The Gift of Changing Woman.* New York: Henry Holt, 1993.

To the Apache of Arizona and New Mexico (who called themselves "Ndee," "the people"), "tradition and history prepare the way for the future" (p. 32). Seymour, an urban easterner, sets out to learn about these traditions, principally the "Changing Woman" ceremony that celebrated a girl's coming into womanhood. After engaging in background research, listening carefully to Apache elders, witnessing the ceremony, and studying works by nineteenth- and twentieth-century Apache artists, she related the myth of Changing Woman and recounted how the enactment of the ritual becomes a true recreation of the myth and its spiritual meanings for the girl and her community. The only survivor of a great flood, Changing Woman wandered through the Southwest giving the landscape its spectacular beauty. She also gave birth to two sons, signifying the union between the power of the sky and the mountains. She is the symbol of the female fulfillment to which the initiate aspires. Harmony, balance, and stability are evoked in the ceremony, depicted not only through Seymour's explanatory narration, but also through the words of Apache participants and the stylized, symbolic paintings of such well-known Apache artists as Allan Houser. Students in the junior high grades can compare the story of Changing Woman to other creation myths involving floods and can notice how the story brings past, present, and future; the initiate and her family and community; and human, animal, and spirit beings into a timeless unity. The communal nature of the ceremony can be compared to the solitary male initiation journeys depicted in Terri Cohlene's *Turquoise Boy* and Paul Goble's *Star Boy.*

Sleator, William, reteller; illustrated by Blair Lent. *The Angry Moon.* New York: Little, Brown, 1970.

In adapting this well-known Tlingit myth from the northwest coast, Sleator emphasizes two themes frequently found in books for younger readers: the separation of two close friends and the dangerous, heroic journey of a small child away from home, into a perilous and unknown region, and back home. When Lapowinsa mocks the moon for having strange marks on its face, she is taken away, and Lupan must find her. After constructing an arrow ladder in the sky, he makes a frightening ascent and is rewarded by a spirit grandmother with four gifts that he uses in rescuing his friend. The story they tell on their return home, "was passed down from one generation to another, and is remembered to this day" (p. 48). Sleator does not emphasize the cultural values of the story; instead he stresses the testing of the hero and the heroic qualities he exhibits along the way. Lent, who has illustrated legends from a variety of non-European cultures, uses color to contrast the natural world of the earth and the spirit world of the skies. In the illustrations, the children are very small, an indication of their vulnerability in threatening situations. Children in the early elementary grades can discuss the heroic qualities of the boy and draw parallels between his sky journey and the boy's journey in Gerald McDermott's *Arrow to the Sun*. They should notice how color is used to communicate the danger and loneliness facing the children.

Sloat, Teri, reteller; illustrated by Robert and Teri Sloat. *The Hungry Giant of the Tundra*. New York: Dutton Children's Books, 1993.

As Sloat notes in her introduction to this story she heard from an Yupik (Alaskan) storyteller, traditional tales were designed to instruct and to warn, as well as to entertain. To prevent children from wandering too far into the tundra, parents frequently spoke about Akaguagankak, the always-hungry and not-too-bright giant who liked to seize and then dine on unwary boys and girls. The children in this tale are so busy having fun that they do not hear their parents call to come home for supper and, moving onto the tundra, are captured by the giant. When he discovers that he does not have the knife with which to prepare his feast, Akaguagankak removes his trousers, stuffs the children inside, and hangs the bundle in a tree. With the aid of a magical chickadee and a magical crane, the children escape and make it home. Not so their pursuer, who also enlists the crane's aid, but is dumped into the river, never to be seen again. The illustrations reveal the vast landscape in which it is so easy to become lost and humorously depict the dull-witted giant. Early elementary students can draw parallels between this book and *Hide and Sneak*, a cautionary tale by Canadian Inuit author Michael Kusugak. They can also notice the similarities and differences between this story and Paul Galdone's *The Little Girl and the Big Bear*, a Russian tale in which a child, lost in the woods, escapes her not-too-clever captor.

Stan-Padilla, Viento, reteller and illustrator. *Dream Feather*. Millbrae, CA: Dawne-Leigh Publications, 1980.

This interesting and unusual picture book by Yaqui artist Viento Stan-Padilla seems to be a mixture of Jungian psychology, New Age spiritualism, traditional agrarian religious customs, and coming-of-age vision quests. Chosen by the spirit of the sun to be his generation's carrier of the seed that represents spiritual power and corn, a boy travels at sunrise through the rocks of a cave and the earth, past stalks of young corn, into the sky, through the clouds, to spheres colored to represent the rainbow's spectrum, and, finally, to "the light of the Crystal Star" (n.p.), where he receives the seed, which he takes back to the cave. While elders sing of his journey, the boy leaves the cave, reentering the world in possession both of the seed and his new name, "Dream Feather." Although there are no notes indicating any specific traditional tribal sources for the narrative, and the illustrations seem to be a combination of generic Native designs and New Age crystals, helixes, and rainbows, the story is most applicable to the southwest, as indicated by the corn plants, the mountain caves, petroglyphs, wampum belts, and the eagle feather found in the illustrations. Six wordless doublespreads show the boy progressing through different colored circles, each a step of "pure color, each step a note in the ancient song" (n.p.). Junior high students who have read such books as McDermott's *Arrow to the Sun* and John Grinnèll's "The Legend of Scarface" (in *Blackfoot Lodge Tales*), who have studied various Native traditions, such as the vision quest of initiation and the acquisition of true names, or who have researched southwestern agrarian rituals and beliefs about the sun, may engage in their own interpretations of the sometimes cryptic text and mysterious pictures. They should pay careful attention to the spatial relationships between the boy and the sacred eagle feather and the changing colors and configurations of the six circles.

Steptoe, John, reteller and illustrator. *The Story of Jumping Mouse.* New York: Lothrop, Lee and Shepard, 1984.

In this loose adaptation of an unidentified plains story that he heard as a child, African-American children's author-illustrator John Steptoe presents the quest of a tiny mouse to reach the far-off land frequently mentioned in the elders' tales. Undeterred by warnings that the journey will be long and perilous, he is temporarily stopped when he reaches a stream. However, Magic Frog, impressed by the mouse's hope, ferries him across and gives him long legs and a new name, Jumping Mouse. The ensuing trek across the desert, over another stream, and into the mountains is fraught with danger and hardship, and at least once he is tempted to give up. However, his kindness to others, giving selflessly his sight and sense of smell to animals in greater need of them, brings him to his destination where he is reunited with his friend Magic Frog, who once again transforms and renames him. Steptoe's illustrations, in pen-and-ink and pencil, do not evoke any Native backgrounds, being completely naturalistic; but they do give a strong sense of the vastness, beauty, and danger of the landscapes through which the hero passes, as well as the various emotions he experiences. As the author admitted on the dust jacket, the story "is a statement about my own hopes and dreams," struggling against poverty to become a successful artist. It resembles a number of European children's books about small, unlikely heroes. However, elements of plains culture can be found. For example, the difficulty of crossing the stream parallels the people's difficulty using their bull boats to cross rivers, many of which contained powerful, evil spirit-serpents. The story may originally have explained the origin of kangaroo mice and eagles (the supreme, most revered of birds) and the significance of names. Early elementary students can list in sequence the various creatures Jumping Mouse meets and the qualities of character his responses to them reveal.

Taylor, C.J., reteller and illustrator. *The Ghost and Lone Warrior: An Arapaho Legend.* Montreal: Tundra Books, 1991.

In this legend, set in the time when horses had not yet arrived in the northwestern American plains, a group of hunters travel to distant mountains in search of buffalo to feed their hungry village. When his ankle is injured, Lone Warrior must stay alone, enduring pain, braving the storms of winter, keeping a fire going, and foraging for food. His courage and determination are rewarded as he is able to shoot a buffalo; but his good fortune seems short-lived when a ghost arrives at his camp demanding food. All is well, however, for the visitor is the spirit of a famous chief, an ancestor who has been testing the young man's worthiness to be the leader of his people. In many ways, the narrative parallels the stages of the vision quest, the journey of initiation taken by young men in most traditional plains cultures. Alone on a hill or mountain, facing physical hardship and hunger, they purified themselves, proving their readiness to receive spiritual visions to guide them in their adult years. Lone Warrior's selflessness (he urges the members of his party to leave him and to search for food for the village), his generosity (he shares his food with the ghost), his skill with bow and arrow (despite the pain of his injury he is able to shoot true), and respect (he thanks the spirit of the slain animal) make him an appropriate leader for his hunting culture. Taylor's oil paintings evoke both the physical landscape and the spiritual dimensions of the tale. Students in the middle grades can list the various tests Lone Warrior passes and discuss the qualities of character these prove. Beginning with the illustration of the blizzard, they can notice the amount of red color—symbolizing life and new beginning—in each picture. Why, they may ask, is the skeleton, associated with death and endings in European culture, clothed in a red robe?

Taylor, C.J., reteller and illustrator. *How Two-Feather Was Saved from Loneliness: An Abenaki legend.* Montreal: Tundra Books, 1990.
As the very informative endnote explains, this legend from the far eastern woodlands combines three origin, or pourquoi stories: the discovery of fire, the growing of the first corn, and the beginning of human villages. Mohawk author-artist C.J. Taylor tells of the testing of Two-Feather, who searches for a friend to end the loneliness he feels in a world with only a few, scattered human beings in it. Because he obeys the spirit-woman, following where she leads, making fire, and trusting her when she commands him to drag her through the hot ashes, he is given the gift of corn and founds a village where people find companionship in their new agricultural life. Taylor's oil paintings reinforce the thematic and emotional elements of the legend. The opening illustration of a bleak winter landscape devoid of people is a contrast to the concluding scene of villagers celebrating the corn harvest in the brightly colored late summer setting. Green pervades the illustrations in the middle of the story, symbolizing both the corn maiden and the vitality of life she embodies. Students in the middle elementary grades can discuss the qualities of character Two-Feather reveals while following the Corn Goddess and can compare the opening and closing illustrations. They can compare this story with Taylor's *The Ghost and Lone Warrior*; Joseph Bruchac's "The Coming of Corn," in *Keepers of the Earth*; and William Toye's *The Fire Stealer*, noticing similarities in the heroes and differences in the various traditional cultures' explanations of elements so important in their lives.

Taylor, C.J., reteller and illustrator. *Little Water and the Gift of the Animals: A Seneca Legend.* Montreal: Tundra, 1992.

C.J. Taylor has turned to the mythical period, when human beings and animals could talk to each other, in this legend of the origin of the sacred medicine songs and dances of her people. When a mysterious illness strikes his people at harvest time, Little Water, who is a good friend to the animals, especially wolf, goes to the forest to ask his friends to share their healing powers. Knocked unconscious in a fall, he is rescued by the animals, who communicate to him while he dreams. The cures they give him, which quickly heal Little Water's people, are still practised by the Little Water Society of the Iroquois Confederacy. This pourquoi legend illustrates not only the importance of hunters having respect for game but also the spiritual kinship that exists between human beings and animals. Taylor's oil paintings emphasize this spirituality, particularly in the scene in which the helping animals are depicted in a vortex swirling above the head of the unconscious youth and in the final illustration where the healthy villagers gathering their harvest are seen opposite the ghostly faces of the animals who have shared their healing magic. Students in the middle elementary grades can discuss the interrelationship theme and can notice the importance of sacred rituals in the healing process. They can also discuss the positive image of wolves in contrast with the depictions in European stories and can relate the wolf in this story to the one in Paul Goble's *Dream Wolf.*

Te Ata, reteller; adapted by Lynn Moroney; illustrated by Mira Reisberg. *Baby Rattlesnake.* San Francisco: Children's Book Press, 1989.

In this cautionary story adapted from a tale told by Chickasaw elder Te Ata, Baby Rattlesnake ignores his parents' advice that he is too young to have a rattle and, having forced the elders to give him one, then ignores warnings of the impropriety of fooling the other animals with his new toy and the danger of using it to frighten the daughter of a human chief. As is the case with many traditional Native peoples, the rattlesnake nation does not force its view on the child, but allows the child to make mistakes and thus learn in the process. Baby Rattlesnake learns not only the wisdom of his elders, but also the necessity of using a gift for the correct reasons: rattles are warning devices, not toys to amuse the immature. Australian illustrator Mira Reisberg has used cut paper and bright primary and secondary gouache paints to depict the various events and lighthearted tone of the story. A silent lizard, not mentioned in the text, seems to be thinking about the events taking place; the borders are used to expand on the emotional aspects of each scene. The only question about the illustrations is the use of Navajo clothing and Pueblo dwellings in a story originally told by a Chickasaw living in the Oklahoma Territory. Children in the early elementary grades can notice the child's repeated ignoring of warnings and can discuss the lessons original listeners would have received. The possible thoughts of the lizard can be articulated. Viewers of the pictures might ask why his direction on the page changes during the last few illustrations.

Toye, William, reteller; illustrated by Elizabeth Cleaver. *The Loon's Necklace.* Toronto: Oxford University Press, 1977.

In this picture book version of a legend known along the northwest coast and across the Arctic, the loon, the bird associated with the shaman, the possessor of supernatural healing powers, plays a central role in the affairs of human beings. Unable to hunt for his family because of his growing blindness, an old man is victimized by an old hag, who steals his food and abducts his son. The boy escapes and leads his father to the lake where the old man is taken beneath the water by his friend Loon and given back his sight. In gratitude, the old man gives the bird his white shell necklace, which its descendants still wear. Thwarted, the hag turns herself into an owl, a bird of ill omen on the northwest coast, so that she can torment the family with her screaming. However, the family departs, listening to the laughing, happy calls of their benefactor. In addition to stressing Loon's role, the story discusses the need for balance. The hag wants more meat than she needs; but the man wants only enough sight for him to be able to hunt for his family. Cleaver's woodcut and collage illustrations emphasize the evil power surrounding the hag, a being of the dark forest, and the supernatural healing powers of Loon as it swims beneath the aquamarine lake. Students in the middle elementary grades can discuss the theme of balance in the story and can notice the similarities and differences between this story and the Inuit version, "The Blind Boy and the Loon," in *Tales from the Igloo* by Maurice Metayer. The role of the loon can be compared to that of the magpie in Nancy Van Laan's *Buffalo Dance.*

Troughton, Joanna, reteller and illustrator. *How Rabbit Stole the Fire.* Glasgow: Blackie, 1979.

This Cherokee story shares many elements with fire-acquisition legends of other Native cultures. Powerful beings possess the fire, which must be stolen by trickery. In the chase that follows, a group of animals carry the fire, which is then hidden in a tree. The culture hero explains how to release it by rubbing sticks together. Rabbit, while he lacks the strength, cunning, bravery, and fierceness of other animals, is "leader . . . in mischief" (n.p.). Enthralled by his clever dancing, the sky people let down their guard, and, his headdress afire, Rabbit flees. In carrying the fire, the other animals receive their distinctive physical characteristics. The theme of cooperation between the animals (all found in Cherokee territory), the importance of the small, but tricky hero, and the explanation of the method of getting fire from the wood links the story to its people. While the illustrations reflect the narrative, the sky people look more like Iroquois from upstate New York than Cherokee from North Carolina or Georgia. Children in the early elementary grades can compare this story to the California fire myth, *Fire Race*, by Jonathan London, noticing similarities and differences in character and incident. Upper elementary and junior high students can research traditional Cherokee hair styles and face and body paint designs to see if Troughton's illustrations are accurate.

Yolen, Jane, reteller; illustrated by Barry Moser. *Sky Dogs*. San Diego: Harcourt Brace Jovanovich, 1990.

Drawing on one of the major Blackfoot myths, the arrival of the first horses to the northern plains, and on cultural beliefs about Old Man, the creator-hero of the Blackfoot, Jane Yolen creates an original story in which an old man, He-who-loves-horses, tells a group of children about how, when he was a young orphan, his reaction to a momentous event in his tribe's history led to his receiving his name and assuming a place in the council of warriors. Too far from the village to hide when three horses carrying sick members of the Kutani tribe approached, he was the first to touch one of the animals and, later, to learn how to groom, train, and then ride horses into battle. Yolen accurately depicts aspects of nineteenth-century Blackfoot culture. In telling how his people confer names, the aging man is engaging in the accepted practice of recounting deeds of personal bravery and of boasting of his nation's greatness. Although choosing a realistic rather than mythic-supernatural account of the coming of horses, she accurately depicts the awe, reverence, and fear of the mythic hero Old Man. Students in upper elementary and junior high grades will enjoy comparing Yolen's approach with Paul Goble's in *The Gift of the Sacred Dog*. They can discuss how the boy's actions enabled him to earn both his name and his place in the council, and they can examine the people's attitudes toward their culture hero. Students might wish to speculate about the sickness of the Kutani people, from farther west. Could it have been smallpox, which the white people brought to America along with horses?

Young, Ed, reteller and illustrator. *Moon Mother: A Native American Creation Tale*. New York: Willa Perlman Books, 1993.

This Native creation myth from an unnamed culture group offers parallels to both the Book of Genesis and modern theories of evolution—but with significant differences. When a spirit person arrives on the earth, he admires the grass, flowers, trees, rivers, and lakes and decides to settle. Lonely, he creates birds, fish, animals, and then men, "images of himself" (n.p.). However, after he leaves the people on their own so that he can join a newly arrived woman spirit person, the human beings begin to fight with each other, and, when they seek their creator's advice, they discover that he has departed from the earth, leaving behind a baby girl, the mother of all subsequent human beings. The woman spirit person's face can still be seen in the full moon, and a new born baby's cry is the result of its unhappiness at being separated from her. Although neither the text nor the illustrations make it possible to specify the tribal source of the story, it seems to have similarities to myths of several groups of the Southwest. It also reflects general Native concepts. Although, as in Genesis, men and then women are the last to be created, in this story women are not born from men, but are the product of a union between the two spirit persons. The face in the moon is a constant reminder of the links between spirit and human beings, sky and earth worlds. Young's pastel illustrations, with their contrasts of lights and shadows, emphasize the almost mystic spirituality and create the sense of an earlier time when human and spirit people interrelated more freely. Students in the junior high grades can attempt to find the culture group from which Young's adaptation came and can, then, compare this creation myth with those from other parts of North America

PICTURE BOOK FICTION AND POETRY ABOUT NATIVE PEOPLES

Baylor, Byrd; illustrated by Tom Bahti. *When Clay Sings.* New York: Atheneum, 1972.
Byrd Baylor, who has written several children's books celebrating the landscape of the Southwest and the joys of those who live in harmony with its rhythms, responds here to fragments of clay pots and bowls dating back to the long-past Anasazi, Hohokam, Mimbres, and Mogollon cultures of Utah, Arizona, New Mexico, and Colorado. Thinking about modern Native children who might find pottery shards, she invites them to consider how the vessels and the designs reveal the physical, social, and spiritual lives of the people. Basing her hypotheses on actual designs and real pieces of pottery, she creates rhythmic, poetic prose that evokes a distant life: the women singing reverentially to the living clay as they shape it; the celestial bodies they observed and represented on its surfaces; children playing; hunters and their prey; spirit beings; shamans and dancers. She also thinks of the sacred songs the users of this clay must have sung, words of power used to please the winds and rains, the animals and spirits. Bahti, using shades and mixes of brown, yellow, and gray-black that were the colors on pots and designs, harmonizes his visual text with Baylor's verbal one. Curving lines and design patterns balanced on the page not only depict the things of which Baylor writes, they also suggest balance and interrelationship between human beings and the rest of the animate, inanimate, and spirit worlds. This quality was as important an aspect of the pots as their suitability for practical daily use. The book is a symbolic act of archaeology. Just as Baylor imagines children finding and piecing together bits of pottery, so she and Bahti piece together the designs to gain an understanding of the many dimensions of the lives of these traditional peoples. Upper elementary and junior high students can interpret details of the illustrations and text to arrive at their own generalizations about these cultures.

Blades, Ann. *A Boy of Taché.* Montreal: Tundra Books, 1973.
Based on an incident that occurred while Blades was teaching in northern British Columbia, this story depicts the coming of age of a Carrier boy. Making the hero younger than he was in reality, thus emphasizing his courage, Blades narrates how, on the first beaver-trapping expedition of the spring, Charlie must travel alone down the dangerously swift river to seek medical aid for Za, his seriously ill grandfather. At the story's conclusion, his mission successfully accomplished, Charlie takes over the old man's hunting and trapping duties.

Written in a simple, factual manner and illustrated with watercolors of an almost primitive style, the story captures not only the physical environment and lifestyles of the people but also the underlying universal aspects. The presence of the beautiful and rugged landscape in nearly every picture emphasizes the determination and courage with which the people face and adapt to the world around them. The springtime setting symbolizes the new life to come. Za notices and does not shoot a pregnant beaver; Charlie must become a man, using adult skills to navigate the river in his quest to keep Za alive. The old man, like the wise old person of traditional tales, teaches the boy what he will need to know on his rescue mission and in his future life. The final illustration, in which Charlie and an old neighbor face the horizon watching the rescue plane fly into the distance, symbolizes the unity of past and future in the present moment. Charlie is watching his grandfather, the possessor of wisdom from the past, make his last trip from the trapping grounds. He is also looking into his own future, which will draw on this past. Students in middle elementary grades can discuss the steps of Charlie's growth to maturity and can compare his journey to that of such mythic characters as the boy in Paul Goble's *The Gift of the Sacred Dog*. They can study the illustrations, noticing the importance of the rugged landscape, and can consider why Charlie's shirt is colored a bright yellow.

Bruchac, Joseph; illustrated by Paul Morin. *Fox Song*. New York: Philomel Books, 1993.
In this simple, yet lyrical and evocative story, seven-year-old Jamie awakens and tries to hold on to her dream about her recently deceased Abenaki great-grandmother. Lying in bed, she recalls events from the four seasons in which the old woman had taught her about nature and about the interrelatedness of life and death. In the summer, for example, Jamie had learned that burning off dead berry bushes guaranteed plentiful new growth the next year. In winter, the old woman knows that a fox's tracks are leading the vixen toward her mate so that there will be young in the spring. Awakening, the girl goes to the maple tree under which she had so often sat with her great-grandmother. Amid the falling leaves that had reminded her mentor of departed old people, she sings the song the great-grandmother had given her, sees a fox watching her, and realizes "that she would never be alone." In this present moment, she understands that her future will be guided by the wisdom of her past. Morin's oil paintings are realistic, portraying the landscape in each of the four seasons, and symbolic, their luminescence communicating the spirituality embodied in the old woman's teachings. Of particular interest is the opening illustration, with a dream-catcher on the wall and a birch bark basket on the dresser. Jamie will be able to hold on to her dream of the past, thus overcoming her grief and carrying with her the old lessons. The basket, with its designs of birds, animals, and ferns symbolizes the respect for the natural world she will carry within. Children in the early grades can discuss the lessons Jamie remembers, can compare this story about the death of a loved one with Miska Miles's *Annie and the Old One*, and

can discuss the lessons they themselves have received from old people in their lives. Those in the middle elementary grades can notice the circles, literal and symbolic, found in the illustrations and the text.

Campbell, Maria; illustrated by David Maclagan. *Little Badger and the Fire Spirit.* Toronto: McClelland and Stewart, 1977.
On her eighth birthday, Ahsinee goes to spend the summer with her grandmother and grandfather, eagerly anticipating the stories she knows the old man will tell. As she watches him light his pipe, she asks about the origins of fire. Set in the time when animals and people talked to each other, the grandfather's tale explains how Little Badger acquired the fire that enabled his people to survive winter's killing cold. Seeking the wisdom of his teacher and friend Grey Coyote, the blind hero learns that he is to be taken by members of his village to a distant mountain where he must enter alone into the cavern of the fearsome Fire Spirit. Displaying courage, kindness, selflessness, and wisdom, he befriends and passes four animal guardians and earns the Fire Spirit's admiration and the gifts of fire and sight. In this original story, Campbell, a Canadian Métis, uses elements of the traditional narrative of initiation, the four-fold testing of many legends, and the close relationship between human beings and animals central to Native belief. To these she adds the symbolism of the drum, the beats of which come from the hearts of all living beings, and the frame narrative, in which an aging couple helps a child learn about her cultural past. Maclagan's illustrations, in full color and black-and-white, emphasize the dangers the hero faces and the personal transformations he undergoes. Children in the early elementary grades can compare the size and placement of the hero and the colors in early and later illustrations and can discuss the qualities of character the boy reveals during his journey. Students in middle and upper elementary grades can compare and contrast the hero's four encounters with the animals with the four kiva tests of the boy in Gerald McDermott's *Arrow to the Sun* and can discuss the symbolic meanings of the drum.

Carlstrom, Nancy White; illustrated by Leo and Diane Dillon. *Northern Lullaby.* New York: Philomel Books, 1992.
This simple, lyrical lullaby, intended to be sung to a young child, evokes a sense of Alaskan land and skyscapes and the animals and inanimate creatures who inhabit them. Beneath Papa Star and Mama Moon, near Grandpa Mountain and Grandmother River, slumber animals referred to as Great Uncle, Auntie, Cousin, Sister, and Brother. Each of these animals is garbed with traditional clothing, headgear, and masks appropriate to the various Native peoples who live in the area. In the background of the illustrations is a log cabin, the dwelling of the small Native child who is the narrator of the lullaby. Although the book does not specifically relate to Native cultures and seems, in fact, to have been created for the author's own child, it does celebrate the sense of the interrelatedness of all beings central to the beliefs of many Alaskan peoples. The Dillons' illustrations emphasize this point. Younger students can discuss the significance

of giving extended family roles to the various beings. Those in the upper elementary grades can research traditional Native clothing and masks from Alaska and can make a list of the various cultures depicted in each illustration. They can then research designs and costumes from Native peoples of their own area and can reillustrate the lullaby using the results of their findings.

Cumming, Peter; illustrated by Alice Priestley. *Out on the Ice in the Middle of the Bay.* Toronto: Annick Press, 1993.

Stories of bear-human confrontations are found across most of the northern hemisphere, for in many cultures the bear is seen both as a threat and as the animal who most closely resembles people in both shape and size and in habitat. In the Arctic, these confrontation stories are frequently based on fact as Nanook, the polar bear, who possessed a powerful inua or spirit, did not fear human beings and frequently stalked them. Set in the contemporary Arctic, *Out on the Ice in the Middle of the Bay* tells what happens when a human girl and a bear boy leave their dozing parents and encounter each other at the base of an iceberg in the middle of the bay. Parallel texts depict the actions and reactions of both pairs of parents and children and emphasize the security each child finds at the conclusion of the adventure. The iceberg around which the encounter takes place is a kind of neutral territory, a dividing area between the terrains of the human beings and polar bears. Priestley's colored pencil illustrations evoke the hues of a northern afternoon in late November, and pastel reds, yellows, and oranges give way to deep blues as night settles over the iceberg, now deserted of both human beings and bears. In many ways, this realistic story is a modern cautionary tale, for Leah, when her father falls asleep, deliberately disobeys his order not to go outside. However, neither animals nor people are injured or killed and neither species invades the territory of the other, a fact that offers an implicit ecological lesson. Children in the early elementary grades can discuss the characters of Leah and her father, considering the responsibility of each for the near disaster. They can also discuss the similarities and differences between this story and Robert McCloskey's *Blueberries for Sal.* Children in the middle elementary grades can write and then perform a play of the story for younger children, with those not acting reciting the rhythmic text, half of the group saying the lines relating to the human beings, the other half, those relating to the bears.

Eyvindson, Peter; illustrated by Rhian Brynjolson. *Jen and the Great One.* Winnipeg: Pemmican Publications, 1990.

In this ecological fable, a young girl listens to her friend the Great One, a giant fir tree, tell about his life and the time when he was surrounded by other great ones. The arrival of Businessman, who believes that money talks and who does not hear the message of how the trees help maintain an ecological balance, signals the end of a world in which all elements of nature exist in harmonious balance. However, with the aid of Jen and her friends, who plant the seeds from the Great One's cones, there is hope for the future. Although the written text does not mention it, the illustrations indicate that Jen and several of her friends are Native, which is appropriate given their people's traditional respect for the natural world. The destroyers of the forest, who think of the green of money rather than of trees, are white people. Students in the early elementary grades can discuss the ecological theme of the story and relate it to traditional Native beliefs found in other narratives. They should discuss the two types of green and notice how the disappearance of natural green in the illustrations reveals the advance of technology. This story can be compared to *Song for the Ancient Forest*, by Nancy Luenn.

Eyvindson, Peter; illustrated by Wendy Wolsak. *The Wish Wind*. Winnipeg: Pemmican Publications, 1987.

Tired of winter, Boy ignores Wish Wind's invitation to play and, in spite of warnings to exhibit patience, demands that he be taken into spring. Quickly tiring of that season, he is transported into summer, where, ignoring Wind's cautionary advice, he demands to escape the heat. Discovering that he has aged during the autumn, Boy, now Old Man, learns the value of patience and asks for one more wish. It comes true as he awakens from his dream and accepts the invitation to play. Although the text does not state it, Wendy Wolsak's illustrations indicate that Boy is Native. His impatience and self-centeredness place him in opposition to traditional beliefs in which human beings were expected to live in harmony with the cycle of the seasons. Students in the early elementary grades can compare Boy's response to each season with Jamie's in Joseph Bruchac's *Fox Song* and his misuse of wishes with a similar situation in *The Fisherman and His Wife*, by the Brothers Grimm.

Highwater, Jamake; photographs by Marcia Keegan. *Moonsong Lullaby*. New York: Lothrop, Lee & Shepard, 1981.

Highwater has created a rhythmic prose-poem that embodies many Native cultures' beliefs about the spirit powers of the moon and her influence on the creatures who live under the night sky. Sitting by a campfire, the elders sing to children, celebrating successful hunting and gathering. A variety of birds, small animals, plants, and trees are bathed by the moon's light and touched by the life-giving song. Holy people, lonely and grieving men and women, lovers, parents, and children experience the moon's calming influence. So, too, does the sun, whose night sleep is soothed by her melody. Keegan's photographs, representing the objects itemized in the song, use various intensities of light to emphasize the spiritual powers of the moon. Although modern science presents the moon as being lifeless, casting only reflected light, for most traditional peoples, she—not it—was of tremendous spiritual importance. The gentle rhythms of Highwater's prose are appropriate both for a lullaby that provides night-time assurance for young listeners and for a hymn of religious awe for adults who recognize that they are not alone in the night, but under the protection of a beneficent being. Children in the early elementary grades can notice the difference between this moon poem and those of English-European writers and can compare the lullaby with Carlstrom's *Northern Lullaby*. In the middle elementary grades, the book can be used as an introduction or conclusion to a study of such Native myths as *Moon Mother* (Young), which describes the moon's power and its significance in the lives of people and other created beings.

Jacobs, Shannon K.; illustrated by Michael Hays. *The Boy Who Loved Morning*. Boston: Little, Brown, 1993.
In her introduction, Jacobs notes that this story, a reflection of her respect for Native spiritual traditions, does not depict any specific culture groups. However, the landscape, presence of tipis, references to diminishing buffalo herds, and emphasis on the spiritual significance of dawn all suggest the middle and northern plains. Partly under the influence of his grandfather, a boy has learned to celebrate the coming of dawn by playing his flute. He performs this ritual alone, because the old man is preoccupied with the many problems besetting his people. On the mesa, surrounded by his three spirit friends—Coyote, Snake, and Crow—the boy thinks of his forthcoming naming ceremony and of playing the flute at it in order to make his grandfather proud. However, his own pride in his talent increases so much that he forgets to revere the world in which he lives, destroying the balance of day and night by using his skills to call up the sun in the middle of the night. Power and pride cause him to lose his spirit friends. Only when the grandfather, aware of his own relative neglect of the boy, offers wise advice does the boy recognize his faults, regain his friends and his humility, and receive a new and appropriate name. Hays' illustrations, acrylic on linen canvas, are dominated by gold, yellow, and orange colors appropriate for both the early morning time and the geographical setting. The ghostly presences of the animal spirits are indicated by outline drawings through which the land appears, emphasizing their connection with the natural world. Students in the upper elementary grades can compare the scenes that take place on the mesa, discussing how the boy's choices of names and the animals' reactions indicate his changing attitudes and the correctness or incorrectness of those attitudes. This story can be compared to "The Legend of Scarface," by George Bird Grinnell, in its discussion of the significance of the sun to plains peoples and the importance of animal friends and helpers.

Keeshig-Tobias, Lenore; illustrated by Polly Keeshig-Tobias. *Bineshiinh Dibaajmowin/Bird Talk*. Toronto: Sister Vision, 1991.
In this bilingual Ojibway-English story, Little Brown Bird feels lonely in the big city to which she and her older sister have moved while their mother attends college. She is also sad because the school children, playing cowboys and Indians, refuse to believe that she is Indian. Looking at the family photo album, she remembers her grandfather teaching her Ojibway words and her mother's Native interpretation of Columbus's arrival in the New World. When the family goes to the park and she hears children speaking in many different languages, she thinks of the dawn when many birds awaken, each species singing in its own language. The image of the birds runs subtly through the story suggesting the

variety of Canadian cultures. She is "Little Brown Bird," and that night, she returns happily to her home, which she calls her nest. This simple story is a celebration of the multicultural nature of Canada's urban centers. Early elementary children can discuss the meaning of the bird metaphor and can, like Little Brown Bird, discuss elements of their language with other students.

Ortiz, Simon; illustrated by Sharol Graves. *The People Shall Continue.* San Francisco: Children's Book Press, 1988.

This prose poem by Acoma Pueblo poet Simon Ortiz traces the history of Native peoples from the myth-time of creation to the present day renaissance of traditions and beliefs. In spite of the diversity of their origins and lifestyles, the peoples cooperated and shared, and all held the belief that the Earth, the source of life, must be respected. The narrative then outlines the destruction of the old cultures: the arrival of greedy Europeans, the removal of tribes to distant reservations, the breaking of treaties, the creation of residential schools, and the urbanization of many individuals. Although there is no mention of the destructive effects of disease and Christianity, and although one might question the statement that the different traditional groups were peaceful toward each other, the book does present the major aspects of post-contact history. It concludes with a celebration of the modern resurgence of Native pride. An embodiment of modern Pan-Indian thought, it presents an alternative view to the pattern of North American history many children encounter. Vivid illustrations by Sharol Graves depict the various hair and clothing styles of Native Americans. For upper elementary and junior high students studying novels about various periods of Native history, this book provides a valuable overview.

Prusski, Jeffrey; illustrated by Neil Waldman. *Bring Back the Deer.* San Diego: Gulliver Books, 1988.

About a family from an unspecified hunting culture in the eastern woodlands, this original story draws from beliefs and customs of many tribes to present what might best be called a generic initiation or coming-of-age story. With his father gone on a hunting trip, his grandmother preoccupied with caring for his mother and a newborn sister, and his grandfather too old to leave the lodge in search of food, the boy must go alone into the cold winter landscape. After listening to the shamanistic wisdom his grandfather gives regarding the power of dreams and fire and the importance of knowing and becoming the animal hunted, the boy sets out. He becomes progressively isolated from his family, losing his father's trail and then his own spear and knife. When, along with a wise, lone wolf, he stalks and then chases a buck, he discovers himself back home, reunited with all the members of his family, including his father. His hunt has been transformed into a vision quest; he has become one with the animals of the forest, and his thought, "I am myself" (n.p.), reveals his new awareness and maturity. He has found his power. Although the story draws on customs, beliefs, and ceremonies of eastern woodlands and hunting cultures in a general way, its vagueness robs it of authenticity as a depiction of Native beliefs. In some ways, it resembles "New Age" appropriations of imperfectly understood traditions. Waldman's illustrations, which use blue and pink pastels set against a black background and which depict shapes of animals in the clouds, enhance the visionary, almost mystic quality of Prusski's original work of fiction. Although the family's lodge looks Ojibway or perhaps eastern Algonquin, there are no visual motifs to aid readers in specifically locating the story. An explanatory note by the author and/or illustrator would have helped. Students in junior high school who have studied traditional Great Lakes and woodland cultures can relate visual and verbal details of the story to specific culture groups, noticing overlaps and, if they find any, inaccuracies and then can evaluate the book's validity in portraying Native realities.

Rogers, Jean; illustrated by Rie Muñoz. *King Island Christmas.* New York: Greenwillow Books, 1985.
While some Eskimo groups still observe traditional customs, a large number are Christians, incorporating many of their older values into western religion. On tiny King Island in the Bering Sea, the villagers are worried that high seas will prevent a new priest from arriving in time to lead them in the Christmas celebrations. In Eskimo fashion, they meet as a group to seek a solution to their problem. When the priest is brought from the freighter and returned to the village, a feast is held and the newcomer distributes gifts. The illustrations, by an artist who, like the author, has lived in Alaska for many years, portray the cooperative spirit, with large groups of the island's residents seen on every page; the bright colors communicate the friendliness, cooperation, and joy of the season that overcomes the darkness and cold outside. This is a fresh, original variation of a standard type of story: the miracle of the Christmas spirit. While happiness, cooperation, generosity, and unselfishness are found among nearly all people celebrating this festival, each culture and physical environment creates unique customs and stories. Students in the early elementary grades can compare this Christmas celebration to the one found in Jean Speare's *A Candle for Christmas.*

Sis, Peter. *A Small Tall Tale from the Far Far North.* New York: Alfred A. Knopf, 1993.
Although not a tale about Eskimo people, this story details a Czechoslovakian wanderer's encounter with and appreciation for the Bering Strait Eskimos. Jan Welzel, whose existence and books about his travels have been questioned by some, seeks freedom from the dreary life of his homeland by travelling east across Siberia. Trapped by a mysterious magnetic mountain, he is rescued by Eskimos who nurse him back to health, make him a part of the community, and teach him their ways. When the goldrush brings Europeans into the Eskimos territory, Welzel seeks to help his new friends and leads the invaders toward the magnetic mountain. Beneath the tall-tale humor of the narration—contemporaries compared Welzel to Baron von Munchausen, the famous author of outrageous and funny fictions—are serious themes. Welzel, like the poor child

in many European folktales, seeks a new and better life by making a long, solitary journey to a land where he finds fulfillment living in a community based on joy and sharing. His illustrations—in colored inks, watercolors, acrylic gold, and rubber stamps—reinforce his themes. His homeland is depicted in pen-and-ink with pale washes, while his Arctic home is filled with roseate and gold hues—the gold of the Eskimo community, a contrast to the precious metal sought by Europeans. The illustrations of Eskimo life are filled with a helter-skelter of tiny details of joyous interaction, a contrast to the static figures of his own village and the regimented formations of the advancing prospectors. Students in upper elementary and junior high grades can discuss the contrast between the two lifestyles and can notice how the details and colors of the illustrations reveal these lifestyles.

Speare, Jean; illustrated by Ann Blades. *A Candle for Christmas.* Vancouver, Canada: Douglas & McIntyre, 1986.

Set in an unnamed reservation in northern British Columbia, this night-before-Christmas story is about Tomas, a young boy anxiously awaiting his parents' return home. He has been staying with Nurse Roberta while they help his uncle at a distant ranch. After decorating the tree at his cabin, the boy dreams of walking outdoors following a giant candle that illuminates the darkness. When his parents return, his mother reports having seen a huge light that guided them on their travels. Did Tomas have a dream? Did the mother see the lights of the settlement? Was it all coincidence or a miracle? These questions are implicitly raised, but not answered. The true miracle is that the boy is reunited with his family in the family home. Blades' simple, but vivid watercolor illustrations convey many of the emotions of the story. Taken as a group, the pictures provide a series of contrasts: between the nurse's home, with its light-colored, almost pale color schemes and linoleum floor, and Tomas's cabin with its rich brown, rough-hewn wood floors and brightly colored tablecloth and bedspread; and between the indoors of both houses and the white-gray winter outdoors, where people and buildings seem small against the winter landscape. The final illustration, with mother, father, and son sitting on the checkered quilt facing the Christmas tree, signals the end of Tomas's loneliness and the establishment of a sense of family love and home. Students in the early elementary grades can consider Tomas's dream/vision, discussing the nature of its "reality" and can compare the two homes and the inside and outside settings.

Wheeler, Bernelda; illustrated by Herman Bekkering. *Where Did You Get Your Moccasins?* Winnipeg, Canada: Pemmican Publications, 1986.

An outgrowth of a project at the Manitoba Education Native Writer's Work-shop, this simple story by Cree-Saulteaux author Bernelda Wheeler describes the experience of a young boy who proudly brings a new pair of moccasins to school. The story is cumulative, as Jody answers each of a series of questions about them by adding words, phrases, and sentences to his previous answers. The children and readers learn that his grandmother had used traditional methods in preparing the hide of the deer shot by his father. In a sense, the new moccasins are a symbol of his family and cultural heritage, which he proudly displays in the very different environment of an urban, multicultural school. The story ends with a humorous, unexpected twist. To the question, "Where did she get the beads?" (p. 25) comes a simple and different reply: "From the store" (p. 26). Herman Bekkering's charcoal illustrations add dimensions to the text, depicting the urban environment in which the boy lives and the contrasting rural and forest settings and revealing the wondering admiration of the students and Jody's sense of pride. Students in kindergarten and the early elementary grades can be asked to form an answer to the final question before hearing it and can discuss the surprise ending. They can consider Jody's pride and, after reading this story and Maryann Kovalski's *The Cake that Mack Ate*, can create their own cumulative story describing the process of making a prized personal possession.

Yerxa, Leo. *Last Leaf First Snowflake to Fall.* Toronto: Groundwood/Douglas & McIntyre, 1993.
Using rich, evocative collages and rhythmic free verse, Ojibway artist Leo Yerxa presents two universal themes: the transition from late fall to early winter and the experience of a child's first overnight forest sleepover with a parent. The two leave their cabin to paddle the canoe across quiet waters that reflect the sky to a small island and then walk into a deep swamp. "[T]he only nishnawbe [Ojibway] to visit this place" (n.p.), they sleep beneath their canoe as the first snow of winter falls. At dawn, the young narrator "walked into the light of a new season" (n.p.). The rhythmic language captures the quiet simplicity of the event and awe and joy the child feels as she becomes aware of her place in the changing patterns of nature. The collages, created from tissue paper dyed with acrylics, watercolors, and inks, give the narrative an almost mythic and dream-like atmosphere. The human figures are small, just one element of the natural world into which they enter and become a part. Students in the middle elementary grades can study the five doublespreads, noticing the natural details and creating their own poetic texts. They can also compare this story with Charles Larry's *Peboan and Seegwun*, the Ojibway myth of the transition from winter to spring. The experience of dawn can be compared to that in Uri Schulevitz's *Dawn*.

REFERENCES

Barber-Starkey, Joe; illustrated by Paul Montpellier. 1989. *Jason and the Sea Otter*. Madeira Park, Canada: Harbour Publishing.

Bruchac, Joseph, reteller. 1993. *Flying with the Eagle, Racing the Great Bear: Stories from Native North America*. Mahwah, NJ: Bridgewater Books.

Campbell, Joseph. 1949. *The Hero with a Thousand Faces*. Princeton, NJ: Princeton University Press.

————. 1988. *Historical Atlas of World Mythology*. Vol. 1, Part 2. New York: Harper & Row.

Clark, Ann Nolan; illustrated by Velino Herrera. 1941. *In My Mother's House*. New York: Viking Press.

Goble, Paul. 1969. *Red Hawk's Account of Custer's Last Battle*. New York: Pantheon.

————. 1972. *Brave Eagle's Account of the Fetterman Fight*. New York: Pantheon.

————. 1973. *Lone Bull's Horse Raid*. Scarsdale, NY: Bradbury Press.

————. 1978. *The Girl Who Loved Wild Horses*. Scarsdale, NY: Bradbury Press.

————. 1980. *The Gift of the Sacred Dog*. Scarsdale, NY: Bradbury Press.

————. 1983. *Star Boy*. Scarsdale, NY: Bradbury Press.

————. 1984. *Buffalo Woman*. Scarsdale, NY: Bradbury Press.

————. 1985. *The Great Race of the Birds and Animals*. Scarsdale, NY: Bradbury Press.

————. 1987. *Death of the Iron Horse*. New York: Bradbury Press.

————. 1988a. *Her Seven Brothers*. New York: Bradbury Press.

————. 1988b. *Iktomi and the Boulder*. New York: Orchard Books.

————. 1989a. *Beyond the Ridge*. New York: Bradbury Press.

————. 1989b. *Iktomi and the Berries*. New York: Bradbury Press.

————. 1990a. *Dream Wolf*. New York: Bradbury Press.

————. 1990b. *Iktomi and the Ducks*. New York: Orchard Books.

————. 1991. *Iktomi and the Buffalo Skull*. New York: Orchard Books.

————. 1992a. *Crow Chief*. New York: Orchard Books.

————. 1992b. *Love Flute*. New York: Bradbury Press.

————. 1992c. "On Beaded Dresses and the Blazing Sun." In *Sitting at the Feet of the Past: Retelling the North American Folktale for Children*, edited by Gary D. Schmidt and Donald R. Hettinga. Westpoint, CT: Greenwood Press.

————. 1993. *The Lost Children*. New York: Bradbury Press.

Goodchild, Peter, editor. 1991. *Raven Tales: Traditional Stories of Native Peoples*. Chicago: Chicago Review Press.

Gregg, Andy, reteller; illustrated by Cat Bowman Smith, 1993. *Great Rabbit and the Long-Tailed Wildcat*. Morton Grove, IL: Albert Whitman.

Martin, Rafe, reteller; illustrated by David Shannon. 1992. *The Rough-Face Girl*. New York: G.P. Putnam's Sons.

McDermott, Gerald. 1972. *Anansi the Spider*. New York: Holt, Rinehart, Winston.

————. 1973. *The Magic Tree*. New York: Holt, Rinehart, Winston.

————. 1974. *Arrow to the Sun: A Pueblo Indian Tale*. New York: Viking.

————. 1975a. "On the Rainbow Trail." *Horn Book* 51 (April): 123-31.

————. 1975b. *The Stonecutter*. New York: Viking.

————. 1977. *The Voyage of Osiris*. New York: Windmill/E.P. Dutton.

————. 1979. *The Knight of the Lion*. New York: Four Winds Press.

————. 1980a. *Sun Flight*. New York: Four Winds Press.

————. 1980b. *Papagayo: The Mischief Maker*. New York: Windmill/Wanderer.

————. 1986. *Daniel O'Rourke*. New York: Viking/Kestrel.

————. 1988. "Sky Father, Earth Mother: An Artist Interprets Myth." *The New Advocate* 1: 1-7.

————. 1992. *Zomo the Rabbit*. San Diego: Harcourt Brace Jovanovich.

————. 1993. *Raven*. San Diego: Harcourt Brace Jovanovich.

————. 1994. *Coyote: A Trickster Tale from the American Southwest*. San Diego: Harcourt Brace Jovanovich.

Stott, Jon C. 1979. "An Interview with Gerald McDermott." *The World of Children's Books* 4 (Fall): 1-4.

————. 1984a. "Horses of Different Colors." *American Indian Quarterly* 8 (Spring): 117-25.

————. 1984b. "Profile: Paul Goble." *Lanugage Arts* 61 (December): 867-73.

————. 1994. Private conversation with Gerald McDermott. May 12, 1994.

Te Ata, reteller; adapted by Lynn Moroney; illustrated by Mina Reisberg. 1989. *Baby Rattlesnake*. Emeryville, CA: Children's Book Press.

Waterton, Betty; illustrated by Ann Blades. 1978. *A Salmon for Simon*. Vancouver, Canada: Douglas and McIntyre.

Young, Ed, reteller and illustrator. 1993. *Moon Mother: A Native American Creation Tale*. New York: Willa Perlman Books.

Native Tricksters and Legendary Heroes in Children's Stories

Adaptations of traditional stories constitute the majority of children's books about Native peoples. This should not be surprising. Since the middle of the last century most adults have believed that folktales, suitably altered, are appropriate for young readers. In addition, "social studies" experts wished to introduce children to the different, sometimes "queer" customs, fashions, and beliefs of cultures from other times and other places. However, the popularity of such types of stories does not ensure that each adaptation is an accurate reflection of the original story and the culture from which it emerged. Between the generations of oral presentation and their appearance on printed pages, Native stories undergo many steps or stages of transmission that allow for considerable alteration of content and intent. Anyone who has played the parlor game of whispering a written statement in someone's ear and then receiving a written version of the statement after it has been whispered around a circle will be aware of the possibility of error in each stage of transmission. However, the parlor game involves only a small group of people all speaking the same language and takes place in a small space and during a short period of time. The transmission from oral tale into children's book includes a movement across languages and through long periods of time and involves people whose treatment of the story is influenced by a wide variety of motives and attitudes.

When asked to pinpoint the original story on which their adaptation is based, most children's authors must give a highly qualified answer. With a very few exceptions, the retellers neither speak the language of the culture from which the tale has come, nor have heard an oral, albeit English, version of the story told by a Native person. Usually, the adaptations are built on research into anthropological books about the various cultures and their narratives, and often the adaptations are composites of several versions of the story found in these studies. Thus, it is difficult to state with certainty the nature of the stories from which the children's books came.

However, the following generalizations about the hypothetical originals can be made. At first, of course, the stories were presented orally, usually in a Native language. Storytellers were able to use voice pitch, tone, and volume, along with facial expressions and body language, to communicate various elements of their narratives. They would have used the unique resources of their specific Native tongues to the fullest, employing sounds and rhythms that enhanced the dramatic aspects. Moreover, they would have chosen levels of style appropriate to the serious or comic quality of the tales, levels no doubt established over generations of tellings. Each retelling, while adhering to the basic elements of the narrative, would have been unique, with the teller, aware of his audience and the situation of the performance, adapting the components in various degrees. Traditional stories were not static, for they evolved, not only slightly from telling to telling, but also in larger ways over the years as a result of changed social conditions and contacts with the customs and tales of other cultures.

In their original telling, the stories might seem extremely short, almost cryptic to a modern listener from outside the culture. However, as a Papago woman is reported to have explained to a white scholar transcribing one of her poems: "The song is very short because we understand so much" (Ramsey 1977, xxii). Members of this informed, involved audience would not have been limited to adults, for the concept of a specific children's literature was foreign to traditional Native cultures. Young auditors would have responded to what they understood. Undoubtedly, they frequently dozed off or let their minds wander when what they heard was either boring to them or beyond their levels of comprehension. They would, perhaps, have unconsciously assimilated elements beyond their understanding, pulling them from memory later when time, age, or experience permitted comprehension. Finally, most of the traditional stories, especially those considered sacred, would have been told during the winter season when there was more leisure time and, more important, when the spirit beings who might be offended by poorly told stories were likely to be dormant. The telling of stories was a shared, communal event, an expression of group identity that depended on common knowledge of both content and language and was unique to each tribe or culture group. Certainly coming close to this social and oral linguistic experience is extremely difficult, if not impossible, for the modern, non-Native children's author.

The usual stages of transmission increase the already great difficulties. The first print versions of most Native stories were written by white people who, listening to materials presented in what, to them, were second languages, may have missed the nuances of style and vocabulary only long familiarity with a language can bring; or by whites listening to Native translators whose command of English may have been limited. Moreover, they may have been given versions of narratives that either presenters or translators wanted them to hear, versions that disguised or even omitted elements of a sacred or spiritually powerful nature. Some tellers may have altered the tales to meet collectors' expectations of what Native tales should be.

The actual transcription of the stories transmitted was frequently influenced by factors that could further distance the tales from their performance originals. In addition to the simple problems inherent in translating any language into another is the fact that a language is an embodiment of thought processes and world views unique to its speakers. There are frequently no words in one language to express the words of another simply because the two cultures do not share the same concepts. Contemporary anthropologist Clifford Geertz has summarized the problems of transmission, transcription, and translation this way: " 'Translation' . . . is not a simple recasting of others' ways of putting things in terms of our ways of putting them, . . . but displaying the logic of their ways of putting them in the locutions of ours" (Geertz 1983, 10). Translators frequently experienced a stylistic dilemma. Franz Boas, the early twentieth-century scholar who is often called the "Father of Modern Anthropology," wanted almost literal, word-for-word translations to use "as raw data for an extensive analysis of myth motifs and cultures" (Maud 1993, viii). The result of such an approach among scholars who were not literary stylists was often plain, in a word "dull," prose. Literary artists, such as the late nineteenth-century authors Charles Godfrey Leland and Silas Rand, who rewrote northeast coast legends, sought to make their adaptations compatible with the tastes of their readers. Today these renditions often seem quaint, mannered, and old-fashioned. Moreover, they sometimes tidied up and tamed tales containing scatological and sexual references offensive to white readers and spiritual elements inimical to Christianity. Recent transmitters of Native stories, such as Jerome Rothenberg and Dennis Tedlock from what is referred to as the "School of Ethnopoetics," have created poetic English versions of traditional tales in which typographical features, page layout, and the rhythms of phrases attempt to recreate the characteristics of an oral performance in the original language. While this method of transmission may create results closer to the originals, it is still vulnerable to many of the dangers inherent in the process of transmission.

The next stage of transmission involves recasting the stories into forms suitable for audiences of non-Native children. Since most members of these audiences would be familiar with English and European folktales, or fairytales as they were usually called, this stage involved making Native stories resemble European ones as closely as possible. Even these European tales had been rigorously edited for children. Only those deemed comprehensible and nonthreatening to young readers and appropriate for nurturing their social and moral development were adapted. Offending elements were excised or altered. For example, as John M. Ellis has shown, the Brothers Grimm changed Hansel and Gretel's mother to a stepmother so as not to alarm children about their own mothers. Accordingly, Native tales containing unacceptable religious, moral, scatological, and sexual elements were either dismissed or altered drastically. Characters and events were made to resemble those of European tales. Supernatural beings were sometimes changed into fairies and elves; narratives of boys and girls, often orphans, courageously overcoming obstacles and growing to adulthood were popular; animal stories were frequently retold. The moral virtues emphasized were not generally related to the values of specific cultural groups, but to supposedly universal attributes of human nature, these usually being the same as those widely accepted among European peoples. The stories were generally longer than versions Native children would have heard. Being unfamiliar with physical and cultural backgrounds, readers required fuller, more detailed expositions and descriptions. Moreover, there were frequent passages of character analysis and recountings of inner thoughts, elements that would not have been found in Native tales, in which characters were representative types, not individuals, as is the case in much European children's literature.

In recent adaptations, greater efforts have been made to bring readers to the indigenous qualities of the stories rather than to make the stories conform to the readers' cultural and literary backgrounds and expectations. Some non-Native writers have heard the stories from Native tellers, and most engage in extensive research about the traditional cultural elements inherent in the narratives. Today, many Native peoples are themselves writing versions of the stories they have grown up with. Nonetheless, all of these recent books, like their predecessors, are vastly different from the oral originals. They are fixed, print versions, static renditions depending on writing to convey what have now, within the pages of a specific book, become unchanging conflicts, themes, and characters. Although these may be read aloud to groups of children, they can also be read silently by one person. The dynamic interplay between teller/creator and listener/recreator is usually absent. No matter how accurate and sympathetic these adaptations may be, they and their narrative voices are very different and far removed from the original narratives and narrators.

In selecting children's versions of traditional Native tales, adults must ask several important questions. What, in all probability, would the original version of a specific story have been like? What cultural values would it have embodied? What were the stages of its translation, transcription, and adaptation from oral story to children's book? What are the personal backgrounds of the authors, and what background research have they engaged in? How have these influenced the writing of the story? How has the story been influenced by the authors' conceptions of the audience and what is suitable and appropriate literature for it? How have authors been influenced by current publishing fashions and concepts about the nature of traditional Native peoples? And, finally, what is the meaning that emerges from the book as it is written? In order better to answer these questions and examine the stages of transmission, the remainder of this chapter will consider children's book portrayals of two representative character types found in Native literature: the trickster and the culture hero. Coyote is a trickster whose adventures and misadventures have been told widely across the plains, in the Southwest and the interior plateau, and along the Oregon and California coasts. Nanabozho, the culture hero of the Ojibway peoples of the upper Great Lakes, was first introduced to non-Native audiences in the 1830s by Michigan Indian Agent Henry Rowe Schoolcraft and soon after made tremendously popular and misnamed Hiawatha by New England poet Henry Wadsworth Longfellow.

TRACKING THE TRICKSTER: COYOTE AND HIS COUSINS

The trickster figure is found in traditional stories from around the world. To West Africans he is Anansi; to southern African Americans, Br'er Rabbit. In Greek mythology, he appears as Hermes (Mercury); in Norse mythology, as Loki. The Bible calls him Satan. In medieval England he was incarnated as Robin Hood. Across Native North America, he has a variety of names: Napi, the Old Man (Blackfoot); Iktomi, the Spider (Lakota); Nanabozho, the Great Rabbit, who is also a culture hero (Ojibway); Saynday (Kiowa); Wesakajuk (Cree); Glooscap (Micmac); and in many cultures, Coyote, the Wanderer. In all his forms, he possesses a dominant trait, extreme cunning, which he sometimes uses to benefit others, but most frequently to fulfill his selfish desires, and which he sometimes misuses, causing great harm to himself. The various Native American tales about the trickster reveal characteristics related to specific cultures. However, the tales also reveal enough common traits to make a generic profile of the trickster possible. The existence of common traits suggests either that the various culture specific groups of trickster stories all derive from a common source, or that neighboring culture groups exchanged trickster stories.

A few brief quotes from twentieth-century scholars and authors will indicate essentials of the trickster's nature. Jarold Ramsey has called him "all man's epitome" (Ramsey 1983, 25), while Gary Snyder identified him with "something in ourselves which is creative, unpredictable, contradictory" (Snyder 1975, 260). To Karl Kerényi, he is "the spirit of disorder, the enemy of boundaries" (Kerényi 1972, 185), and to Gerald Vizenor, "The Trickster of Liberty" (Vizenor 1988, title page). Kenneth Lincoln believes him to be "reality's 'credible' fool" (Lincoln 1983, 196), and Carl Jung sees the trickster as a representative of the "undifferentiated human consciousness, corresponding to a psyche that has hardly left the animal level" (Jung 1972, 200). Pancho Aguila terms him the "chameleon trickster of change" (Aguila 1982, 34), while Kenneth Lincoln focuses his attention on the character's "divine demonism" (Lincoln 1983, 123). Contained within these phrases are recognitions of the complex and contradictory nature of the trickster and reflections of the wide variety of attitudes toward him held by both traditional audiences and modern commentators.

Most trickster stories begin with some variant of the phrase "Trickster was going/walking/trotting/travelling along." Generally, he travels alone, revealing a general restlessness, seeking to fulfill his basic needs: food, sex, a sense of self-importance, and a desire for power over other beings and the natural environment. Ramsey has noted that he is on the margins of his society; although he may have a wife and children and casual relationships with his group, he acts only for himself and opposes "restraint or altruistic, responsibly domestic, or executive motives" (Ramsey 1983, 26). Never part of a noble or ruling clique, he nevertheless seeks control over others for his own, rather than the general good. As the solitary wanderer, the trickster figure may well reflect the single human being motivated by an instinct for survival, travelling through a world in which he does not really belong, using his wits to achieve his own physical and psychological well-being. Even after a defeat, which sometimes results in his death, he quickly recovers to begin again his search for his own fulfillment.

His marginality and self-centeredness, his restless wandering and seeming homelessness, his tenuous relationship with a social group to which he does not belong but on which he partially depends for the satisfaction of his needs have frequently been noted by scholars and commentators and have often been interpreted in opposing ways. Psychologist Carl Jung saw in these aspects representations of human beings in a lower state of moral and social evolution. The character symbolized elements that later were controlled by social organizations seeking general rather than individual good. The stories reminded listeners of what each one, as an immature child, had been and of what human beings had been in some earlier era and illustrated the dangers of being trapped in or regressing to an infantile, animal-like state. However, other commentators have viewed the trickster's character, situation, and actions in a more positive light. Ramsey, for example, suggests that, in societies where the tribal norms, the general will, and accepted rules of behavior tended to stifle individuals, the trickster represented the vital principles of each person that are a necessary counterpart and complement to social conformity. All people have unique, inner identities that are as important as, and sometimes in conflict with, their socially defined identities.

Part of the complexity of the trickster figure arises from the fact that he plays a variety of roles in the narratives and sometimes more than one role in a single story. In some tales he is a creator, although secondary in importance to a supreme or first being. In this role, he is almost a tag-along, wanting to appear important, providing such necessities as fire, but sometimes giving questionable gifts, the most obvious being death. In trying both to gain acceptance and to fulfill his ego needs, he messes up the world of the original creator.

In other stories, he is a transformer, altering existing plants, animals, and geographical features, giving them the characteristics they still possess; that is, he takes the earlier world and gives it its present form. His motivations for transforming are sometimes altruistic, sometimes completely selfish. For example, the Blackfoot trickster Napi provides mountain goats with a certain type of hoof because he wants them to be able to travel on steep and rocky terrain. But Iktomi, the Lakota trickster, gives the duck its awkward, waddling gait because it had disrupted his plan for a huge feast. The trickster has also acted as a culture hero, slaying monsters who threatened the people. In some versions of their creation myth, the Navajo people attribute this deed to Coyote, but show him to be as pleased with his accomplishment as he is with its benefits to others. Most frequently, the trickster's adventures focus directly on his search for food, sexual gratification, and ego fulfillment. Often lazy by nature, he either will manipulate others so that they, in effect, do the work for him or will himself perform extensive, arduous labors to meet his objectives. In the Cree version of the story of the trickster who captures and kills an excessive number of ducks for a huge feast, Wesakajuk flatters the birds, whom he thinks are stupid, into constructing the lodge which will, in fact, become their death house. In an Ojibway version, Nanabozho himself works under the hot midday sun to build a wigwam, with the result that he later falls asleep and loses his entire banquet. In the former case, the trickster is an extremely clever manipulator using language to create a disguise, that of a respectful friend of the ducks, to get much with little effort. In the latter, he is a self-defeating buffoon.

Scholars have noted the conflicting, contradictory qualities of the trickster's character, motivations, and actions and have offered a variety of explanations for them, explanations that are generally hypothetical, often contradictory and conflicting, and, at best, only partly convincing. Traditional Native audiences, however, seem to have been untroubled by trickster's incredible variety. This was probably because, given the social situation in which a specific story was told, they expected a certain type of story and because early in each story would be found indications as to which of his familiar roles the trickster would assume. There is another, perhaps more significant reason for their easy acceptance of this variety. The trickster, as many scholars have suggested, represented, in exaggerated story form, the mixed nature of human beings; in responding to his adventures, audiences were projecting elements of themselves onto him. He could be a buffoon or a wise man, altruistic or selfish, heroic or villainous. He was, indeed, to repeat Ramsey's phrase, "all man's epitome" (Ramsey 1983, 25).

For what purpose did traditional peoples repeatedly retell these stories? They were interesting, entertaining narratives, that, like oft-repeated jokes or frequently watched videos, did not lose their appeal. And they were humorous; laughter was usually the immediate response to them. However, this laughter had serious implications. As Paul Radin observed about the Winnebago trickster cycle, "it is difficult to say whether the audience is laughing at him, at the tricks he plays on others, or at the implications his behavior and activities have for them" (Radin 1972, xxiv). Auditors might feel superior to the buffoon; they might fear that they, like his victims, could be tricked; they might nervously giggle and secretly wonder whether they possessed some of his negative characteristics.

Ramsey has noted the moral importance of the trickster tales in what he has termed "shame societies" (Ramsey 1977, xxxi), that is, culture groups in which moral instruction, as well as punishment for transgressions, was indirect and implicit. The tales gently presented lessons that members of the audience could apply to themselves without public ridicule and that children could use as guides for their own maturation and socialization processes. Laughter, like a spoon full of sugar, could make the moral medicine more palatable. Navajo storyteller Yellowman explained to J. Barre Toelken, his Anglo friend, the importance of tales for his children in this way: "Many things about the story are funny, but the story is not funny. . . . If my children hear the stories, they will grow up to be good people; if they don't hear them, they will turn out to be bad" (Toelken 1969, 221).

In addition, the stories had psychological functions important for the maintenance of a healthy, dynamic relationship within a group. Many of the trickster's activities are anti-social. Frequently, he violates sexual taboos, seducing maidens, cohabiting with his mother-in-law, and attempting to commit incest with his daughters. Although at times he succeeds, at others, he suffers painful genital mutilation. Sometimes, his actions mimic and mock those of the shaman, the powerful and feared spiritual authority of the group. This person frequently consulted spirit and animal helpers for advice; trickster seeks guidance from his feces, whose appearance is frequently preceded by strange noises and "spiritual" winds. The shaman travelled down into lakes, streams, and oceans, and up into the heavens on vision quests; trickster hitches a ride with migrating geese and dives into a stream after the reflection of berries—with disastrous results. Hearing and reacting to his audacious and foolish actions provided auditors with "safety valves," brief therapeutic escapes from the social rules and spiritual authorities that controlled their lives. Paradoxically, these tales also reaffirmed these controls; by breaking them, with harmful results for himself and others, trickster implicitly reaffirmed their importance for the well-being of the individual and the group.

Most of trickster's adventures take place in what has been termed the "Myth Age" (Ramsey 1977, xxiv), a time existing before the world assumed its present shape and in which human beings, animals, and spirit powers related freely with each other. However, the stories were not static. Not only did they change as they came into contact with similar stories from other cultural groups and according to the inclinations of individual storytellers and the specific situations of each performance, but also as the physical and cultural conditions of each group changed through time. Jung noted that "The fact that its [a story's] repeated telling has not long since become obsolete can, I believe, be explained by its usefulness" (Jung 1972, 207). Jung was referring to a story's ability to fulfill universal psychological needs. However, the "Incredible Survival" of trickster, as Anglo poet Gary Snyder has termed it (Snyder 1975, 255), occurred also because the stories met the specific needs of various Native American culture groups. Not only does trickster return to life after dying in some of his misadventures, but stories about him reappeared after European peoples moved across the continent displacing Native cultures and attempting to eradicate social and religious customs. Comanche people, for example, tell how trickster outwits the cowboys, missionaries, soldiers, and traders who invaded their lands in the late nineteenth century. These stories helped to "build up emotional self-confidence. . . . What better way than to allow Coyote, the worst bungler of them all, to trick the . . . most common agents of White culture" (Buller 1983, 256). Nearly a century later, such Native authors as N. Scott Momaday, Leslie Silko, Simon Ortiz, and Gerald Vizenor have created characters based on traditional tricksters, showing that figure's importance to Native peoples working to define themselves, their roles, and their values in a modern, urbanized, white-dominated world. Paula Gunn Allen, a Laguna Pueblo novelist-poet-critic, has written that Coyote "has been taken up by contemporary American Indian poets as a metaphor for all the foolishness and the anger that have characterized American Indian life in the centuries since invasion. He is also a metaphor for continuance. . . . it is this spirit of the trickster-creator that keeps Indians alive and vital in the face of horror" (Allen 1986, 158). Interestingly, among modern Native peoples, trickster in his more positive aspects is generally portrayed as Native; in his negative ones, he is often white. Judy Trejo, a Paiute, notes that her people "refer to young Anglo boys who sneak around gawking at young Indian girls as coyotes" (Trejo 1979, 196).

Because the focus of this analysis and evaluation of adaptations for children of trickster tales will be on Coyote, it is appropriate to consider his specific role and character in traditional stories. As noted, his are the most widely distributed of the trickster stories, from the California coast to the upper Midwest, from central British Columbia to Central America. What are the reasons for his widespread popularity? Part of the reason must arise from the almost ubiquitousness of the actual animal on which his physical appearance is based. Now seen in New York's Central Park and the back alleys of suburban Los Angeles, near the Arctic treeline and on the mountains of New Mexico, the coyote was often observed near the lands of the traditional peoples who told stories about him. Usually seen trotting alone, he was a cunning hunter; moreover, he could adapt himself to a variety of physical environments and was an amazing survivor, apparently invincible to the relentless attempts of white settlers to exterminate him. However, as much as the depictions of the trickster draw on characteristics of the actual animal, he is, as William Bright emphasizes (Bright 1987, 340), essentially human in his personality.

Coyote possesses all of the general trickster traits noted above. However, these are adapted to reflect beliefs of specific culture groups. Mac Linscott Ricketts has argued that the character was treated with greater seriousness in hunting cultures than in agricultural ones: "the more strongly the tribe has been influenced by an agricultural way of life, the less important is the place of the trickster-fixer in the total mythology of the tribe, and the more he tends to be known only as a trickster" (Ricketts 1966, 328).

Thus in the agricultural Pueblos of New Mexico and Arizona, Coyote is most widely portrayed as a buffoon and a mischief maker, an object of ridicule. However, to the Pueblo peoples' near neighbors, the Navajo, who were originally hunters and are now herders, he is a menacing figure who plays a central role in their most sacred rituals. This is particularly interesting because it is believed that after the Navajo had migrated to their present homelands, they "borrowed" Coyote stories from nearby Pueblos, adapting them to their purposes. In *Coyote Waits*, Tony Hillerman's detective novel featuring Navajo detectives, one of the characters remarks: "They say Coyote is funny, some of those people say that. But the old people who told me the stories, they didn't think Coyote was funny. Coyote was always causing trouble. He was mean. He caused hardship. He hurt people. He caused people to die" (Hillerman 1990, 70). An alcoholic who had been given whiskey by greedy and manipulative white men and then murdered a man believes he has been possessed by the evil spirit of Coyote who, as the title implies, lies in wait for just such opportunities to perpetrate evil. Hillerman's novel captures an essential Navajo belief about Coyote: his malign nature and power.

For the Navajo people, traditional and modern, the goal of a good life is to be in harmony with the universe, to be a part of the fragile balance that pervades all elements of the human, natural, and supernatural worlds. Sickness and evil, closely linked to each other, are the results of individuals falling under the influences of powerful witches. Stories and ceremonies have healing, restorative power for the people actively responsive to them, and both the rituals and stories about Coyote focus on attempts to maintain, disrupt, or regain the balance. Religious scholar Karl W. Luckert has traced the trickster's changing role in Navajo culture. When the people were mainly hunters, Coyote was a revered being whose cunning made him a successful hunter whose aid they sought. However, to the later herders, he became an enemy, as was his animal counterpart, who preyed on their flocks. Seeing him as the cause of their misfortunes, the Navajo developed the Evilway Ceremony designed to drive off the bad influence. Coyote became associated with witchcraft and, after the introduction of Christianity, Satan, who preyed on the Lord's flocks. In more secular stories, he was the fool whose misdeeds illustrated and warned against negative behaviors.

In 1987, J. Barre Toelken, a long time researcher of Navajo tales and a close friend of several Navajo storytellers, after witnessing Navajo reactions to a lecture he had given about Coyote, reported his startling encounter with the sinister implications of Coyote.

> The stories about Coyote are themselves considered so powerful, their articulation so magical, their recitation in winter so deeply connected to the normal powers of natural cycles, their episodes so reminiscent of central myths, their imagery so tightly connected with reality, that elliptical reference to them in a ritual can invoke all the powers inherent in their original dramatic constellations. (Toelken 1987, 390)

The Coyote stories, which provided humor and entertainment, were used to educate children, by negative example, about their adult roles in a balanced, harmonious universe. A judge in one of the Navajo courts supposedly stated that "Coyote stories should be told at the homes again, . . . and the stories should be followed up by instructions as was done of old" (Haile 1984, 20). They could also evoke healing or destroying forces. In the evil aspect, the qualities of witchcraft—"competitive [and] acquisitive" (Toelken 1987, 396)— could be unleashed on the person telling the stories, destroying harmony. By analysing the deeper levels of these stories, Toelken was told that he faced great danger to himself or members of his family and could even become a witch himself. Accordingly, he has resolved to stay away from discussing these potentially evil-producing aspects of the stories, leaving them, as they should be, in the hands of those Navajo people equipped with the knowledge, wisdom, and skills for dealing safely with them.

Just how culture-specific the Coyote stories are can be seen by comparing the Navajo attitudes with those of the Hopi people, who also live in northern Arizona, their lands completely surrounded by the much larger Navajo reservation. Both groups inhabit the same physical environment, but speak different languages and hold different religious beliefs. Later arrivals, Navajo herders may have been influenced in some of their customs and beliefs by the agrarian Hopi, but their view of Coyote is vastly different. The basic differ-ence has been summarized as follows:

> In the course of the history of religions, archaic gods who are in the process of being replaced by newer divinities have . . . only two alternate survival routes open to them. These include continuation of being taken seriously, but as an evil devil-being, and, survival as a harmless fool at the level of an entertaining fairytale figure. In Navajo tradition, which hap-pens to thrive still close to the culture stratum of hunters, Coyote is taken very seriously, both as a demonic witch-person and as a god. In the present volume of Hopi stories he roams still as a hunter, but at the level of comfortable harmlessness. (Malotki and Lomatuway'ma 1984, vi-vii)

In the introduction to *Gullible Coyote/Una'ihu*, Ekkehart Malotki has summarized Hopi attitudes. The word for the animal, *issaw*, is also the word that approximates the English slang expression "sucker." The people have no use for the animal's pelt or the meat, although in the winter they hunt coyotes, as much for sport as for controlling the species' population. To them the coyote is both a poor hunter and a wasteful scavenger, ravaging their fields. They have no kachina dolls representing coyote, although there are many representing other spiritually powerful and more respected animals; and no shaman will take Coyote as a helping spirit. Although in earlier times, Coyote may have possessed stronger powers of evil, the Hopi now consider that the greatest danger he possesses is an ability to transmit his gullibility and stupidity to a hunter who has killed him or to the hunter's children. Coyote is also adulterous, a quality the members of the Coyote clan, who are frequently viewed with disdain by other Hopi, are thought to share. Stories about him usually present these degrading qualities. Even in stories where he acts as a helper, he is usually a bungler. In acquiring fire, for example, he drops a flaming brand when it scorches his fur and the stick must be carried back to the community by other animals. Helping Spider Woman arrange the stars in the sky, he becomes excited and impatient and flings them into the heavens in a jumble. "Coyote is likened to the Hopi clown whose sacred duty it is, among other things, to hold up a mirror to the foibles, evil intentions, and wrong-doings of the Hopi audience" (Malotki 1985, 20).

The differences in the Navajo and Hopi views of Coyote can be seen by comparing a popular story told by both peoples, the narrative about Coyote and Horned Toad (or Lizard). In outline, the stories are similar: Coyote enters Horned Toad's garden and swallows Horned Toad, who, wandering about in Coyote's innards searching for an escape, causes his swallower's death. Horned Toad then emerges from his captor's anus. The simple moral is the same for both versions: cruel actions motivated by selfish greed will lead to disaster for the perpetrator. However, significant differences in details between the versions create different cultural themes.

In the Navajo version, Coyote, who has a garden, leaves it to invade his neighbor's. After accusing Toad of stealing from him, he swallows the little animal and goes to sleep in his victim's hogan. Later, he threatens the victim with real death, saying he will precipitate himself off of a cliff. When he dies as a result of Horned Toad's cutting out his heart, Coyote is revived by the winds and thunder. Returning home feeling very ill, he informs his family that he is going away to die. His intention is to return much later in disguise so as to be able to seduce his daughter. Clearly, Coyote in this story is unrepentantly evil, falsely accusing someone else of the very act of thievery he is contemplating, attempting to murder another, and scheming to commit incest. Death, deeply feared by the Navajo, is treated lightly by him and, real or pretend, is something used to achieve selfish, not common goals. Coyote seems aware of the evil spirits that would surround a dead person's hogan, for when he thinks he hears ghost noises, he remarks: "Is there any wonder about it, when one occupies a ghost's house" (Haile 1984, 48). But he seems oblivious to the awesome implications of the suicide he proposes and trivially feigns death for lustful purposes. The physical illness he feels on returning home is symptom-atic of spiritual illness, a basic Navajo belief that he recognizes when he remarks: "No wonder! When people (always) despise and hate a person, how can one be in good health" (Haile 1984, 48). No Holyway curing ceremony can ever help this evil being. Even though he is given a second chance, as it were, being brought back to life by the supernatural powers of the wind and thunder, he remains unregenerate.

In the Hopi version, Coyote Woman is a lazy hunter, while Horned Lizard is a hard-working watermelon farmer who feels obligated to invite Coyote (whom he at first mistakes for a Navajo) to lunch. Horned Lizard is swallowed by his guest, who wishes to provide for her family without the need of arduous hunting. Suffering great pain because of Horned Lizard's wanderings among her vital organs, Coyote Woman reveals her gullibility: when she gives him directions to an exit, her anus, she sends him through her intestines and bowels, which he tears apart, causing her death. In some ways, the story is a parody of the Hopi emergence myth. Like most Pueblo peoples, the Hopi believed that people arrived from a subterranean world to this one through the *sipapu*, a hole in the earth. The remark that Horned Lizard's "mind was set on locating the hole where he could emerge" (Malotki 1985, 154) would certainly strike Hopi listeners as a parody of one of their most important spiritual narratives. At the end of the story, Coyote Woman is dead and is not reborn (at least until the beginning of the next story). The values of the agrarian Hopi way of life, symbolized by Horned Lizard, are victorious. The lumps on his back, acquired when watermelon seeds stick to him during his intestinal journey, are present reminders of his triumph. Coyote, although lazy and greedy, is seen as an embodiment of unacceptable and foolish behavior rather than of powerful evil.

Needless to say, creators of children's versions of trickster stories do not include scatological or sexual episodes. However, they may use stories containing these episodes, altering what they deem offensive selections and thus deviating from the intentions or meanings of the originals. Adaptors may include the moral and religious elements but in presenting these may render them in terms more familiar to and within the supposed range of comprehension of young non-Native readers, thereby robbing the stories of their sacred significance. Whether or not adaptors imply the elements of evil that Toelken has found in Navajo stories is debatable. The major questions to ask about adapted versions are: How closely and how well do the children's stories present the narrative details, conflicts, and characters and the cultural values inherent in the originals? Is the culture specifically identified? Are the sources of the adaptations identified?

Three recent children's books present versions of California myths depicting Coyote's role in the creation of the world and its transformation into its present state. As folklorist Stith Thompson has noted, despite the variety of cultures and languages in the region, the various groups' origin myths have many elements in common (Thompson 1977, 305). Floating alone or with a companion on a watery void, the creator shapes a world out of earth brought up from the depths and brings plants, animals, and human beings to life. Coyote, although he bestows the gift of fire, is generally a secondary figure, quarrelling with the creator and disrupting his work. However, hard work, pain, disease, and death enter the world through Coyote's agency.

Betty Baker, a white author of several children's novels about traditional Native life, has amalgamated several of these myths in *And Me, Coyote!* Although she does not cite her sources, the dustjacket notes that her story is based "on Native American creation myths from central and southern California." Floating in the water with World Maker and his blind brother, Coyote obeys the creator, who commands him to sneeze and shake his fur, thus creating the land and food. However, he claims an equal role in the operation and angers the brother, who spitefully releases sickness into the world. In order to help Coyote, who complains of poor hunting conditions, World Maker places the sun, moon, and stars into the sky. Finally, when the creator sets about to fashion human beings, Coyote demands that they "be smart like me" (Baker 1982, n.p.) and, of course, takes credit for the job. Baker omits the delight that Coyote feels in some versions as he gazes at the newly formed woman and the widely distributed episode in which he causes death and then regrets his decision when his son is the first to die. Thus, negative elements of his character and the idea of his cosmic blundering are omitted. He appears merely as foolish for his ill-founded pride in his role in the creation.

In *Back in the Beforetime: Tales of the California Indians*, Jane Louise Curry also amalgamates stories from several tribes. A well-known writer of fantasy novels, Curry began collecting legends while a graduate student studying in England. Intended for a general and, therefore, largely white audience from ages 8 to 12, the collection of 22 tales begins with the creation of the world and ends with the creation of human beings. Coyote appears in 15 tales, providing such useful services as causing the sun to travel east to west each day, acquiring fire, and freeing salmon from imprisonment by evil witches. More often, he is up to his tricks, attempting to feed his appetites and ego and usually failing because of his selfishness. The theme of cooperation underlies the narratives: when creatures work together, the results are positive and everyone benefits. Gracefully told and quick moving, the stories are entertaining and their morals never too obvious. Yet they are also somewhat bland, with those about Coyote never really capturing the trickster's cheeky insouciance and resilience.

The major problem with the collection becomes obvious after one reads the brief "Author's Note" at the end of the book. Curry reports that the tales are taken from tribes all over California and that she has selected "those legends which could be woven together to tell the larger tale of Creation from the making of the world to man's rise to lordship of the animals" (Curry 1987, 133). Her object has been to construct a mythology like that of the Bible or the Icelandic Elder Edda, and she has departed from a Native point of view in the phrase "man's rise to lordship over the animals," giving human beings a role that is European in its focus. Moreover, in yoking together stories from diverse areas and from groups possessing different lifestyles and languages, she has homogenized the rich variety of California's traditional Native cultures. If their myths are spiritual responses to specific environments, this collection, which, incidentally, gives no sources for the stories, does not make this evident. Curry has also taken the liberty of joining together myths from different tribes to tell "a composite tale" (Curry 1987, 133). Her motivations, she says, come from the fact that she is "a storyteller rather than a folklorist" (Curry 1987, 133). In the interest of telling good stories, she loses much in the transmission.

Fire Race: A Karuk Coyote Tale is a northern California version of a tale found in many Native cultures: the acquisition of fire by theft from selfish, often supernatural beings. Coyote faces and successfully solves three major problems: how to enter the dwelling of the three wasp sisters, the fire's wary guardians; how to get fire back to the other people; and how to liberate fire from the tree in which it has been placed by one of his helpers. What is interesting in this version, retold by Jonathan London with the assistance of Pomo/Miwok storyteller Larry Pinola, is the completely positive portrayal of Coyote. Scholar William Bright notes that in a (very similar) Karuk version he collected, "it is clear that Coyote enjoys the stealing for its own sake and the joy of the trickery involved" (Bright 1993, 84). In *Fire Race*, however, "Wise Old Coyote" is aware of the misery of his friends and calls a meeting in which he stresses the necessity of cooperation if they are to succeed. Before he departs, he outlines the plan he has carefully formulated. In contrast, another version by Barry Lopez states that when he arrives at the place where the fire is kept, Coyote has no plan. He defecates, liberating his three sisters who live in his stomach, seeks their advice, and then takes all of the credit for himself. While the scatological aspects would be unacceptable in a modern children's book, they do have the effect of diminishing Coyote's wisdom and emphasizing his vanity. In *Fire Race*, Coyote is far more clever and altruistic. His first problem is solved when he flatters the Yellow Jacket sisters and tells them to close their eyes. This done, he grabs the burning stick and organizes a relay in which each animal carries the fire until too tired to go any farther and then passes it on. For the usually self-centered and individualistic Coyote, this exhibition of cooperation is unusual. Finally, when Frog spits the hot coal into a willow tree, Coyote shows his friends how to liberate it by rubbing two branches together.

Why should *Fire Race* depict Coyote as an admirable culture hero instead of as a vain self-seeker? A reason may be found in the "Afterword" written by Karuk essayist Julian Lang. "Both children and adults were taught through stories about the special relationship that we must keep between ourselves and the natural world" (London 1993, n.p.). Coyote's character and actions help the people to "remember and respect each other" (London 1993, n.p.). When members of the audience see the animals spoken of in the story, they will remember the moral lessons. As in most Coyote stories, then, the hero provides a moral example, but in this case, for a modern audience living in a natural world threatened by lack of cooperation, a positive one.

Coyote Places the Stars, a recent picture book by Harriet Peck Taylor, presents a Wasco (Oregon) version of one of the trickster's most significant activities: giving the heavens their present appearance. Star stories are important in the mythologies of all Native American culture groups. The myths explain the nature, origins, and interrelationships of the stars in ways that reflect the values that the cultures place on certain types of human conduct and relationships. In addition, many of the stories deal with travels by both star beings and human beings between the sky and earth worlds. Unlike modern European peoples who view the stars as distant, inaccessible, and, at best, slightly knowable masses of matter and energy, most traditional Native peoples believed in a vital universe in which they were frequently related to stars who were similar to them, although usually superior. Their cosmos was unified, and they were part of a linked, vital whole. Thus, the stories were truly mythic, for, as well as inculcating moral and social values, they represented a time when the two worlds and its peoples were more closely linked than they usually were at the times of the stories' telling.

Taylor's adaptation is a clear example of how altering a source or omitting sections from it can radically change its meaning. She lists her sources as Barry Lopez's *Giving Birth to Thunder, Sleeping with his Daughter: Coyote Builds North America* and *They Dance in the Sky: Native American Star Myths*, by Jean Guard Monroe and Ray A. Williamson. They, in turn, based their adaptations on a version first published in 1953 by Ella E. Clark in *Indian Legends of the Pacific Northwest*. Clark credits an oral version first collected earlier in the century, so her written rendition is most likely closest to the Wasco source. The myth is one of a series told along the Columbia River in which Coyote, sometimes for positive, but generally for negative reasons, transforms the world into the form it now exhibits.

Clark's story begins with Coyote living with a family of five wolves who generously share their food with him. With the family and its dog, he climbs into the heavens on an arrow ladder he has created, so that all can get a closer look at two animals the family has seen in the sky. However, thinking that the wolves, who are staring at the grizzly bears they find in the sky, make a good picture, he maroons them, climbing down the ladder, which he dismantles behind him. However, at this point, Coyote becomes worried: "Who will know about the picture if I die? . . . I want the new people [the soon to be created human beings] to know that it is my work" (Clark 1953, 154), and he commands the meadowlark to fly above the earth singing his praises, something that the bird still does. Coyote makes a second trip, this time with benevolent motives. Warned that the rapidly increasing number of stars could fall to earth causing the world to turn to frost, he arranges the Milky Way and the rest of the constellations—the first being the Big Dipper, which comprises the wolf brothers, their dog, and the two bears. In addition to being a pourquoi story explaining the origin of the constellations and the meadowlark's song, the tale presents the conflicting moral qualities of Coyote's nature. An unproductive member of his adopted family, he cruelly abandons them so that he can enjoy the picture they make, and he vainly assumes that his role will be remembered. However, on his second trip, he is a hero, working for the safety of the earth, if only, perhaps, to make it a more comfortable place for himself.

Coyote Places the Stars omits the first journey and provides Coyote with vastly different reasons for making the second one. Climbing to the heavens on an arrow chain, he decides to arrange the stars into patterns representing his animal friends. Returning home, he calls the animals together and, although he explains that they are viewing his handiwork, "I hope that all who see it will remember Coyote and all the animals of the canyon" (Taylor 1993, n.p.). When the animals celebrate his achievement with a feast, he pledges, "I will always be your friend and the friend of your children's children" (Taylor 1993, n.p.). To this day, his nocturnal howls are a call to human beings to look at the constellations and, it seems to be implied, to remember the animals they represent. Obviously, the omission of the first journey removes from the story the negative elements of Coyote's character that audiences of the original version would have observed and learned from. In the journey he does make, although he displays a touch of vanity, he also reveals a sense of friendship and sensitivity toward the other animals that transforms the tale into a parable of good will rather than of self-centeredness. This Coyote is a good neighbor, a member of the group, not a devious loner of whom the other animals should be suspicious and even fearful. The statement that his howls are a call to human beings to notice and then to remember the animals seems almost to imply a modern ecological message: see the constellations, remember the animals, and then be a friend to them, just as Coyote was.

Two collections of well-known Navajo Coyote tales have been published specifically for Navajo children. *Coyote Stories of the Navajo People*, a project of the Rough Rock Press, a branch of the Navajo Curriculum Center, contains 14 tales based on legends contributed by elders, edited by school officials, and reviewed by "many other Navajos" (Roessel 1991, n.p.). *Navajo Coyote Tales*, which contains four of the same stories and adds two others, presents simplified, easy-to-read versions that, according to the back cover, "were collected directly from the Navajo by William Morgan and translated into English" (Morgan 1988, n.p.). The two books' vastly different styles reflect their different purposes and help to create different meanings for the four stories retold in both books. The tales are extremely well known and would, no doubt, be familiar to their intended audiences. As Toelken has noted, Coyote stories, including several in these books, formed an integral part of the detailed and complex Navajo creation myth. So powerful are they, he notes, that even brief allusions to them can evoke spiritual forces central to the great healing ceremonies (Toelken 1987, 396). The tale in which Coyote loses his eyeballs in a juggling game is important in the curing of eye diseases, and the story in which he swallows Horned Toad is used in ceremonies relating to internal disorders. Moreover, Coyote's excesses, weaknesses, malicious intentions, and foolishness represented aspects of behavior that could disastrously disrupt the fragile balance of the world in which the people lived. Obviously, the two books omit off-color aspects of the traditional stories. However, do they embody the serious medical, moral, and religious aspects of the traditional tales? And if so, how are these aspects presented?

An examination of each volume's preface and version of the well-known story about Coyote and Skunk will suggest answers.

The "Foreword" to *Coyote Stories* states that, although it is hoped the tales will benefit non-Navajo students, they are primarily designed to "help Navajo children achieve a positive self-image" (Roesel 1991, n.p.). While this statement may partly allude to the importance of having Navajo rather than Anglo stories in the classroom, it most probably refers to the effect of the stories themselves, which will inculcate and reinforce cultural values. In his introduction, Gary Witherspoon, the Director of the Navajo Curriculum Center, notes the tales' central place in the various ceremonies, and emphasizes that "They are considered actual occurrences and not the results of artistic imaginations" (Roessel 1991, n.p.). They are also told in homes during the winter, usually by older men, and the elders who contributed to this volume request that, in recognition of their spiritual reality and power, they be read or studied only "between the first frost in the fall and the first thunder in the spring" (Roessel 1991, n.p.). Although written in English in a prose style similar to that of other books the children no doubt read, the tales are clearly presented with full awareness of the crucial role they play in fostering the well-being of the students and the society of which they will become adult members.

In the "Introduction" to *Navajo Coyote Tales*, Robert W. Young, identified only as a "Specialist in Indian Languages," begins by lamenting the decline in "the last decade or so" (Morgan 1988, 1) of the Navajo tradition of storytelling. Not only does he seem unaware of the existence of *Coyote Tales*, first published nearly two decades earlier than this book, he also presents a limited account of the purposes of Navajo storytelling. These tales, he says, alleviated the tedium of long winter nights and presented morals through the narration of adventures of "personified animals" (Morgan 1988, 2). This opinion does not take into account the real and powerful spiritual aspects of the characters or the fact that children would also have heard the stories or parts of them when they attended the sacred healing ceremonies. After noting similarities in theme and purpose between these and traditional European children's stories, Young states that the selected vocabulary and sentence structure are designed to reinforce reading skills. "Consequently, the form and language of the tales vary radically from that which characterized the original version. But the subject matter . . . is wholly Navajo" (Morgan 1988, 2). However, he does not note that the repetitive style of a basal reader is very different from the deeply rhythmic, ritualized repetitions of the great Navajo chants. If, as Toelken (1969) has emphasized, form and style are essential to all levels of meaning in a Navajo story, these versions lack both the spirit (whatever Young means by that term) and deeper significance of the originals. They do represent, however, one non-Native view, and a disputed one at that, of what constitutes an appropriate textbook for beginning Navajo readers. Teachers using the book might want their students to display their newly acquired school skills to parents; it is doubtful if Navajo parents would be quite so pleased hearing children read from it as teachers might hope.

"Coyote and Skunk" is a Navajo variant of a story found all across the Great Plains: the narrative of how the gluttonous and devious trickster is tricked out of an excessive feast he has prepared for himself. Among the people of the northern plains, the trickster loses water fowl, and the story is an illustration of the consequences of violating the hunting rituals that concerned showing respect for animals and not killing more birds than needed. As Toelken has shown (1969), the Navajo version embodies many deeply held Navajo beliefs; these beliefs would have been implicit in the telling, and young members of the audience would have been expected to understand them. Familiar with the events of the story, they would have been responding in ritual fashion both to what they heard and what they intuited.

The tale begins as Coyote uses his powers to wish a heavy rain to float him to an area near the home of prairie dogs. In the version collected by Haile, he desires the water to cool him off; in Toelken's version (1969), as the first part of a scheme to seek revenge on the prairie dogs, who have mocked him. In either case, it is implied that Coyote employs his powers and uses the precious rain for selfish reasons. As Skunk wanders by, Coyote asks him to cover him with worm-like grasses and to report to nearby animals that he is dead and that they should celebrate with a dance, during which Coyote plans to club them to death. Toelken suggests that the dance the animals perform would be like a healing ceremony designed to rid them of the negative, evil forces associated with Coyote, even when he is dead. After Skunk blinds the animals with his spray and Coyote kills them, the fire is prepared, with Skunk doing all the work in Toelken's version. Coyote lacks the cooperative spirit he had earlier encouraged in Skunk. The trickster suggests the two have a race, with the winner in Toelken's version getting the fattest animals. Skunk, with ideas of his own, ambles behind a bush, while Coyote races by, a flaming stick tied to his tail. He does not see Skunk because of the smoke raised by the stick. The fire, Toelken suggests, would be a parody of the well-known tale of Coyote's acquisition of fire. Doubling back, Skunk eats the choicest prairie dogs and hides. Coyote returns in a grand flourish designed to illustrate his racing prowess and first decides to wait so as not to display his greed. Then he decides to devour the feast. After discovering the trick, he pleads for food, committing a tremendous breach of Navajo etiquette, and is offered bones and offal, the rewards of the scavenger not the hunter. Not only has he revealed his vanity, greed, and indecorum, he has performed the more reprehensible acts of not helping with work and wasting precious rain, and, more significant, he has misused supernatural powers and feigned death, activities very dangerous in his culture. His attitude toward water is also reflected in his killing of the prairie dogs, for they were related to the coming of rain. Toelken quotes this Navajo saying: "If you kill off the prairie dogs, there will be no one to cry for rain" (Toelken 1987, 391).

The text prepared by the Navajo Curriculum Center includes all of the important elements of these traditional versions and adds three others that are significant. Coyote is made more gluttonous, suggesting the race so that he can get all, not just the best meat. When he discovers the meal missing, he begins to dig frantically, cool calculation having been replaced by panic. He appears even more foolish and reprehensible. Moreover, Skunk agrees to the race because he has already formulated his plan to double back. The trickster is tricked, justice has been achieved, and a kind of balance restored to the world. While young students might not be completely aware of the implicit significance of all the details they read, they will have become more fully aware of incidents that will assume greater meaning to them when the stories are repeated as part of their moral and religious training.

By contrast, "Coyote and Skunk Woman," from *Navajo Coyote Tales*, includes only the basic points of the story. Coyote, being hot, calls up the rain to float him "to many prairie dogs" (Morgan 1988, 28). When Skunk arrives, coyote asks that the animals be brought to the scene, which is quickly done. After the spraying and clubbing, the two build a fire and Coyote suggests the race. Skunk hides, returns, eats the feast, and leaves the bones for Coyote. Neither character is given motivation for its action; the bulk of the short text consists of repetition of words and phrases. While most of the phrases are repeated four times, this repetition is not intended to emphasize plot or to imply a reverse use of the number four so important in legend, but rather to increase the readers' ability to recognize key written words and phrases. An interesting example occurs when Skunk wanders near Coyote's body. "Sssst" (Morgan 1988, 29), the trickster says four times, a sound similar to "Psst" and designed to attract someone's attention. In the version recorded by Toelken, Coyote repeats "Shilna'ash" (Toelken 1969, 216), four times, a term roughly equivalent to "old buddy" (Toelken 1969, 233), as he begins setting the other animal up, pretending friendship so that he will have help in executing his plans for revenge and much food. Native readers of the Morgan adaptation would gain from it a greater familiarity with English words they might encounter in other books than with elements of their own heritage.

Another Navajo Coyote adventure is *Ma'ii and Cousin Horned Toad*, retold and illustrated by Navajo artist Shonto Begay. Dedicated to "the spirit of *Dineh*/To the elders. . . , To the youth" (Begay 1992, n.p.), this *Ma'ii Jol Dlooshi* or "coyote out walking" (Begay 1992, n.p.) teaching story, is, the author notes, designed to "show us proper ways to conduct ourselves" (Begay 1992, n.p.). And, as is typical of Navajo teaching stories, the narrative shows, rather than states, presenting Coyote's thoughts and actions so that readers can intuit the moral lessons. Such an approach is not only an appropriate Navajo technique, it is also a useful one for a book put out by a major mainstream children's publisher (Scholastic) and intended for a largely non-Native audience. Uninitiated readers can proceed through the narrative without being slowed down by exposition and can imply either non-culture-specific morals or morals that relate to their own cultures. Notice, for example, that Coyote does not die and that Horned Toad does not escape through the predator's anus. Inclusion of these details would not have shocked traditional or most contemporary Navajo audiences. However, omission or revision does not drastically alter either the general or culture-specific themes and avoids the risk of offending the adults who select and purchase most books for children.

Because Begay's fine illustrations complement but do not generally expand the meanings of the words, we can analyze how the written narrative, which includes the basic details of the traditional tale, serves its Navajo teaching function. Hot and hungry, Coyote decides to mooch a meal from Horned Toad. "He liked his stomach full, not noisy" (Begay 1992, n.p.), the narrator notes in a phrase that ironically foreshadows Coyote's later predicament and that would certainly amuse Navajo readers familiar with the story. Meanwhile, Horned Toad displays exemplary conduct, working happily and hard in his garden and reverentially singing for rain and for the joy of sharing the good harvest that the rain will bring. The contrasts between the two characters are firmly established. Arriving at Horned Toad's, Coyote breaches several laws of Navajo etiquette: he pushes his way through the corn; roughly shakes his host's hand; rudely interrupts him; begs and lies; greedily devours the meal that Horned Toad, "being the nice fellow he was" (Begay 1992, n.p.), has prepared; demands more; and does not say thank you.

At this point, Coyote's devious, selfish, perhaps even evil nature surfaces. Believing the farm will provide him with an endless supply of food that he will not have to share or work for, he sings a song that is in contrast to his "cousin's." He thinks he has been blessed because he is a child of Ye'ii. If this is so, it is not a blessing, for Ye'ii was the grandfather of the wicked monsters of Navajo mythology. Crying out in feigned pain, he implores Horned Toad's help, again breaching etiquette, swallows his host, and settles contentedly to sleep, a dangerous move considering that, in Navajo belief, the spirit of a dead person, in this case one Coyote thinks he has murdered, could well be lingering nearby, ready to cause harm. Awakened by an unknown voice calling "shil na aash," (old buddy), a term he had used in his encounter with the prairie dogs, he thinks that he is hearing the spirit of someone he has killed and shamefully displays panic and fear. It is Horned Toad planning his escape. He out-tricks the trickster, expressing reluctance to leave his new home inside Coyote's stomach, a place where he can have plenty of food without having to work hard—the kind of location Coyote earlier wished for himself. Coyote threatens to expel his unwanted guest by drowning, burning, or crushing, remedies that would be harmful to himself, as well as to Horned Toad. Sore and terrified, he faints and his cousin emerges from his mouth. As Karl W. Luckert has noted about another version of this tale, Coyote's physical illness is an outcome of a spiritual sickness, and he is in need of a healing ceremony, one, of course, he does not undergo (Luckert 1979, 20-22). Regaining consciousness, the villain flees, never to bother Horned Toad again. To this day, Begay tells readers, when people encounter a horned toad, they put it over their hearts: "We believe it gives strength of heart and mind" (Begay 1992, n.p.). The story and its sacred beliefs still live.

One final element should be noticed: Begay's use of four-fold repetition. Coyote eats four meals, the third being his host; sleeps four times, the final time in a dead faint; and hears the word "Shil na aash" four times. However, these repetitions are a parody of sacred repetition, just as Coyote's actions are an inversion of etiquette and accepted behavior. In one of his excessive feasts, Coyote devours his eventual nemesis. His first three sleeps result from overindulgence, the fourth from panic and self-inflicted injuries. The four muffled sounds come not from evil spirits of dead people, but a still-living victim who will be his eventual vanquisher. Coyote's actions and Begay's stylistic devices invert normal Navajo order and literary style, but with a restorative moral purpose.

The incredible survival of Coyote in Native oral and written literature and his continuing presence in new children's stories are reflected in four recent children's books. In her illustrations to John Bierhorst's *Doctor Coyote: A Native American Aesop's Fables*, Wendy Watson depicts the hero riding a pickup truck, wearing blue jeans, hunting with a .22, and sitting in an aluminum lawn chair. Gretchen Will Mayo, in *Meet Tricky Coyote!* includes the episode of the outwitted white cowboy and has a picture of a frame house. White Minnesota writer Phyllis Root has created *Coyote and the Magic Words*, an original story about the creative power of language, in which Coyote is "many things: a teacher, a hero, a fool, even a storyteller" (Root 1993, n.p.). Of recent stories, *A Coyote Columbus Story*, by Cherokee professor and novelist Tom King, comes closest to embodying both traditional and contemporary Native interpretations of the character.

The book appeared in 1992, the quadracentennial of Columbus's arrival in the Caribbean and a year in which Native and non-Native historians, novelists, and film makers provided vastly differing assessments of the explorer's motivations and deeds. King offers a modern creation myth that explains Columbus's existence and activities: "Coyote . . . fixed up this world. . . . Some of these things were pretty good, and some of these things were foolish" (King

1992, n.p.). Here is the traditional bungling transformer. However, some of his creations, including prune juice and afternoon naps, are modern. Coyote's passion, playing softball, is also a popular sport among contemporary Native peoples and is the reason for her creating animals and Native peoples. (Perhaps to appeal to readers of both sexes, King has made Coyote female!) She follows the old ways, using the power of song to bring animals and people into being but does so to have others with whom to play softball. The animals refuse to play and the human beings, bored with losing because she constantly shifts the rules in her favor, depart to shopping malls and cruise ships. In desperation, she creates Columbus, who will not play because he is too busy trying to find India and items to sell. Coyote realizes her mistake, admitting that she must have performed the song incorrectly, but it is too late. The invader has seized a number of Indians to take back to Europe. Confronted by angry animals and the remaining Indians, Coyote tries unsuccessfully to "un-sing" Columbus and, instead, creates Jacques Cartier, the French explorer. Undaunted by her previous bunglings, she invites the newcomer to play ball.

Younger and older Native readers familiar with the character of Coyote and the elements of Coyote stories and aware of the animal's continued survival among modern storytellers will have little trouble recognizing and responding to the thinly veiled literary and social satire. Coyote is revealed as a counter-productive bungler, and her creation, Columbus, as a money-hungry kidnapper. The Indian people are found to be easily seduced by the consumer goods and services Coyote has also created. "If the softball glove fits," Coyote might say, "wear it!"

And so, the trickster continues to trot along as he did long ago, responding and sometimes adapting to changed conditions and sometimes being done in by his own weaknesses and these changes, but always surviving. And so, too, do the stories, moving from tribe to tribe, from generation to generation, from oral performance to written text, adapting form and content to new social circumstances and literary fashions. Renewed and renewing, the history of the telling of these stories is a symbol of the lives, traditions, and histories of the people who created and still create them.

THE HISTORY OF A CULTURE HERO'S BIOGRAPHY: NANABOZHO/HIAWATHA

Like Coyote, Nanabozho (variously referred to as Nanabush, Manabozho, Manaboju, Weynaboozhoo, and other names) was both a culture hero and a trickster. However, this mythological character of the Ojibway people of the north central woodlands plays a much more important and noble role than Coyote does. Like Glooscap, the central figure of the Micmac legends of the northeast coast, he was a great leader of his people and gave virtually all of the natural landscape and the animal beings their distinctive features. Stories about him were first published in 1839 by Henry Rowe Schoolcraft in *Algic Researches* and achieved wide popularity when they were included in Henry Wadsworth Longfellow's *The Song of Hiawatha*. Thereafter, they frequently appeared in adaptations of Schoolcraft's and Longfellow's works, in collections of anthropological studies, and in books written by Native peoples recalling stories they had heard as children or had told to their own children. The history of the telling and writing of these myths is, in many ways, representative of the life of Native tales from the times they were orally told to the present, when they are being retold and published by descendants of the original tellers.

The Ojibway (Chippewa as they are called by the United States government, or Anishinaubaeg—the People—as they refer to themselves) live in Ontario, Manitoba, Minnesota, Wisconsin, and Michigan, from the eastern shores of Huron Bay to the western tree line. From the time of their arrival in the area, probably in the early sixteenth century, until the influx of European missionaries, trappers, and settlers in the early eighteenth century, they lived primarily as hunters and gatherers. Game provided meat and clothing materials; maple sugar was harvested in the spring and wild rice in the fall. They also planted some squash and corn. Living in a land where the weather changed drastically from summer to winter months, they adapted their activities to the different seasons and to the life cycles of the plants and animals on which they depended. The Midewewin ceremonies, their greatest religious observances, were held in spring and fall; during the winter they told stories and sacred myths. The arrival of white people profoundly altered their traditional ways. The vagaries of the fur trade, the development and then disappearance of the lumbering industry, the so-called civilizing influences of Christianity and white schooling, and the ravages of disease and alcohol reduced most of the Ojibway to poverty and a state of dependency on white people. Only within the last few decades have they begun to achieve a degree of economic stability and to recover their social and spiritual traditions.

An important way of understanding the traditional and still vital culture of the Ojibway is through the study of tales about their culture hero, Nanabozho. As Canadian Ojibway anthropologist and author Basil H. Johnston has stated, "Read my literature, and you will get to know something of my thoughts, my convictions, my aspirations, my feelings, sentiments, expectations, whatever I cherish or abominate" (Johnson (*sic*) 1992, 107). Many of the stories about Nanabozho recount isolated episodes detailing his adventures and misadventures and their consequences. Travelling in Wisconsin in 1855, German scholar Johann Georg Kohl found that "all along Lake Superior, you cannot come to any strangely formed rock, or other remarkable production of nature, without immediately hearing some story of Menaboju connected with it" (Kohl 1985, 415). However, as Kohl's observations, as well as those of Schoolcraft and twentieth-century anthropologists, reveal, there is a biographical pattern to the legends.

Although individual details vary within specific Ojibway groups, the general outline of the myth of the culture hero is as follows. Nanabozho was the son of the West Wind (a powerful manito or spirit being) and a human maiden, who died giving him birth. He was raised by his grandmother, Nokomis, and early exhibited his special powers, including his ability to transform himself into rocks, trees, and animals. Learning about his mother's death, he journeyed west to seek revenge on his father. The two fought a tremendous battle, after which the West Wind told his son to return to the people to teach and guide them. Once when a close friend (in some versions his brother, in others, an adopted son or a close animal companion) was killed by evil underwater serpent manitos, he travelled beneath the water to kill their king. The remaining evil beings caused a great flood that covered the earth, and Nanabozho found refuge at the top of a tall tree. From there he directed a muskrat to dive to the bottom of the waters to bring up dirt, which he then used to create a new earth. Near the end of his days, Nanabozho departed from the people, promising to return some day. In some versions, he went to live with his father in the west; in others, he still lies in a state of suspended animation, as the Sleeping Giant, a huge rock formation near Thunder Bay, Canada, at the western end of Lake Superior. In other tales, he continued to wander the northwoods, fighting the logging operations of Paul Bunyan and finding himself powerless against the federal bureaucracy during the Great Depression of the 1930s.

In addition to having given the earth its present form after the deluge, Nanabozho gave the Ojibway people the secrets of the sacred Midewewin ceremonies. In individual, self-contained episodes, he endowed plants, animals, and landscapes with their distinctive physical characteristics, sometimes as a reward, sometimes as a punishment, occasionally in a fit of anger because someone or something thwarted his selfish desires. He was sometimes a buffoon, as when he dove into a stream after the reflections of berries; often he was gluttonous and suffered for it. He also broke sexual taboos, as when he feigned his own death in order to return in disguise and marry one of his daughters. There are scatological elements in some of the stories. Clinging to the tree during the flood, he defecated in fear and struggled to avoid swallowing the feces floating around his head. One time he asked his anus to keep guard over food he was cooking and did not recognize bursts of flatulence for the warnings they were.

The cultural significance of Nanabozho's character and actions have been analyzed by many scholars. When he first published the legends, Schoolcraft observed: "Whatever man could do, in strength or wisdom, he could do. But he never does things above the comprehension or belief of his people; and whatever else he is, he is always true to the character of an Indian" (Williams 1991, 65). A careful observer and keen student of Ojibway customs, Schoolcraft saw in Nanabozho a symbolic representative of the cultural lives of the people. While knowledgeable of and, to a degree, sympathetic towards them, Schoolcraft considered Native peoples inferior to Europeans: "A mythology appears indispensable to a rude and ignorant race like the Indians" (Williams 1991, 297). Surprised that they were even sufficiently advanced to possess a mythology, he felt that they were clearly in need of the intellectual and spiritual gifts the advancing Europeans could bestow on them. Thus, although correct in believing that the myths revealed the culture of the Ojibway who told them, Schoolcraft mistakenly sought in them evidence of this group's supposed primitive inferiority.

Clearly a different approach to the relationships between the myths and the tellers is required. Such is found in the writings of Basil H. Johnston, who has retold the legends and written scholarly works on his people's traditional customs and beliefs. For the Anishinaubaeg, the world possessed four closely interrelated levels (Johnston 1976, 21). From the sun and moon, the first creations, came plant life; then came animals, and, finally, human beings. Only by existing harmoniously with the first three created groups could human beings achieve fulfillment. Accordingly, teaching and learning about their place and role in the creation was essential for humans. In this process of teaching and learning, stories were of great importance. "So precious did the tribe regard language and speech that it held those who abused language and speech and truth in contempt and ridicule and withheld from them their trust and confidence" (Johnston 1990, 12). Nanabozho, in many of his adventures, misused language. However, by listening quietly, children learned the wisdom they would need when, in their adult lives, they interacted with the earth and the other created beings. Although they might only gradually come to understand this, each story possessed four levels: "enjoyment, moral teaching, philosophic, and metaphysical" (Johnston 1976, 70).

Johnston states that the Great Spirit sent Nanabozho to the people as an intermediary and a teacher, and in many of the stories he performs just such a role. However, in accepting human form, he also took on human limitations, and, like other young people, he needed a wise instructor, his grandmother Nokomis. After the battle with his father, he is warned that "your own powers are limited and may betray you" (Johnston 1976, 19). Indeed, many of his adventures reveal his limitations and, by extension, those of listeners to the stories. Living in a culture where hunting skill and spiritual reverence to the animals were essential, Nanabozho was often "too impulsive, too impatient, too vain to follow direction or proven ways" (Johnston 1983, 42) and frequently went hungry. In sum, stories about him "represent and reflect the Anishinaubaeg's conception of what constitutes human nature and human character" (Johnston 1983, 44). Hearing about him at his best and worst, the Ojibway did and still do learn about their own potentials and limitations. For Johnston, the great myths are not examples of the pagan beliefs of an inferior peoples, but reflections of the lives of members of a specific culture seeking to learn from and define themselves in an interrelated world.

From 1839 until past the middle of the twentieth century, Schoolcraft's versions of the Nanabozho legends and Longfellow's appropriation of many of them in *The Song of Hiawatha*, published in 1855, served as the basis for children's adaptations. As noted, Schoolcraft considered Ojibway culture inferior to European, and his opinion is reflected in the myths and legends found in his *Algic Researches* and other publications. Because his part Ojibway wife, who told him many of the stories, was a Christian who had received English schooling, it may be wondered how close to the traditional forms of the tales the versions he received were. In an 1856 edition of his work, he wrote that the stories "have been carefully translated, written, and rewritten, to obtain their true spirit and meaning, expunging passages, where it was necessary to avoid tediousness of narration, triviality of circumstance, tautologies, gross incongruities, and vulgarities" (Williams 1991, 294). Given the heavy editorial hand this passage implies, it seems that Schoolcraft was moving away from the "true spirit and meaning" of the tales. That his knowledge of European literature influenced him is indicated by his reference to Nanabozho as "the Indian Hercules, Samson, or Proteus" (Williams, 1991, 23). His attitudes toward these flawed European mythic heroes may have colored his approach to the Ojibway character. In 1929, folklore scholar Stith Thompson harshly criticized Schoolcraft's approach and its influence: "Unfortunately, the scientific value of his work is marred by the manner in which he has reshaped the stories to suit his own literary taste. Several of his tales, indeed, are distorted almost beyond recognition. . . . A result of Schoolcraft's sentimentality has been the attitude of a large part of the general public toward Indian tradition" (Thompson 1929, xv).

While Schoolcraft does not include the scatological aspects of Nanabozho's adventures and gives considerable attention to his defeating the evil manito Pearl Feather and the underwater serpents, his portrait of the culture hero is surprisingly negative. In comparing him to Hercules and Samson, Schoolcraft is inviting his readers to see parallels between the weaknesses of these Classical and Biblical heroes and Nanabozho. In his prefaces, he notes that although the hero developed qualities admired by the Indians, "he relied largely upon these in the gratification of an ambitious, vainglorious, and mischief-loving disposition" (Williams 1991, 66). Although "Manabozho is regarded by the Indians as a god and a benefactor . . . [t]he conception of a divinity, pure, changeless, and just, as well as benevolent, in the distribution of its providences, has not been reached by any traits exhibited in the character of this personage" (Williams 1991, 80). In the story "Iosco," Nanabozho lives alone, repenting for the "dreadful ravages" (Williams 1991, 143) of his earlier life. In an afterword to this story, Schoolcraft emphatically states that "he is here represented, as in all other known instances, to be a Bad, and not a Good Spirit, and there is no countenance given to the verbal opinion, sometimes expressed, that this personage partakes of any of the characteristics of a Saviour" (Williams 1991, 146).

It is as if Schoolcraft, in order to emphasize the superiority of European, Christian culture over that of the traditional Ojibway, wished to cast Nanabozho in a bad light, even in his most praiseworthy activities. Nokomis hesitates telling him about his father because she fears the young man's "wicked and revengeful disposition" (Williams 1991, 67). Although told by his father to "Go and do good" (Williams 1991, 69), he later plays a cruel trick on his grandmother's lover, physically deforms a bird who foils his plan for a great feast, and, simply because the animal had gotten in his way, kills a badger who had hidden him from evil manitos. Successful in his battle against the evil Pearl Feather, "Glory fired his mind. He displayed the trophies he had brought in the most conspicuous manner, and felt an unconquerable desire for other adventures. He felt himself urged by the consciousness of his power to new trials of bravery, skill, and necromantic prowess" (Williams 1991, 72). While seeking his drowned brother, Nanabozho receives information from a kingfisher, who he then attempts to strangle. For this act, Schoolcraft attributes to Nanabozho the following motivation: "He had found out all he wanted to know, and then desired to conceal the knowledge of his purposes by killing his informant" (Williams 1991, 76). Other versions from the Lake Superior Ojibway explain that the character is angry because the kingfisher is waiting to eat the deceased's intestines if these float to the surface. Schoolcraft is here certainly making Nanabozho morally reprehensible. It is not surprising that he states that Nanabozho loses his power after defeating the underwater serpents, that he and his family then live in poverty, and that he finally resides alone and in disgrace. Nanabozho does not deserve a hero's rewards and death. One is reminded of the fate of Geronimo as portrayed in *Wolf of the Warpath*, published over a century later.

Although both Schoolcraft and Longfellow wrote for white audiences whom they considered morally and intellectually superior to the characters in their works, the portraits of the culture hero the two men created are vastly different. If Schoolcraft used the myths and legends to illustrate the inferiority and essential baseness of Nanabozho in contrast to a Christian hero and savior, Longfellow used Schoolcraft's works to create in Hiawatha a noble man of nature whose teachings to his people were worthy preparations for the coming of the superior religion of Christianity. In the same character, Schoolcraft saw an example of the "Heathen Savage," while Longfellow saw the "Noble Savage." Because Hiawatha was essentially a stereotypical "Good Indian," he was a more appealing figure to mid-nineteenth-century readers than was Schoolcraft's character. In fact, Schoolcraft's adaptations did not receive wide public recognition until *The Song of Hiawatha*, in which Longfellow acknowledged his debt to *Algic Researches*, achieved great popularity.

In a concluding note to "Manabozho," Schoolcraft commented on the fragmentary qualities of the individual stories and the lack of connection between most of them: "To collect all these and arrange them in order would be an arduous labor; and, after all, such an arrangement would lack consistency and keeping, unless much of the thread necessary to present them in an English dress were supplied by invention, alteration, and transposition" (Williams 1991, 79). Longfellow performed just such an arduous labor and, in doing so, influenced later children's adaptations of the Nanabozho legend. He rejected his preliminary title of "Manabozhoo" for the more poetic name of the Iroquois hero, Hiawatha, incorrectly "assuming that both names referred to the same person" (Longfellow 1992, viii). However, he made extensive use of Schoolcraft's material, selecting, arranging, and altering, frequently in significant ways, those tales that appealed to him and related to his literary purposes. Influenced by the English and European romantic movements, he wished to write a poem presenting an American Indian finding in nature a life that was both nobler and simpler than the lives of white, urbanized North Americans and Europeans. Moreover, at a time when the need for a national American Literature was being stressed in major literary circles, he wished to create an American epic, a long, dignified poem employing the conventions of its European models, but presenting indigenous subject matter. The story of Hiawatha/Nanabozho, suitably altered and then narrated in lofty language, would fulfill his aims. Longfellow referred to the completed work as "This Indian Edda" (Longfellow 1992, 161), comparing it to the great mythological poem of Iceland. As a modern commentator has noted, Longfellow was "more interested in establishing its cousinship with the heroic poetry of the Old World . . . than in being ethnohistorically correct" (Longfellow 1992, viii).

Not surprisingly, scatological and sexual aspects do not appear in *The Song of Hiawatha*. Neither does the genteel Longfellow draw on those parts of Schoolcraft's writings in which Nanabozho is a buffoon, cruel deceiver, or vain-glorious self-seeker. Hiawatha does not trick the dancing ducks, get trapped in the branches of a tree, or boast of his achievements. Instead, he is sent to earth by the Gitche Manito as "A Deliverer of the nations" (Longfellow 1992, 8). Longfellow has Native groups from across North America assemble together to receive a gift that will end their quarrelling, and thus he transforms a specific Ojibway culture hero into a generic, Pan-Indian hero. With the exception of his angry journey to find his father, Hiawatha leads an exemplary life. In one episode, which in Schoolcraft's version attributes the hero's actions to another character, Hiawatha provides the Indians with the gift of corn. As people of Longfellow's time considered farming a more civilized activity than hunting, the poet makes his hero an agent of progress. In another episode, one invented by Longfellow, Hiawatha marries a Sioux maiden, Minnehaha, thus creating a bond of peace between two hostile groups. "In his wisdom," (Longfellow 1992, 105), the hero teaches the people the art of picture writing so that they will be able to preserve their past. (Certainly this concept ignores the importance for Native peoples of oral traditions and attaches an importance to writing that is European rather than Native in its implications.) Each of Nanabozho's confrontations as they are enacted by Hiawatha become occasions for the people to benefit. The fight with his father is designed as a test of his worthiness to serve his people; the defeat of Pearl Feather does not lead to boasting but to the distribution of the slain manito's wealth among the people; the death of a beloved friend, Chibiabos, results in the benefits of the Midewewin healing ceremonies. Finally, Hiawatha's departure from his people is not an occasion of enduring sorrow, but of joy, for he has prepared them for the arrival of the Black Robes, the Christian priests who will offer them a means of achieving a more fulfilled spiritual life.

Longfellow's poem became an almost instant success; within four years it had sold over 45,000 copies. For thousands of American school children over the next century, the poem formed their notion of the "Good Indian": wise teacher and benefactor of the people, friend of nature's creatures, and, when the time came, welcomer of emissaries of the new European culture and religion. Abridged and prose versions were published in school readers, and memorization of lengthy passages and performance of episodes from the poem at school plays became common events. So great was Hiawatha's symbolic presence, particularly in children's literature, that in 1938, Alden O. Deming subtitled her book *Manabozho, The Indian's Story of Hiawatha*, almost as if the Native people's narratives were variants of Longfellow's original. What is surprising is that several illustrated children's versions of *The Song of Hiawatha* have been published since 1983 and that, even now, in Michigan's Upper Peninsula, the location of so many Ojibway myths, most people know who Hiawatha is, but have never heard of Nanabozho.

In *Hiawatha*, Susan Jeffers, whose illustrated adaptation of Chief Seattle's speech was discussed in Chapter 1, selected and illustrated just over 100 lines from "Hiawatha's Childhood," Part III of Longfellow's poem, a section that she loved as a girl. In this section, Nokomis teaches Hiawatha about the natural world and the boy refers to the living creatures as "Hiawatha's Brothers" (Longfellow 1992, 23). Jeffers emphasizes the benign quality of nature and leaves out references to the betrayal of Nokomos by a jealous woman; the seduction, abandonment, and death of Hiawatha's mother Wenonah; and the grief Nokomis experiences. The illustrations reinforce the important role of women in the education of the future hero. In the first two pictures, the spirit of Wenonah keeps guard over the grandmother and the infant. Nokomis is in each illustration, offering love and support, but gradually allowing the growing child to venture forth on his own. At the conclusion, she stands apart as Hiawatha sits among his animal brothers, and she is smaller on the page than she had been in previous illustrations. The boy is now ready to enter manhood, and, on the back endpapers, he walks alone into the forest on his first hunt.

Jeffers' illustrations certainly complement and clarify the text she has chosen and reinforce the positive image of the growing child and his environment. Hiawatha is clearly set forth as a "noble child of nature." However, in her introduction, she makes statements that compound the misrepresentations of Native people already present in Longfellow's poem. She reports that the poet "had known the chief of the Ojibwa tribe" (Jeffers 1983, n.p.). This would have been George Copway, only one of many Ojibway chiefs, each from a different band of the widely spread culture group. She correctly states that Longfellow's poem is a composite of stories from a variety of sources, but then says, "One such story concerned an actual man named Hiawatha" (Jeffers 1983, n.p.). However, Longfellow did not include material about the fifteenth-century Iroquois leader, but used material about the mythical figure of the same name whom he mistakenly believed to be the same person. This picture book will bring young readers closer to the intent of the lines taken from Longfellow's poem. But it will also perpetuate a well-meaning stereotype and will not help its audience experience the cultural values and beliefs of the traditional Ojibway people of the south Lake Superior shoreline.

Hiawatha's Childhood, for which British artist Errol Le Cain won the prestigious Kate Greenaway Award for illustration, reprints the same lines chosen by Jeffers. However, Le Cain's illustrations create a different mood than Jeffers'. Jeffers' naturalistic pictures, which contain many light colors and much white space, present the happy childhood of a realistically depicted Indian boy. Le Cain's illustrations, bordered with stylized birchbark designs and containing traditional Native religious symbols and often employing dark, even somber hues, present a mythic child growing up in a world filled with frightening supernatural beings and forces. A setting sun spreads almost lurid orange-red colors over the landscape, and a stylized sun figure adorns the inside of the wigwam. Supernatural figures appear in the tail of Ishkoodah, the comet, and in the frigid winter forest. Five fiercely staring owls foreground a picture in which the wigwam home is depicted as very small in the background. Even the natural world is violent. While Nokomis sings a lullaby in which Hiawatha is referred to as a baby owl, a large owl flies past, a small animal hanging from its beak. This is the natural and supernatural world that the adult culture hero must understand and confront on his own; but at this point he is close to and often clings to his grandmother. Only toward the end of the selection, as Hiawatha ventures alone into the world of nature to learn its secrets, do the illustrations become lighter. He no longer needs Nokomis; a bird perches tamely on his finger; bears and wolves stand in a circle listening to him speak; he watches squirrels and beavers; and he rides on the back of a reindeer. In Le Cain's final illustration, which prints the phrase "Hiawatha's Brothers," human, animal, and supernatural spheres are linked. Hiawatha, still seated on the reindeer, is surrounded by his bird, animal, and insect friends. Nokomis watches proudly from the trees; the sun shines from above. Orange-red colors are again present, but they do not overwhelm the landscape as they had earlier. A unity has been achieved, and this phase of Hiawatha's education and maturation has been completed.

While the mood and implications of Le Cain's illustrations are different from Jeffers' and may even be closer to Ojibway mythology than were Longfellow's words, *Hiawatha's Childhood* is not without problems. On a literal level, the picture accompanying the phrase "shining Big-Sea-Water" shows a very small lake surrounded by the hills and reflecting the hues of the setting sun. On a mythical level, depicting people riding horses in the comet's tail is more appropriate to a plains' vision quest; the comet's face resembles a northwest coast ceremonial mask; and the owls' headfeathers are like those in stylized modern Eskimo prints. Le Cain may have embodied the sense of a spirit-filled world, but the symbols he chose to do so are not always Ojibway. Such mixing of symbols can only reinforce an uninformed reader's notions of a generic, homogenous North American Native culture.

While young readers of Longfellow's *The Song of Hiawatha* or of shortened adapted versions were learning about the natural childhood of the "Noble Savage," young readers of adaptations of Schoolcraft's story of Nanabozho received toned-down versions of the flawed hero. Such was the case in Cornelius Matthews' "Manabozho, the Mischief-Maker," published in 1867 in *The Indian Fairybook*, a volume reprinted in 1877 as *The Enchanted Moccasins*. In the two stories preceding "Manabozho, the Mischief-Maker," Nanabozho appears as a giant "who was at times quite thick-headed and dull of apprehension" (Matthews 1877, 212). The adapter, who in his preface had noted the similarities between European and Native tales, is here recasting the Ojibway figure in the mold of the dim-witted giants of such English folktales as "Jack-the-Giant-Killer." The title, "Manabozho, the Mischief-Maker," along with the opening sentence—"There was never in the whole world a more mischievous busy body than that notorious giant Manabozho" (Matthews 1877, 215)—not only establishes a negative attitude toward the character, but diminishes his powers from those of one capable of malice to those of one who is merely an annoyance and a nuisance.

The story includes four episodes taken from Schoolcraft's account: the father-son battle, the battle with Pearl Feather, the winter hunting with the wolves up to the point of the drowning of the wolf, and the story of Nanabozho's dinner with Woodpecker, in which he tries, with disastrous results for himself, to imitate his host's method of procuring food. In many cases, Matthews uses sentences and paragraphs taken directly from Schoolcraft. However, his omissions are very telling. The most significant are the killing of both the giant sturgeon and the serpent king who had drowned his friend, the flood, and the remaking of the world. As folklorist Richard M. Dorson has noted, "Chippewa mythology centers around the conflict between sky and underwater powers" (Dorson 1952, 16). The latter were considered evil and, in defeating them, Nanabozho performed heroic acts for his people. Matthews totally ignores the fact that, however flawed, the central character does have a major impact on his world.

Like Schoolcraft, Matthews introduces the episode of the dinner with Woodpecker by noting that Nanabozho, now without most of his magical powers, is virtually destitute. However, whereas Schoolcraft says that the powers left him after the battle with the water serpents, implying that the hero made a great sacrifice during the titanic struggle, Matthews says they departed after the drowning of Wolf. This change is the most significant alteration in the adaptation, for it radically changes the nature of Nanabozho's character. Matthews follows Schoolcraft in having Nanabozho travelling alone with Wolf at the end of the winter, but adds, "The old spirit of mischief was still alive within him" (Matthews 1877, 241). Accordingly, he tells his companion that, in order to avoid enemies, he should travel across the spring ice that, he falsely says, "is always safe" (Matthews 1877, 242). Schoolcraft, by contrast, has him warn Wolf about the dangers of crossing the lake ice. That Matthews' Nanabozho should lose his power at the moment that Wolf drowns provides the implicit moral that a thoughtless love of mischief not only causes tragedy for another, but also brings a severe punishment on oneself: Nanabozho is bereft of an essential part of his being. As was the case of the boy who cried wolf too often, the results of Nanabozho's deceptions are not what he expected. Such a moral is more in keeping with the fashion of nineteenth-century children's literature, in which improperly behaving children met hideous, gruesome ends, than with Ojibway thinking about the trickster or even with Schoolcraft's interpretation of the event.

A final point about Matthews' adaptation of Schoolcraft may be made: he added details to those details he borrowed. In order to wrest from his reluctant grandmother the secret of his parentage, Nanabozho behaves like a spoiled child, beginning "a loud lamentation, which he kept increasing, louder and louder, till it shook the lodge, and nearly deafened the old grandmother" (Matthews 1877, 217). He later grows so big that, "if he had at any time taken a fancy to one of the . . . trees for a walking-stick, he would have had no more to do than to pluck it up with his thumb and finger" (Matthews 1877, 218-19). When he converses with his father, "a whole day to deliver a single sentence . . . was quite an ordinary affair" (Matthews 1877, 219). And while he is supposed to be fasting in preparation for his battle against Pearl Feather, he devours "twenty fat bears, six dozen birds, and two fine moose" (Matthews 1877, 227). Whereas Schoolcraft magnifies Nanabozho by linking him to great but flawed Biblical and Classical heroes, Matthews trivializes him by describing his activities in terms similar to those used by writers of the humorous, preposterous tall tales popular at the time. Not only does Matthews depart from Schoolcraft, his humor is vastly different in both nature and purpose from that frequently found in Ojibway tales about their culture hero.

In *Manabozho: The Indian's Story of Hiawatha*, Alden O. Deming combines both the Longfellow and Schoolcraft traditions. An editor's introduction notes the relationship between the two authors but states, "The stories that have been selected for this book have all been taken from Mr. Schoolcraft's works" (Deming 1938, v). This statement is accurate only if it means selected from Schoolcraft's stories as altered by Longfellow. Nearly three-quarters of the episodes are taken from *The Song of Hiawatha* and Deming's book reads like a condensed paraphrase of Longfellow. With one exception, Manabozho is as praise-worthy and exemplary as Hiawatha. The exception is when he deceives the dancing ducks, an event not narrated by Longfellow and a low point in the hero's friendship with the animals. However, when he kills the serpents who drowned Wolf, he regains their confidence.

Deming's mixture of the two traditions is seen in the hero's wooing of and marriage to Minnehaha. Deming uses Schoolcraft's brief mention of Manabozho's infatuation with the daughter of a nearby arrow maker and then switches to Longfellow's account of the hero's relationship to a Dakota maiden. The editor notes that Schoolcraft "learned their languages so that he could understand their stories" (Deming 1938, v), a vast over-simplification of Schoolcraft's' activities, and then notes that Miss Deming lived among the Indians and as a child "listened to some of the very stories which she has here related" (Deming 1938, vi). Whatever the identity of the unspecified tribes she knew, Deming did not, when she came to write this book, listen to their tongues as Schoolcraft listened to Ojibway tongues before he wrote his stories. Rather, she listened mainly to Longfellow and further adulterated his versions of Schoolcraft's adaptations. In doing so, she not only confused the characterizations of the hero by those two writers but reinforced the "Noble Savage, Child of Nature" stereotype.

Like Deming, Dorothy M. Reid, author of *Tales of Nanabozho*, winner of the Canadian Association of Children's Librarians' Book-of-the-Year award, has created a biography of the culture hero. Published in 1963, the book draws on Schoolcraft and Longfellow, as well as anthropological collections of Canadian Ojibway tales and a volume of Algonquian Indian tales by Egerton Young, a nineteenth-century Canadian children's author. However, Reid makes the episodes she selects relate specifically to the Thunder Bay, Ontario, region where, for many years, she was a children's librarian and storyteller. In her "Preface," she discusses "The Sleeping Giant," a large rock formation in Lake Superior believed to be the body of the Ojibway culture hero. The stories that follow explain who this being was, the key events of his life, and how he came to rest in a state of suspended animation in the waters just east of Thunder Bay.

Readers familiar with Schoolcraft, Longfellow, anthropological collections, and earlier children's adaptations will recognize most, if not all, of the episodes in *Tales of Nanabozho*: the miraculous birth, the battle with the West Wind, the death of his brother and the ensuing flood, the battle with Pearl Feather, the killing of the giant sturgeon, and the encounters with members of the plant and animal worlds. However, unlike Schoolcraft or Matthews on the one hand, or Longfellow or Deming on the other, Reid does not present her hero as being either essentially evil or virtuous. Instead, she creates a biography in which the mischievous, foolish, and sometimes petulant boy and young man gradually evolves into the hero who, imperfect though he is, generally seeks to help his people.

Throughout his life, Nanabozho exhibits qualities of anger, impatience, pride, and greed. In his earlier years, these are revealed in his misadventures and his responses to them. Seeking a feast of berries, he dives foolishly into a stream after their reflection; carried into the air by a flock of geese he has attempted to capture, he falls into a bog but brags of his flight; when his shoulders do not warn him that his dinner is about to be stolen, he angrily punishes them. In his youth, his creative problem solving is hastily thought-out, and he refuses to accept responsibility for his failures. However, he does use his wits to capture fire for his aging grandmother, Nokomis, even if he is not above boasting about the deed. In each of these cases, he gives the landscape and animals their present characteristics; for example, geese still fly in a V formation, and ganders still bear the mark of the angry kick he gave one of them.

The "Mighty One" (Reid 1963, 45), as Reid frequently calls him, makes his first major step toward maturity during his encounter with his father, the West Wind. On learning about his mother's death from Nokomis, he sets out to kill his father. "As Nanabozho realized the strength of his father, his heart filled with pride. Then his mind darkened once again with his vengeful purpose. Had not the West Wind deserted Wenonah and been the cause of her death? Had not his father given power to his older brothers and nothing to him? His rage almost choked him" (Reid 1963, 37).

Selfish pride and justifiable anger seem to motivate him equally. However, after the battle, Nanabozho learns that he has a mission—to use his strength and knowledge to help his people—and he returns home contented. But he does not completely lose his selfishness, becoming entrapped in a birch tree that he angrily whips when he loses another feast and scorning a partridge whom he considers a lowly, insignificant animal. Yet, in this latter instance, he recognizes his mistake and acknowledges the bird's virtues.

Nanabozho's second great battle, with the evil spirits who have drowned his brother, marks the next stage of his maturation. His twin, who had died in infancy, is returned to life by the West Wind, who wishes his son to have a companion. With a new responsibility, the culture hero performs many good deeds for his people. However, after his brother's death, his anger returns. He tries to kill a kingfisher who hopes to feast on the drowned body but then accepts the bird's apologies and makes peace with it. His anger against the spirits is justifiable, for these evil beings, his sworn enemies, have acted from pure malice. After the flood, Nanabozho remakes the world for the stranded people, later saves his grandmother from other evil beings, kills a giant sturgeon so that she may have much needed oil, and gives the people cures for illness. Along the way, he generously rewards those trees and animals who have assisted him. He also acquires a wife, Minnehaha, or Laughing Water, a character Reid found in Longfellow's *The Song of Hiawatha*.

The final five chapters of *Tales of Nanabozho* tell of the coming of the white people, how the culture hero leads the Ojibway to their present home near Thunder Bay, and his transformation into the Sleeping Giant. The Ojibways' peace and contentment is shattered when news is received of the arrival of Europeans along the St. Lawrence River. Informed in a dream vision by the Gitche Manitou, the Great Spirit, that the newcomers must not be harmed, he learns that he must lead an escape to the west. He represses his anger and urge to destroy the Europeans and heads the trek to Thunder Bay, where he befriends the supernatural thunderbird who helps him protect the people. Nanabozho performs many good deeds, including punishing a mean-spirited raccoon, teaching the secrets of picture writing, destroying the evil Pearl Feather, and saving a beleaguered maiden. He is even able to appreciate his own foolishness when he realizes that a fierce face that startled him is really the reflection of his own begrimed face in the water. This is something he could not do when, as a boy, he dived for the reflected berries.

As Nanabozho's life on earth draws rapidly to a close, he is transformed into the Sleeping Giant, a victim both of the advancing white people and his own impulsive anger. Informed by an evil Sioux (as the author terms him) warrior of the existence of rich deposits of silver in the area, the Europeans sail the length of Lake Superior. Nanabozho drives them away with a great storm, which also makes it impossible for the women to fish. Sorrowful, despondent, and frustrated, he finds that his wife has not prepared an evening meal, and the two quarrel. "The rage that had been in Nanabozho's heart for many days exploded once again and he flung his wife out of the wigwam and up on the cliff" (Reid 1963, 121), where he turns her into a stone formation that can still be seen. When the Europeans arrive, he forgets the Gitche Manitou's injunction against harming them, causes a storm that drowns several, and is turned into a stone himself by the Gitche Manitou. When the Great Spirit needs him again, he will be revived.

Because it reveals the character's complex, mixed nature, Reid's biography of the culture hero is closer to the Native understanding of Nanabozho than were the accounts of either Schoolcraft or Longfellow. However, even though she states that she "tried to make my own versions true to the spirit of the original material" (Reid 1963, 10), the extent of her cultural accuracy needs to be examined. In her "Preface," she notes that the people "delighted" (Reid 1963, 9) in recounting his adventures, and that "the story-tellers never tired of inventing tales of his exploits" (Reid 1963, 9–10). While they may have taken some delight in the telling and listening, they would probably have also experienced awe and reverence, for many of the stories would have had profound spiritual implications. Moreover, narrators would not have considered that they were inventing the tales; rather they would have been adapting and transmitting aspects of their sacred mythological history. In arranging the episodes into a biographical sequence, she is following the lead suggested by Schoolcraft and practiced by Longfellow. She is also casting her children's version into the form of the European hero journey made popular for younger readers in adaptations of such legends as those about King Arthur. The education of the apprentice hero and his final rest in suspended animation bear striking resemblance to elements in the British leader's life. Finally, her focus on Nanabozho's character development may have been influenced by anthropologist Paul Radin's analysis of a Winnebago (Wisconsin) trickster cycle. In *The Trickster*, first published in 1956, seven years before her book, Radin used a psychological approach to account for the moral and social development of the hero that he found in the stories he collected.

While the written, English-language tradition of Nanabozho/Hiawatha stories was developing and flourishing in the nineteenth and twentieth centuries, the Ojibway continued to transmit their stories orally. Victor Barnouw gathered and analyzed Wisconsin myths and tales in 1941 and 1942; and, in 1946, Richard M. Dorson collected a number of tales from Michigan's Upper Peninsula. Sister Bernard Coleman recorded Nanabozho tales in Wisconsin and Minnesota in the late 1950s. Reading these collections, one is surprised to discover how many of the episodes collected a century earlier by Schoolcraft, Kohl, and others were still told orally. Given the effects of the advancing logging industry, with its physical displacement of Native peoples and destruction of their traditional lifestyles; Christianity, with its attempts to repress Native spirituality; and residential schools, with their inculcation of the English language and related reading materials, the survival of the stories attests to their vitality.

Thus it is not surprising that, with the renaissance of traditional Native spiritual values over the last 25 years and the increased accessibility for Native peoples to print media, many Ojibway have written Nanabozho tales. In 1971, the well-known Canadian artist Daphne "Odjig" Beavon created 10 short books of Nanabozho tales as a supplement to a Canadian publisher's reading series. In a brief introduction reprinted in each volume, Beavon recalls her father and grandfather relating stories to her when she was a child, mentioning that the hero often performed good deeds, but could also be "rather naughty" (Beavon 1971, n.p.) and expressing the hope that "the moral truths that were so important to Indians will continue to exist in years to come" (Beavon 1971, n.p.). Most of the familiar stories are retold: the hero falls from the air trying to trap geese, loses his eyeballs while juggling them, and has cooking ducks stolen from him. He also punishes a rabbit and raccoon for their misdeeds, giving them their distinctive physical features, and regulates the cycle of the seasons. Underlying these stories are moral lessons that a series of questions following each story invites readers to relate to their own lives. Beavon illustrates the tales in the "Legend Painting" style, which emphasizes the spirituality inherent in each of them.

In *The Mishomis Book: The Voice of the Ojibway*, Edward Benton-Benai, a Wisconsin Ojibway educator, retells several stories about Nanabozho, whom his group calls Way-na-boo-zhoo. Designed specifically for Native students, he states that "this book is the result of many periods of fasting, meditation, consultation, dreaming, and listening to the quiet voice of the Creator who speaks not to the ear but to the soul" (Benton-Benai 1988, iii). One of the most interesting myths in the collection is about the hero's encounter with his father, Mudjikeewis. It is told, as are the other stories, by Mishomis, the Grandfather, who lives on Madeline Island near the Wisconsin shore of Lake Superior, a place he is "preparing . . . to be a place of rebirth for traditional Indian ways" (Benton-Benai 1988, 1). Compared to Schoolcraft's version, which is only five paragraphs, Benton-Benai's is very long: 22 pages of small type printed in double columns. The length is a result of the author's detailed presentation of the events of the journey to the west, including Mishomis' explanations of the continuing moral, social, and spiritual significance of these events.

The long journey to the west shows the stages of growth Way-na-boo-zhoo must undergo before he achieves maturity in the meeting with his father. Married at the time of his departure from the eastern seacoast, he is willingly given his freedom to leave by his wife, who realizes that individuals must be permitted to achieve fulfillment on their own terms. Along the way, he learns to respect the power and goodness of the rivers and is guided by a buffalo, a grizzly bear, and a sasquatch, a supernatural giant, each of whom teaches him about his relationships to all living beings. Having acquired determination, courage, and wisdom, he is ready to encounter his father. Proud of his son, Mudjikeewis is also sad, for he realizes that the two must fight in order to end father-son conflicts among the people. Because he respects the courage the young man reveals during the battle, Mudjikeewis agrees to answer questions and so begins the hero's final major phase of education. He is told that his transcontinental trip has been between birth (the east) and death (the west) and that he is to be a teacher and example to human beings. Mudjikeewis presents him with the sacred peace pipe to bring back to the people.

On the return journey, the young leader learns from the Whirlwind that foolishness has a place in creation and begins to think about "blending foolishness and seriousness in his life" (Benton-Benai 1988, 54). Although Benton-Benai does not recount any of his character's foolish escapades, he is clearly indicating how these tales, which would be well known to his audience, relate to the hero's serious role in Ojibway mythological history. When he experiences an earthquake, Way-na-boo-zhoo, on his own, is able to control his fear and learn from the event, something he had been unable to do on the outward journey. He also realizes that the rest of his life on earth will be a continuous learning experience. Returning to his homeland, he "felt a happiness, warmth, and fulfillment that he had never experienced before" (Benton-Benai 1988, 59). He is ready to begin his role as leader of his people.

Unlike Benton-Benai, who emphasizes the hero's role as an example of positive character development, Canadian Ojibway author Basil H. Johnston, whose discussions of Ojibway culture have been examined earlier, explores the hero's mixed nature. *By Canoe & Moccasin: Some Native Place Names of the Great Lakes* presents the hero's journey from Tahquamenon, his home near Sault Ste. Marie, to the Great Plains and beyond, and then back home. After Nanabozho nearly drowns diving for the reflection of berries, the author comments: "Though he could perform marvellous deeds as a spirit, Nanabush as a human being could commit the most stupid of blunders. He knew matters that men did not know and was ignorant of some of the most basic of human knowledge. Besides, he lacked a certain degree of common sense" (Johnston 1986, 40). Thus, on the one hand, he defeats a giant beaver whose dam has flooded parts of Wisconsin and turns an old woman into a woodpecker because of her selfishness. On the other, he twice runs away in fear from evil spirit beings and requires the help of small animals to overcome them. He mistakes bullrushes for dancers, gets trapped in a moose skull, and falls from the sky into a muddy lake. In addition to presenting the character's mixed nature, Johnston links stories from different Ojibway groups, creating a composite hero whose character is seen after a reading of individual tales from these various regions. Northern and southern Ontario, Michigan, Illinois, Wisconsin, Minnesota, and Manitoba are the places visited, and the Native place names from these areas are present reminders of the deeds the hero performed and the characteristics he exhibited.

Most depictions of traditional Native life and stories are found in the picture books and folktale adaptations created by Native and non-Native authors and illustrators. However, there are also many novels presenting the old ways and the relationships between those ways and contemporary Native life. These novels usually focus on the struggles and conflicts faced by Native peoples attempting to preserve their traditions and cultural identities in the face of the advancing European invasion. They reflect both Native and European points of view on a crucial aspect of North American history. Chapter 4 examines how several novels present these conflicts.

COLLECTIONS OF TRADITIONAL MYTHS AND LEGENDS
Adult Collections

Bierhorst, John, editor. *The Red Swan: Myths and Tales of the American Indians.* New York: Farrar, Straus and Giroux, 1976.
In gathering 64 tales from the Arctic to Mexico, scholar John Bierhorst has attempted "to present a comprehensive view of the world . . . as perceived through the lens of American myth" (31). At times he has reprinted his sources as he found them; at other times, when he felt the original intent was obscured by the "literary styles" of non-Native adaptors, he has rewritten them. Beginning with myths about "The Dream Father" and "The Body of Our Mother," he concludes with those of "Returning Life" and "Death and Beyond." Underlying his selection process is his desire to indicate the idea of "crossing the threshold" (7) or moving toward a fuller individual and social identity. While there are familiar stories such as "Sedna and the Fulmar," which can be compared to Beverly Brodsky McDermott's *Sedna*, there are also many stories that have not yet been adapted for children. Reading this collection, along with the extensive introduction and detailed notes and Bierhorst's companion volume, *The Mythology of North America* (1985), adult readers will gain a fuller understanding of the role of mythology in defining the lives of Native individuals and culture groups and will thus be able to judge how well or poorly children's adaptations have reflected the cultural basis of individual myths.

Erdoes, Richard and **Alfonso Ortiz,** editors. *American Indian Myths and Legends.* New York: Pantheon Books, 1984.
Richard Erdoes, a German-born scholar of the American West, and Alfonso Ortiz, an anthropologist born and raised at San Juan Pueblo in New Mexico, have collected 166 stories that reveal "a universal concern with fundamental

issues about the world in which humans live" (xiv). Grouped into such thematic sections as "The Eye of the Great Spirit: Tales of the Sun, Moon, and Stars" and "Counting Coup: War and the Warrior Code," each story is preceded by an explanatory note and followed by an indication of its source. Erdoes and Ortiz have collected many of the stories themselves; others are retellings of earlier transcriptions or adaptations. Unlike Stith Thompson, who reprinted selections from scholarly journals, the editors have recast many of their stories in one prose style, thus giving the entire collection a unified tone. Readers of children's books will recognize alternative versions of Manitonquat's "Muckachuck" ("Glooscap and the Baby"), Goble's *Her Seven Brothers* ("The Quillwork Girl and Her Seven Star Brothers"), Gregg's *Great Rabbit and the Long-Tailed Wildcat* ("Adventures of Great Rabbit"), and other tales, and will find it interesting to examine differences between the adaptations. An appendix briefly discusses the 78 tribes or culture groups from which the stories originated. Although the book has been praised for the range of its coverage and for the collaboration of a non-Native and Native team of scholars, it has been criticized for its fairly free renditions, designed for a non-Native audience. A valuable reference, both for the extent of its collection and background notes and as an example of a method of adapting oral materials, it should be used in conjunction with Stith Thompson's more scholarly *Tales of the North American Indians*.

Feldman, Susan, editor. *The Storytelling Stone: Traditional Native American Myths and Tales*. New York: Dell, 1991.
Intended as an introduction for the general reader, this collection of stories of Native culture groups north of Mexico gathers its 52 selections under the headings "In the Days of Creation," "Trickster," and "Tales of Heroes, Supernatural Journeys, and Other Folktales." In her introduction, Feldman emphasizes that "Mythic ideas are embodied in ritual, architecture, and social organization, as well as in stories. Myths, therefore, cannot be treated as independent creations of fancy" (14). The stories, she thus implies, cannot be fully understood in isolation and must be considered as one part of complex, tightly interrelated patterns by which Native peoples defined their physical, psychological, social, and spiritual lives, both collectively and individually. However, the title story indicates the great importance of narratives. In it a young man out hunting alone meets a talking rock that gives him tales in exchange for game. While Europeans tend to view rocks as the lowest elements of the created world, for most Native peoples they were the most enduring, venerable, and, sometimes, sacred products of the creator. Therefore, that a stone should be the provider of stories attests to its great value. Students in upper elementary and junior high should become familiar with this myth and its significance so as to understand that the Native stories they hear are far more than mere entertainments and should be treated with the respect given them by original audiences. Feldman's introduction gives a clear overview of the main elements of traditional stories and provides footnotes that link her general

points to specific tales in the collection. A useful bibliography lists the sources from which she takes the stories, usually unaltered, and notes other collections from the major culture groups.

Thompson, Stith, editor. *Tales of the North American Indians.* Bloomington, IN: Indiana University Press, 1929.

Stith Thompson, one of the major folklore scholars of the twentieth century, gathers 96 "representative versions of each of the better-known tales" (vii) under such headings as "Mythological Stories," "Trickster Tales," "Journeys to the Other World," and "Animal Wives and Husbands." As the versions are those collected by anthropologists and originally published in scholarly journals, they offer interesting comparisons to those retold by modern Native storytellers and those specifically adapted and illustrated for children. Adults and junior high students can notice similarities and differences between "The Offended Rolling Stone" and Goble's *Iktomi and the Boulder*; "The Theft of the Light" and McDermott's *Raven* and Bill Reid's *The Raven Steals the Light*; and "The Arrow Chain" and Sleator's *The Angry Moon*. Readers can notice how incidents and narrative styles are altered in children's versions and how these changes influence the tone and meanings of the adaptations. Thompson supplies extensive notes that direct interested readers to other, similar versions of a story, both within the story's original culture area and in other culture areas. Using these notes, teachers and those older students who are better writers might wish to locate and then adapt other versions of stories familiar to them. These can then be read aloud to younger students.

General Collections of Stories Adapted for Children

Brown, Dee, reteller; illustrated by Louis Mofsie. *Teepee Tales of the American Indian Retold for Our Times.* New York: Holt, Rinehart, and Winston, 1979.

The author of *Bury My Heart at Wounded Knee*, a history of late nineteenth-century white-Native relationships, has gathered 36 stories originally collected by anthropologists in the early part of this century. "Because the language was sometimes archaic, the incidents disconnected, the plots and meanings often obscure, I have retold most of them as I believe they would be told by an English-speaking American Indian tale teller of today" (10). The book is a tribute both to such scholars as George Bird Grinnell, Ruth Benedict, and Alfred L. Kroeber, who, Brown feels, kept the tales from vanishing, and to the Native peoples who originally told them. Unlike other general collections, which frequently begin with creation myths, Brown begins with stories about a time "When Animals Lived as Equals with the People" and ends with "Ghost Stories." However, given the rich diversity of cultures reflected by the stories, it is unfortunate that Brown focusses on his belief that "the stories deal with the same strengths and weaknesses of human beings everywhere" (10). Children in the middle elementary grades can compare the Creek story "How Rabbit Brought Fire to the People" with a similar story, *How Rabbit Stole the Fire* (Troughton), from the Creeks' southeastern neighbors, the Cherokee. In upper elementary and junior high grades, students can see how Brown edited his sources by examining "Ice Man and the Messenger of Springtime" in relation to Schoolcraft's "Peboan and Seegwan: An Allegory of the Seasons" (Williams). Just how a modern Native author would have retold one of the stories is seen in C.J. Taylor's *The Ghost and Lone Warrior*. This Mohawk artist used Brown's "The Lone Warrior and the Skeleton" as her source. However, as junior high students will note, she gives greater emphasis to the character development of the hero than did Brown.

Caduto, Michael J. and **Joseph Bruchac**; illustrated by John Kahionhes Fadden and Carol Wood. *Keepers of the Earth: Native American Stories and Environmental Activities for Children*. Golden, CO: Fulcrum, Inc., 1988.

This collection, by Abenaki author Joseph Bruchac and environmentalist Michael J. Caduto, captures the essence of traditional and contemporary Native storytelling. Entertaining stories were not merely sources of amusement; they were living embodiments of the connections between human beings and their natural and supernatural environments. Virtually all traditional tales revealed ways of living with, not in competition with, the landscape and its plant and animal inhabitants, all of which were infused with sacred, spiritual power. The 25 stories and their accompanying ecological activities are intended to bring children into a closer, more interactive relationship with their living surroundings. Arranged under such headings as "Creation," "Fire," "Seasons," "Plants and Animals," each tale is followed by discussion questions, suggestions for hands-on nature activities, and guidelines for "Extending the Experience" of the first two types of involvement. A "Glossary and Pronunciation Key to Native American Words and Names Appearing in This Book" and a large map indicating the major culture areas and locations of specific tribes/nations help readers to relate each story to the human and natural settings out of which it emerges. Bruchac's adaptations of "Old Man Coyote and the Rock," "Sedna, the Woman Under the Sea," "Spring Defeats Winter," and "Manabozho and the Maple Trees" can be compared to versions by non-Native authors Paul Goble, Beverly Brodsky McDermott, Charles Larry, and Dorothy Reid, respectively. A teacher's manual is available for this book, as well as for the companion volumes, *Keepers of the Animals* and *Keepers of the Night*, both published by Fulcrum, Inc. in 1991 and 1994, respectively.

de Wit, Dorothy, editor. *The Talking Stone: An Anthology of Native American Tales and Legends*. New York: Greenwillow Books, 1979.

Dorothy de Wit's collection of 27 tales serves as an example of a book of children's adaptations that, because of some questionable assertions, may misinform younger readers about traditional Native realities and narratives rather than sensitize them to the various cultures. Her divisions are inconsistent. Tales are sometimes gathered under specific culture groups, such as the Iroquois, sometimes by areas, such as the Southwest, and once under the name of a country, Canada. The placement of individual stories is sometimes incorrect. For example, "The Boy-Who-Snared-the-Wind and the Shaman's Daughter," from the Thompson River Indians of south central British Columbia, is included in the "Far North and Eskimo Section." Moreover, the hero of the story carries his belongings in a parfleche, a container most widely used on the plains. In another story, "Wesakajuk," the Cree trickster, is mistakenly identified as a blue jay. And, in her introduction, the editor states that "Storytellers and shamans were careful . . . to use precise wordings so that the tales could be given to others in the form approved of by the spirits of the world" (viii). This observation ignores findings of scholars indicating that, in their oral transmission, stories were frequently altered and often bore the distinctive styles of individual narrators. The trickster is referred to as "peculiar, loveable, foolish, remarkable" (viii). Certainly he was much more than that! Finally, she has often based her versions on the writings of other children's authors known to have deliberately shaped their retellings to meet the tastes and backgrounds of non-Native audiences. Junior high students familiar with the Inuit (Eskimo) legend of Sedna will find it interesting to notice how de Wit's characterization of the young boy Papik, in "The Angakok and the Mother of Seals," casts doubts on the credibility of the shaman's actions. Perhaps because of its limitations, this book should be preserved as an example of the dangers faced by non-Native adaptors of traditional literatures.

Highwater, Jamake. *Anpao: An American Indian Odyssey.* New York: Harper & Row, 1977.

Jamake Highwater has incorporated a large number of traditional tales from various culture groups into his novel about a Pan-Indian character. The story tells of Native life from the time of creation until the coming of white missionaries and the European disease small pox destroyed the old ways and cultures. The events of the hero's life are based on the travels of Scarface, a legendary Blackfoot hero who had been rejected by his people and journeyed to the sun to seek permission from his Sky Father to marry the woman he loved. Highwater uses traditional tales collected by early twentieth-century anthropologists as the sources for individual episodes. Kiowa, Blackfoot, Zuni, Cheyenne, Tlingit, Iroquoian, Papago, Sahaptian, and other tribal narratives are presented and are identified in the notes and bibliography. The author has said that he has drawn on Native traditions to reveal the similarities and interrelationships between North American cultures just as Homer used existing Greek myths to create his great epic *The Odyssey*. Anpao's struggles, disappointments, and triumphs are thus symbolic of Native history through the centuries. The book has been praised for its unifying focus and criticized for ignoring the uniqueness of specific cultures. Students in junior high school who are familiar with most of the tales the author has used can discuss the reasons why Highwater selected them and the results of his changes to them. They can discuss the degree to which he has succeeded in creating an integrated novel representing a generalized Native hero.

Wood, Marion, reteller; illustrated by John Sibbick. *Spirits, Heroes & Hunters from North American Indian Mythology.* New York: Schocken Books, 1982. This book, the collaboration of a British author and illustrator, deals with a wider range of actors than the title indicates. The 25 stories also include animals, heroines, and planters—all very important in the physical and spiritual lives of traditional peoples. Although there is only one story from the Southeast as compared to five from the northern plains, the author has included some of the best-known Native tales and characters. Raven, Hare, Gluscap, Iktomi, and Sedna are represented. "The girl who Married the Bear," "The Big Turtle," "The Theft of Fire," and "The Seven Sisters" are stories that, in one form or another and under various titles, have been frequently adapted for children. The volume has two main strengths. First, stories are introduced by discussions placing them within the contexts of Native responses to the natural and supernatural worlds; thus each tale is seen as an integral part of an holistic response to life. Second, the illustrations—both realistic and stylized—are accurate, both literally and symbolically. Full-color doublespreads present key events, showing the appropriate landscapes and elements of material culture; stylized panels introducing each story depict main episodes and include design patterns from the art of the culture represented. Occasionally there are lapses in the prose, as when Sedna is referred to as a "witch," suggesting a European, not an Eskimo, attitude to this woman of power, or when Sedna says of her prospective husband, "I could do worse," a phrase that sounds very modern and colloquial (21). Students in the upper elementary grades may wish to search for alternate versions of such stories as "Scar Face and the Sun Dance." As these variants may have different titles, it will be necessary to note the specific culture group from which the story comes and to make a list of a few appropriate key subject words. With these materials, students can search the title and subject catalogues of their public library for possible other retellings of a story.

Adaptations for Children of Stories from Specific Cultures

Brass, Eleanor, reteller; illustrations by Henry Nanooch. *Medicine Boy and Other Cree Tales.* Calgary, Canada: Glenbow Museum, 1978. This Cree author-illustrator team has created the best children's versions of Cree legends of the Canadian prairies. The 23 stories explain the origins of horses and the moon, the naming of Saskatchewan's Qu'Appelle valley, the dangers of water serpents, the punishments for improper behavior, and the deeds and misdeeds of the trickster Wesuketchuk. The collection is notable for its portrayal of female characters, some of whom act wisely, while others do not. In "Medicine Boy," an old grandmother tells of her youthful encounter with a supernatural being who teaches her the secrets of designing exquisite clothing. "Abandoned" describes the painful meeting between a woman and her white mother, who had long ago left her with the Cree. A greedy berry-picker loses her infant to a serpent. Ten of the tales are about the adventures of the trickster, whose greed gets him into trouble but who sometimes punishes and rewards animals for their actions. Each narrative contains simple morals that emphasize still relevant lessons for living a good life. Short and simply told, the stories are illustrated with pen-and-ink pictures that enhance the spirituality implicit in many of them. Children in the middle elementary grades can relate the actions of Wesuketchuk to similar ones of other Native tricksters. In the upper elementary grades, the significance of the interrelationships between the characters can be analyzed.

Bruchac, Joseph, reteller; illustrated by Daniel Burgevin. *Iroquois Stories: Heroes and Heroines, Monsters and Magic.* Trumansburg, NY: The Crossing Press, 1985.

In choosing to adapt the stories elders told him as a child, Abenaki author Bruchac notes that "The strength of the traditional tales has not diminished, though the settings of Native American life may change. . . . They entertain, they instruct, and they empower" (4). Beginning with the creation and the deeds of the hero twins, one good and one evil, he proceeds to relate the adventures of animals who received their present physical characteristics as reward or punishment for their actions, and then recounts the journeys under-taken by human beings. The bear has a short tail because of his pride; the vulture, a scruffy coat because of his lack of foresight. A boastful hunter loses his kill, but one who respects animals is saved by his dogs from evil beings. Several of the young men experience dream visions that guide their future lives. In their relationships with other people, only those who are cooperative and generous succeed; others are punished. The focus of the stories chosen is moral, with the characters and the consequences of their actions serving as examples for traditional and modern young audiences. With the exception of the myths about the creation and the hero twins, Bruchac has avoided spiritual materials. "I have been told by many Native American people that it is right that I have not tried to disclose things, to tell stories which were not meant to be told, tales which are special and sacred" (1). Students in early and middle elementary grades, after reading the animal stories, can apply such "character adjectives" as "proud," "generous," and "greedy" to specific animals. In upper elementary grades, students can discuss how the central characters' responses to the human, animal, and spiritual beings they encounter contribute to their future happiness or unhappiness.

Clutesi, George, reteller and illustrator. *Son of Raven, Son of Deer: Fables of the Tse-Shaht People.* Sidney, BC, Canada: Gray's Publishing, 1967.

In his introduction, west coast Nootka author George Clutesi explains his reasons for telling these 12 stories about two of his people's trickster-heroes. Native children have had their traditions and narratives replaced by European tales. "This could be part of the reason so many of the Indian population of Canada are in a state of bewilderment today" (12). The adventures of Ko-ishin-mit, Son of Raven, and Ah-tush-mit, Son of Deer, will provide positive and negative examples of behavior and, thus, will help to restore the old guidelines in children's lives. They may also be helpful to sympathetic non-Native readers. Son of Deer can be a hero, as when he bravely travels to the village of the wolf people, where he uses his cleverness to gain fire for his people. But he can also be a fool. Filled with pride, he doesn't notice that the fire he has brought back is destroying a canoe he is building. Son of Raven's devious and selfish nature accounts for the frequent failure of his schemes. In three stories, he tries unsuccessfully to imitate other animals' methods of procuring food, goes hungry, and is ridiculed. At other times, he is more reprehensible, coveting possessions not his own and killing Ah-tush-mit (who is later restored to life). Clutesi illustrates each story with stylized silhouette drawings. Students in the middle elementary grades can compare Son of Deer's quest for fire with Coyote's in *Fire Race* (London) and Nanabozho's in *The Fire Stealer* (Toye), noticing the different reasons for each group's need for fire. In the upper elementary grades, students can compare Clutesi's Raven from southern British Columbia with Bill Reid's from northern British Columbia (*The Raven Steals the Light*). In his introduction, Clutesi draws comparisons between European and Native children's stories and notes the importance of the number four for Native peoples. Junior high students can study the different values contained in the nursery rhymes he mentions and his own stories. They can also notice how Clutesi's use of four-fold repetition helps in the development of plot and theme.

De Armond, Dale, reteller and illustrator. *Berry Woman's Children.* New York: Greenwillow Books, 1985.

After Raven created the world, he gave Berry Woman the responsibility of caring for the animals and birds. Although people can no longer converse with animals and these cannot remove their fur or feathers to appear as people, Berry Woman's children still possess inua, or souls, that must be respected by hunters. The annual Alaskan Bladder Festival honors her children, who had allowed themselves to be killed. An old Eskimo woman tells her grandchildren about the customs and then talks about 14 birds and animals on whom the Alaskan Eskimo people depended. A brief discussion of the animals' habits and their usefulness to human beings is followed, in several instances, by short summaries of related legends, narratives that link the present animals to their lives in the myth time. Among the better-known myths are those about Raven's creation of the world, the woman who had a crab baby, the girl who married a bear, and the blind boy who was helped by a loon. The discussion of each animal is accompanied by a wood engraving. For children in the early elementary grades, this book serves as a useful introduction to the linked natural and supernatural environments of the Alaskan Eskimos. Middle and upper elementary grade students can study Alaskan wildlife to find out about other of Berry Woman's children. They can then look for legends relating to these animals and create a second collection about "Berry Woman's Children."

Field, Edward, translator; illustrated by Kiakshuk and Pudlo. *Eskimo Songs and Stories.* New York: Delacorte Press, 1973.

This marvellous adaptation of 34 Netsilik Eskimo songs and stories was originally collected in the 1920s by Danish-Eskimo explorer Knud Rasmussen. Using a rhythmic, poetic prose that captures the colloquial oral style of Eskimo storytellers, Field depicts the joys and sorrows, dangers and achievements of traditional life. Included are myths about the creation of day and night, the sun and moon, and thunder and lightning, as well as the story of Nuliajuk (Sedna), the mother of the sea animals. Underlying the collection is the theme of the danger and importance of hunting. "The Lazy Tunrit" and "An Eskimo Taunts His Rival in Singing and Hunting" are ridicule songs directed at men who do not fulfill their required roles. In "Netsersuitsaursuk," a nagging wife taunts her unsuccessful husband; and, in "Orpingalik's Song: In a Time of Sickness," an incapacitated man remembers his past achievements. The vulnerability of children and the infirm aged are depicted in "The Story of Nuliajuk" and "The Death of Kigtak," respectively. "Hunger" deals with an ever-present fear and reveals the sympathy people have for each other, because "We only know that we all want so much to live" (91). Many of the selections emphasize the magic powers that the people felt were inherent in words and the need to use these wisely. Each poem or story is illustrated by a print created by Pudlo or Kiakshuk, both members of the West Baffin Eskimo Cooperative. After listening to several of the legends, students in the upper elementary grades can discuss the moral lessons the stories taught children and can consider how the ridicule songs and stories were indirect means of enforcing appropriate adult behavior. "The Story of Nuliajuk" and "Prayer for Good Hunting" can be examined to reveal the character of the sea goddess and her role in the people's lives.

Fraser, Frances, reteller; illustrated by Lewis Parker. *The Bear Who Stole the Chinook and Other Stories.* Toronto: Macmillan, 1959.

These 14 legends are by a Canadian journalist who, as a girl, knew the Blackfoot people, learned their language, and listened to their stories. Several stories deal with ghosts, departed beings whose presence can still be felt. In "A Song for Lone Warrior," ghosts give a young man a protective song; and, in "The Ghost Pipe," a warrior suffers tragedy when he mistreats a beloved wife whom he has brought back from the dead. In this and other stories, the importance of steadfast and caring relationships between men and women are emphasized. The Sky Beings who influenced the lives of the people appear in "How the Thunder Made Horses" and "The Girl Who Married Morning Star." The Blackfoot trickster figure Na-pe (the Old Man) is often seen seeking great meals and losing them and trying to outwit his devious friend Coyote. The concluding tale, "The Story of the Sun Dance," is a version of the well-known Blackfoot legend about the scarred and deformed young man who proves his worthiness to his intended bride by journeying to the Sun, where he receives the secrets of the Medicine Lodge. These short, crisply told adaptations embody beliefs and traditions that the people still celebrate. Students in the middle elementary grades can compare Na-pe's escapades with similar ones of other plains tricksters. In upper elementary grades, "The Girl Who Married Morning Star" and "The Story of the Sun Dance" can be compared to Paul Goble's *Star Boy*, which combines these two legends. How do the events the authors select communicate their individual interpretations of the myth?

Harris, Christie, reteller; illustrated by Douglas Tait. *Mouse Woman and the Vanished Princesses.* New York: Atheneum, 1976.
In this collection of six Haida and Tsimshian myths from the northwest coast of British Columbia, Christie Harris introduces younger readers to a diminutive but important narnauk, or supernatural being. Mouse Woman, who can assume human or animal form, is a busybody who, nonetheless, watches over and teaches young people who may be courting danger. Her most important lesson, which she states frequently, is that the "obligation of a gift is the great law that keeps all things equal in the world" (65). Although she specifically refers to the gift a young person must offer in exchange for her wisdom or assistance, she also refers to the reciprocal relationships among human beings and between them and the natural and supernatural beings with whom they share the world. She acts as a mediator between errant or threatened young people and the spirit powers, helping the former to act in ways that will restore balance. In each story, a royal princess disappears, sometimes, as in the case of Rh-pi-sunt, in "The Princes & the Bears," because she has shown disrespect for animals; sometimes, as in "The Princess & the Feathers," because of the malevolence of spirit beings. Mouse Woman serves as a catalyst; however, each of the stories emphasizes young people's responsibilities for the outcomes of their adventures. Upper elementary students can discuss the significance in each story of Mouse Woman's concept of obligation and how the central character's response to the concept influences her fate. They can also notice the similarities and differences between the roles and personalities of Mouse Woman and the fairy godmothers of European folktales.

Johnston, Basil H., reteller; illustrated by Shirley Cheechoo. *Tales the Elders Told: Ojibway Legends.* Toronto: Royal Ontario Museum, 1981.
Canadian Ojibway author Basil Johnston, in retelling nine of his people's legends, has hoped to perpetuate two gifts from the culture-hero Nanabush: "Humour and the art of story-telling" (7). Suitable for the middle elementary grades, the tales combine humor and moral lessons. In "The first butterflies," Nanabush gets lazy children to walk by creating butterflies that they chase. "Why birds go south in winter" explains that a foolish loon's wager during a lacrosse game causes a drastic weather change. "Thunderbirds and fireflies" tells of how the carelessness of young lacrosse-playing birds caused the ball to drop to earth, forming Hudson's Bay. Not all the stories feature foolish characters. "How bats came to be" discusses the reward a small animal received for freeing the trapped sun, while "How spiders came to be" details how Nanabush instructed the insects to build webs to trap flies, providing food for themselves and helping the human beings whose food was being ruined by the flies. The

most interesting tale in the collection is, perhaps, "The 'Close-your eyes' dance," a version of the "Hoodwinked Dancers" story found across North America. Johnston includes details that alter some of the basic story's themes. At first, Nanabush is wary of the ducks, for he remembers an earlier misadventure involving them. However, when the fowl foolishly imitate a dance that is sacred to him, he has the idea of deceiving them. In the end, the birds he kills are scorched beyond eating, not stolen, and the surviving ducks ridicule him. Students in the upper elementary grades can discuss the implications of these details in creating the meaning of this particular version. In the middle elementary grades, children can create sentences that specify the morals implicit in the stories.

Manitonquat (Medicine Story), reteller; illustrated by Mary F. Arquette. *The Children of the Morning Light: Wampanoag Tales.* New York: Macmillan, 1994.

In his conclusion, Manitonquat, a Wampanoag (southeastern Massachusetts) elder and storyteller, notes: "These are more than stories, you know. They are the heart of our culture. . . . For they are who we are, our memories and our dreams. . . . if we have our stories we will survive" (72). These gracefully and humorously retold stories will ensure that survival, as readers learn not only of the people's origins, but also of the continuing beliefs the myths embody. "The Morning of the World" outlines the history of the Wampanoag from the time of creation to their arrival at their present home in the Cape Cod region. Elements of many of the tales resemble those of other eastern woodlands peoples: the birth of twins, one good and one evil, to a sky woman who has fallen from the heavens; the creation of the earth on a turtle's back after a muskrat had dived to the bottom of the waters to search for dirt; the struggle with the giant Winter to create the alternation of the seasons; and the reasons for the presence of disease and death. "More Tales of Maushop" discuss the culture hero's regulation of the sun's daily passage across the sky, his seeking the aid of porpoises to drive away the sharks who threaten the people, and his suffering defeat at the hands of "the most powerful spirit there is" (71), the spirit of childhood. The story of "Maushop and the Porpoises" emphasizes the importance of the sea to the Wampanoag people. Other stories embody the people's moral beliefs: the need for hospitality, the importance of following where one's heart leads, and the dangers of losing one's temper and of complaining. Manitonquat captures the oral style in his prose, particularly when he uses contemporary colloquialisms, as, for example, in his description of the meeting of porpoises as "a regular think tank" (58). Mohawk artist Mary F. Arquette's illustrations depict traditional activities accurately and enhance the mythic dimensions of the stories. Students in the upper elementary and junior high grades can make a list of the storyteller's moral statements, can list the implied morals of many of the narratives, and can discuss how the stories reflect the values of these people. The story "The Great Migration and Old Man Winter" can be compared to *How Summer Came to Canada* (Toye) and *Peboan and Seegwun* (Larry).

Marriott, Alice, reteller. *Saynday's People: The Kiowa Indians and the Stories They Told.* Lincoln: University of Nebraska Press, 1963.

This collection of 11 "Winter-Telling Stories" about the Kiowa trickster Saynday is unusual in that it is the work of an anthropologist adapting for children the results of her field work. The trickster performs both good and trouble-causing deeds, but none of them are of a highly serious or scatological/sexual nature. Thus the reteller, while being accurate to the culture, includes only those details she deems appropriate to a young non-Native audience. Saynday-does-good stories include his bringing the sun to the people (his animal friends), liberating the buffalo for the people to hunt, and filing down the teeth of the deer, who are killing and eating the people. He both thinks of the well-being of others and works cooperatively with them. However, in the Saynday-makes-trouble stories, he thinks only of himself, usually about appeasing his enormous appetite, and ends up losing his anticipated feasts. His predicaments—getting his head stuck in a buffalo skull and becoming trapped in a tree, losing a race to an apparently lame Coyote and his soup to a bobcat—are similar to those of other tricksters of the plains. In the last story of the collection, "Indian Saynday and White Man Saynday," Saynday, although acting for selfish reasons, performs a deed most Native audiences would approve of: he tricks a proud white man out of his fancy clothes and fine palomino horse. The informal prose of the adaptations approximates the humorous, colloquial style of contemporary Native storytellers. Students in the middle elementary grades will enjoy noticing the similarities and differences in character and event between Marriott's Saynday and Paul Goble's Iktomi. In studying "Indian Saynday and White Man Saynday," they can create dialogue for what Saynday is really thinking while he talks to the white man.

Metayer, Father Maurice, editor and translator; illustrated by Agnes Nanogak. *Tales from the Igloo.* Edmonton, Canada: Hurtig, 1972.

These 22 superbly retold Copper Inuit (Eskimo) tales from Canada's Northwest Territories contain many of the themes found in traditional Eskimo myths and legends: love and marriage, the uses and misuses of supernatural powers, the heroics of lonely and rejected orphans, shape-shifting, the necessity and dangers of hunting, and revenge and ridicule. Metayer, a long time resident of the north and a speaker of Inuktituk, has captured both the flavor of the traditional tellings and the sense of a world in which spirit beings were present everywhere and could assume human or animal forms at will. He does not shy away from presenting violence—a constant of Inuit life and literature. For example, in "Kajortoq, the Red Fox," the title character tricks two bears into killing each other and then eats them. "The Hunter and the Children" is about an old man who calls down an avalanche on children who are scaring away game. Bears figure frequently—as hunters, hunted, and supernatural beings—and they are always dangerous, as they are in life. Agnes Nanogak's full-color prints depict the major incidents and embody the supernatural forces found in many of the tales. Students in upper elementary and junior high grades can focus on either hunting or bear stories and can examine social attitudes toward the former and the symbolic aspects of the latter for traditional Inuit peoples. In the middle elementary grades, readers can compare "The Blind Boy and the Loon" with *The Loon's Necklace* (Toye), noting how differences in details reflect cultural differences. In the early grades, children can compare the actions of Kajortoq, the sly fox, with those of foxes in various Aesop fables.

Norman, Howard, reteller; illustrated by Michael McCurdy. *How Glooskap Outwits the Ice Giants and Other Tales of the Maritime Indians.* Boston: Little, Brown and Company, 1989.
Glooskap, the culture hero of the peoples of the northeast coast, was, as Norman notes, "a great hero and teacher. He taught the people how they should live, about spiritual power, and how to overcome the obstacles that face mankind" (n.p.). The creator of human beings, he must work constantly to save them from dangerous supernatural beings. After having shrunk the animals to their less-threatening present sizes, he outwits cannibal Ice Giants; regulates Wuchowsen, the storm-causing bird; and, with the help of Fox, sends the kidnapping Panther-Witch back to the moon. In each instance, he must plan his strategies carefully. However, he is not perfect: by tying both of the storm-bird's wings down, he causes the waters to stagnate and thicken; having defeated supernatural beings, he boasts that he is invincible, only to be vanquished by a little baby. In the end, he tires of his role as patient listener to and savior of the people and decides they must care for themselves. However, he very nearly does not reach his "retirement home" because he fails to pay attention to his wolf companions' warnings about the dangers of the rivers they are crossing. Norman's retellings are lively and fast paced; unfortunately, however, he uses the generic term "Indian" to refer to the people. Students in the middle elementary grades can make a list of the enemies Glooskap conquers and suggest what intangible forces they might represent. They can also consider Glooskap's behavior in the light of the introductory statement quoted above. How well does Glooskap fulfill his leadership role? Upper elementary and junior high readers can compare the stories about the Ice Giants, Panther Witch, and the departure from the people with adult versions of these stories that Norman includes in his collection *Northern Tales* published by Random House (1990). How and why has Norman retold the same stories in different ways?

Reid, Bill, reteller and illustrator, with Robert Bringhurst. *The Raven Steals the Light.* Vancouver: Douglas & McIntyre; and Seattle: University of Washington Press, 1984.
Nine Haida legends of the northwest coast are superbly retold by Bill Reid, the foremost contemporary Haida artist, and Anglo poet Robert Bringhurst, and are illustrated with drawings in the traditional style by Reid. Warning! The book contains humorous accounts of Raven's sexual adventures. However, many of the stories can be "safely" presented in junior high school. The authors note that the "purpose of myths . . . is not merely to relate experiences, but to lead to significant changes in the structure of things" (57). Accordingly, in each story a

conflict is resolved and a new order established. Raven brings light to a world of darkness, liberates salmon for the people, and creates human beings. The marriage between a noble bear and a human princess leads to the establishment of the Haida Bear Clan. But Raven's amorous adventures and gluttony cause personal disaster, even as he goes about his solitary wanderings, transforming things along the way. Reid's illustrations do more than just reproduce the appropriate iconography for each story. The careful observer will notice that they embody the key themes and events of the narrative. Junior high students will find it instructive to compare "The Raven Steals the Light" and "The Bear Mother and Her Husband" with Gerald McDermott's *Raven* and Harris's "The Princess & the Bears," respectively, noticing how the Reid versions of the two stories relate more specifically to the cultural values of the Haida people, whereas McDermott and Harris slightly adapt their materials to meet the needs of young non-Native readers.

Sanger, Kay, reteller; illustrated by Tom Sanger. *When the Animals Were People: Stories Told by the Chumash Indians of California.* Benning, CA: Malki Museum Press, 1983.
About these nine tales from the Chumash people of the California coast north of Los Angeles, Sanger notes: "Indian children who listened to these stories found answers to many of their questions about life's mysteries. . . . The stories also taught them how to behave" (i). Taking place at a time "When the animals were still people" (i), they reflect, as she notes, the physical and social culture of the tellers. Young people who ignore warnings or behave selfishly are punished. The ugly color of the centipede's skin is a result of his having boasted about his ability in a favorite Chumash sport, pole climbing. Coyote is occasionally a wise old man, using his cleverness, for example, to help two boys escape from a cannibal giant. But he is frequently the fool as well, falling to earth and dying because he ignores warnings against trying to fly and nearly being boiled alive by a farmer who mistakes him for the raider of a melon patch. This story, with its echoes of Br'er Rabbit's adventures, is one of three that have strong resemblances to other cultures' tales. "Thunder and Fog" is like "Jack and the Beanstalk," while "Duck and Her Daughters" is similar to "Kate Crackernuts." They may, indeed, be Native adaptations of tales that newcomers brought to the area. Students in the middle elementary grades can compare the three tales with their non-Chumash counterparts and can discuss how the Chumash altered the stories to be more applicable to their beliefs and lifestyles.

Scheer, George F., reteller; illustrated by Robert Frankenberg. *Cherokee Animal Tales.* Tulsa: Council Oak Books, 1968.
The majority of these traditional tales of the Cherokee people of the Carolina mountains are pourquoi stories in which animals acquire physical traits because of character strengths and weaknesses. The groundhog loses his tail in a clever escape from cruel wolves; but Rabbit loses his because of his cheating ways, and Possum's is bare because of his vanity. The turkey limps after having been shot in the legs by a terrapin he mocked. Rabbit plays a role in several stories,

thinking only of himself and usually failing in his devious schemes. Many of the tales are similar to African-American stories, no doubt a result of communications between the two peoples, who lived in the same region. Students in the early elementary grades will enjoy recognizing the similarities between "How Terrapin Beat the Rabbit" and Aesop's "The Tortoise and the Hare" and between "The Rabbit and the Tar Wolf" and the African-American story "Br'er Rabbit and the Tar Baby." They can also discuss the relationships between the behavior of the animals in the stories and their own good and bad conduct.

Velarde, Pablita, reteller and illustrator. *Old Father Story Teller.* Santa Fe: Clear Light Publishers, 1989.
Velarde, a renowned artist from Santa Clara (New Mexico) Pueblo, retells and illustrates six stories her grandfather told her long ago. Taken as a group, they form a short mythic history of her people, beginning with their journey to their present home and ending with the story of the first twins, who were able to call the sacred Kachinas to the village. In "The Stars," Long Sash, who now exists as the constellation Orion, guides the ancestors on a long, arduous journey and teaches them "patience, tolerance, and love for one another" (11). However, as a leader separate from the others, he often experiences loneliness. Loneliness and difference, a sense of being excluded and even hated by others is felt by the heroes of other tales. In "Sad Eyes," a boy raised by deer can never readjust to life in his village; "The Enchanted Hunter" is envied for his successes, and evil hunters attempt to destroy him. Transformed into a beautiful maiden by the birds she cares for, the heroine of "Turkey Girl" is mistaken by villagers for a witch. A poetic dreamer and the first twins are mocked by their peers, but become intermediaries between the people and the Kachinas. All of the central figures serve as positive examples for listeners to the tales. Velarde's illustrations, in her "'earth painting' style" (54), are highly symbolic, indicating visually the spiritual significance of characters, objects, and events. Upper elementary and junior high students can make a list of the common traits of the central characters and, using the list, can discuss the nature of heroism and leadership in the stories. An important issue they can consider is the heroes' isolation from the people they guide and serve. Each illustration can be examined carefully and the importance of the iconography for the story's meaning can be discussed. The relationship of visual and written components of the story can be compared to the relationship of these elements in *The Raven Steals the Light* (Reid).

Yellow Robe, Rosebud, reteller; illustrated by Jerry Pinkney. *Tonweya and the Eagles and Other Lakota Indian Tales.* New York: Dial Press, 1979.
When he was old, Chano, who told the author, his daughter, the stories he had heard from his father, stated: "People all over the world have their own way of life, but through their stories we find we can understand them and live with them" (116). In her book, Yellow Robe helps non-Native people understand the traditional ways and beliefs of the Lakota people. Eight stories are placed within the framework of an account of her father's life as a boy. Two themes run

through the stories: the values of cooperation and the dangers of deception. In "The White Fox," a trickster-fox is defeated when a young man gains the help of the spirits of the four winds, and, in "Tonweya and the Eagles," a boy escapes from a rocky ledge because he has been kind to young eagles. However, another boy gets into trouble because he sneakily steals his brothers' sacred hunting objects, and a lying, jealous wife is carried away by wolves. Iktomi, the trickster, loses a duck dinner he had acquired through his deceptions. Discussions of everyday aspects of young Chano's life are the catalysts for his parents to tell stories, tales that teach him right conduct and the nature of the spirit powers in the world around him. Upper elementary students can focus on the two main themes, discussing how the characters' attitudes and actions lead to their being rewarded or punished.

Thematic Collections of Stories Adapted for Children

Bruchac, Joseph, reteller. *Flying with the Eagle, Racing the Great Bear: Stories from Native North America.* Mahwah, NJ: BridgeWater Books, 1993.

This collection by a noted Abenaki author focuses on the theme of initiation. The 16 stories are divided into groups of four, each section representing one of the four "corners" of North America. In several of the stories, there are four tests, four animal helpers, or four days or nights of questing. As Bruchac notes, "four is a number of powerful and magical importance to Native peoples" (x), and both the book's organization and the repetition of the number symbolism emphasize this. These traditional stories were designed both to entertain and instruct. Listening to them, boys about to be initiated would be provided with wisdom and with mythic frameworks and examples to guide them. Adults would be reminded of their own youth and their present responsibilities to the young. Not all of the boys and adults in the legends behave well, and their stories are negative examples. Some of the selections will be familiar to many readers: "How the Hero Twins Found Their Father" (Navajo) and "Star Boy" (Cheyenne), for example. One story is about an historical personage, Crazy Horse, while another is a story a contemporary Eskimo told the author about his own childhood. Underlying all of them is the belief that the rituals of initiation, requiring preparation and usually involving great ordeals, are more than passages to individual maturity. They involve developing a sense of responsibility to and respect for family, tribe, and the natural and supernatural worlds. Bruchac, who in this collection moves far afield from his geographical and ancestral homeland, emphasizes the importance of such a journey: "We learn about ourself by understanding others" (x). In studying these stories, junior high students should note what qualities of character each individual must exhibit or acquire to complete his initiation journey successfully. How is the number four significant in the journey? They can then relate these qualities to the cultural and spiritual beliefs of the peoples originally telling the stories.

Bruchac, Joseph, and **Jonathan London,** retellers; illustrated by Thomas Locker. *Thirteen Moons on Turtle's Back: A Native American Year of Moons.* New York: Philomel Books, 1992.

"Each moon has its own name and every moon has its own stories" (n.p.), an Abenaki grandfather tells a small boy. The authors have chosen stories from 13 nations, the same as the number of segments on Turtle's shell. Most of the stories come from peoples of the eastern woodlands. Each briefly told narrative emphasizes the relationships between the human people and the plant and animal life around them, and many note the deeds of a benevolent creator. Four discuss the food harvested by a specific group in the named moon. Thomas Locker's illustrations accurately depict the landscape, animals, and housing of the different areas and suggest the spirituality inherent in the stories. This book, worth enjoying on its own terms, provides a starting point for research activities in the junior high grades. Readers can find out the names given the moons by the culture group nearest them and can search for stories from that culture relating to each of the moons. They can write and illustrate their own "Thirteen Moons" book, to be shared with younger children.

Lavitt, Edward and **Robert E. McDowell,** retellers; illustrated by Bunny Pierce Huffman. *Nihancan's Feast of Beaver: Animal Tales of the North American Indians.* Santa Fe: Museum of New Mexico Press, 1990.

Adapting materials from nineteenth- and twentieth-century anthropological journals, the authors have written 36 short children's versions of tales from the nine major culture areas. Headnotes outline characteristics of each area and the specific tribes from which individual tales come. Maps locate the tribes and a colored frontispiece map links each story to its place of origin. While some of the legends and myths are not frequently adapted for children, the general themes and subject matter are familiar: the creation of the earth from a flooded world, the acquisition of fire and the determination of the seasons, and the quarrels between animals that frequently resulted in the various species receiving their distinctive physical traits. Although the authors emphasize that the narratives are outgrowths of specific physical and cultural environments, it is possible to notice similarities between the stories of geographically separated groups. A common theme is the need for cooperation that, when achieved, leads to such benefits as warmth and light. When cooperation is not achieved, the animals bear the physical indications of their transgressions. With the exception of "The Flood," a segment of the Navajo emergence myth, most of the stories are relatively uncomplicated and are suitable for early and middle elementary grades. Students should be encouraged to discuss both the universal and culture-specific implications of each story. The frontispiece map can be used as a model for a large wall map on which children can place their own pictures of the story animals near the locations of the appropriate tribes.

Monroe, Jean Guard and **Ray A. Williamson;** illustrated by Susan Johnston Carlson. *First Houses: Native American Homes and Sacred Structures.* Boston: Houghton Mifflin Company, 1993.

Native American dwellings are evidence of the adaptations made by various Native peoples to their environment and symbols of their cultural and spiritual lives. Using available materials—snow, mud, rock, wood and brush, grasses, earth, and hides—they created homes that were perfectly suited to the climates of their areas and provided the appropriate space for their daily and ceremonial activities. The authors describe houses from nine culture areas, omitting the Southeast, where early European invasion and a moist climate led to the obliteration of traditional architectural structures. The different peoples not only displayed ingenuity and skill in gathering building supplies and erecting buildings, they also displayed their beliefs that their domiciles were spiritual, as well as physical, in nature. For example, lacking wood, the nomadic plains tribes used easily transportable buffalo hides to create tipis that faced the rising sun, the source of life, and were shaped in the circular form that symbolized the unified circles of the creation. In their homes and communal buildings, Native peoples told winter stories, many of them sacred myths, explaining the origins of the houses and the activities that took place in them. Several of these myths are included in this book. Students in all grades can acquire a fuller sense of the storytelling environment when they are better aware of the locales in which the narratives were recounted and the house etiquette that accompanied the telling.

Monroe, Jean Guard and **Ray A. Williamson;** illustrated by Edgar Stewart. *They Dance in the Sky: Native American Star Myths.* Boston: Houghton Mifflin Company, 1987.

Like other peoples around the world, Native Americans developed myths about the stars. These explained the creation of the heavens, the origins of specific constellations, and the visits of human beings to the sky worlds and of sky beings to earth. For all Native groups, the narratives reflected their beliefs that the heavens and those who lived in them were closely related to the earth and that all were parts of a unified cosmos. However, as the authors of this collection note, even though there are similarities between stories told by different tribes, each tribe infused its versions with its own moral and religious beliefs. The stories are "allegories or parables that attempt to explain what it means to be human in an often unfriendly world" (x). After two chapters in which different myths about the Pleiades and the Big Dipper are compared, Monroe and Williamson present and discuss groups of stories from specific cultures or culture groups. Because many of these are sacred stories to be told and heard in winter, children in upper elementary grades should study them only during that season. After noticing a specific constellation, students can read one or two of the related myths and discuss the cultural beliefs these embody for each group of tellers. By comparing them to parallel Greek myths, students will be able to understand more fully the differences between Native and European attitudes, not only to the heavens, but also to the types of behavior exhibited by the central characters of the stories.

Taylor, C. J., reteller and illustrator. *How We Saw the World: Nine Native Stories of the Way Things Began.* Montreal: Tundra Books, 1993.

A Canadian Mohawk artist has retold and illustrated nine Native origin stories, four of which are from her general culture area, the eastern woodlands. Each story is designed to reinforce the need to show "love and respect for our Mother Earth" (5), and all of them emphasize the links between the human, natural, and supernatural worlds. The natural beauty of Niagara Falls, still enjoyed by people today, was created when five supernatural girls turned themselves into water so that they could always dive over steep cliffs. Butterflies are a gift to children from the Creator. Because of his earnest desire to help his people, an orphan boy received horses from a water spirit. However, not all the stories deal with gifts and rewards. The small islands along Canada's west coast were formed when a mistreated boy dropped cruel villagers into the sea. The Creator gives Owl dull colored feathers and big eyes because of the bird's impatience and vanity. All the stories stress the necessity of maintaining balance and cooperation and the dangers of ignoring these. The final myth, "How the World Will End," makes the point directly. The Cheyenne state that when people anger Great Beaver, he gnaws faster at the tree supporting the world. We must make him happy by keeping "the earth in balance" (30). Each story is accompanied by a full-page picture that illustrates a central episode and indicates the relationship between the three worlds. Middle elementary students can notice that Taylor has selected stories that illustrate her themes of interrelationship and balance, even though she retells stories from several tribes.. They can also discuss how the details, colors, and styles of the illustrations amplify these themes.

Wolfson, Evelyn; illustrated by Jennifer Hewitson. *From the Earth to Beyond the Sky: Native American Medicine.* Boston: Houghton Mifflin Company, 1993.

Because of the close relationships between spiritual, natural, and human worlds, Native medicine was usually linked to religious beliefs. All parts of the creation contained spirit powers, and illness had spiritual, as well as physical, dimensions. As stories dealt with the three realms and had great power themselves, it is not surprising that they played an important role in the healing practices of the various cultures. As Wolfson notes, "Native Americans understood from their myths, legends, and stories that everything in the universe was alive and filled with feeling and that illness resulted when the spirits felt neglected or offended, when tribal rules were broken, or when people mistreated one another" (7). Although she is writing a study of Native medicine, not compiling an anthology, Wolfson includes several stories to illustrate her main points. The Cherokee myth of how the plants, disagreeing with angry animals who wished to kill greedy and cruel hunters, decided to "create cures for illnesses" (10) precedes a discussion of medicinal plants of North America. The accounts of the sacred vision quests of Crazy Horse, Lame Deer, and Black Elk illustrate an important phase in the training of a healer. The quarrel between the Creator and Hadu'i, an arrogant spirit being, explains the origin of the Iroquois False Face healing society. Wolfson notes that many healing ceremonies were ritual enactments of sacred stories. This book will be a valuable background resource for teachers who wish to emphasize the important function of stories in traditional Native cultures and will be of interest to junior high readers who want to know more about the connections between various aspects of the peoples' lives.

REFERENCES

Aguila, Pancho. 1982. "The Pack." In Coyote's Journal. Berkeley, CA: Wingbow Press, 34-36.

Allen, Paula Gunn. 1986. The Sacred Hoop: Recovering the Feminine in American Indian Traditions. Boston: Beacon Press.

Baker, Betty, reteller; illustrated by Maria Horvath. 1982. And Me, Coyote! New York: Macmillan.

Barnouw, Victor. 1977. Wisconsin Chippewa Myths and Tales and Their Relationship to Chippewa Life. Madison: University of Wisconsin Press.

Beavon, Daphne "Odjig," reteller and illustrator. 1971. Nanabush and the Wild Geese. Toronto: Ginn.

Begay, Shonto. 1992. Ma'ii and Cousin Horned Toad: A Traditional Navajo Story. New York: Scholastic.

Benton-Benai, Edward. 1988. The Mishomis Book: The Voice of the Ojibway. St. Paul, MN: Red School House.

Bierhorst, John, reteller; illustrated by Wendy Watson. 1987. Doctor Coyote: A Native American Aesop's Fables. New York: Macmillan.

Bright, William. 1987. "The Natural History of Old Man Coyote" In Recovering the Word: Essays on Native American Literature, edited by Brian Swann and Arnold Krupat. Berkeley: University of California Press.

Bright, William, editor. 1993. A Coyote Reader. Berkeley: University of California Press.

Brunvand, Jan Harold, editor. 1979. Readings in American Folklore. New York: W.W. Norton.

Buller, Galen. 1983. "Comanche and Coyote, the Culture Maker" In *Smoothing the Ground: Essays on Native American Oral Literature.* edited by Brian Swann. Berkeley: University of California Press.

Clark, Ella E. 1953. *Indian Legends of the Pacific Northwest.* Berkeley: University of California Press.

Coleman, Sister Bernard; Ellen Fronger; and Estelle Eich; illustrated by Ruth Maney. 1962. *Ojibwa Myths and Legends.* Minneapolis: Ross and Haines.

Curry, Jane Louise, reteller; illustrated by James Watts. 1987. *Back in the Beforetime: Tales of the California Indians.* New York: Margaret K. McElderry Books.

Deming, Alden O., reteller; illustrated by Edward Willard Deming. 1938. *Manabozho: The Indian's Story of Hiawatha.* Philadelphia: F.A. Davis.

Dorson, Richard M. 1952. *Bloodstoppers & Bearwalkers: Folk Traditions of the Upper Peninsula.* Cambridge, MA: Harvard University Press.

Ellis, John M. 1983. *One Fairy Story Too Many: The Brothers Grimm and Their Tales.* Chicago: University of Chicago Press.

Geertz, Clifford. 1983. *Local Knowledge: Further Essays in Interpretive Anthropology.* New York: Basic Books.

Haile, Father Berard, O.F.M., collector. 1984. *Navajo Coyote Tales: The Curly Tó Aheedlíinii Version.* Lincoln: University of Nebraska Press.

Hillerman, Tony. 1990. *Coyote Waits.* New York: Harper Collins.

Jeffers, Susan, adaptor and illustrator. 1983. *Hiawatha.* New York: Dial Books.

Johnston, Basil. 1976. *Ojibway Heritage.* Toronto: McClelland and Stewart.

———. 1983. "Nanabush," *Canadian Children's Literature* 31/32, 41-45.

———. 1986. *By Canoe & Moccasin: Some Native Place Names of the Great Lakes.* Lakefield, Ontario: Waapoone Publishing.

———. 1990. "One Generation from Extinction." In *Native Writers and Canadian Writing,* edited by W.H. New. Vancouver: University of British Columbia Press.

Johnson (*sic*), Basil H. 1992. "Is That All There Is? Tribal Literature." In *An Anthology of Canadian Native Literature in English,* edited by Daniel David Moses and Terry Goldie. Toronto: Oxford University Press.

Jung, C.G. 1972. "On the Psychology of the Trickster Figure." In *The Trickster: A Study in American Indian Mythology,* by Paul Radin. New York: Schocken Books.

Kerényi, Karl; translated by R.F.C. Hull. 1972. "The Trickster in Relation to Greek Mythology." In *The Trickster: A Study in American Indian Mythology*, by Paul Radin. New York: Schocken Books.

King, Thomas; illustrated by William Kent Monkman. 1992. *A Coyote Columbus Story*. Toronto: Groundwood Books.

Kohl, Johann Georg. 1985. *Kitchi-Gami: Life Among the Lake Superior Ojibway*. St. Paul, MN: Minnesota Historical Association.

Le Cain, Errol, adaptor and illustrator. 1984. *Hiawatha's Childhood*. London: Faber and Faber

Lincoln, Kenneth. 1983. *Native American Renaissance*. Berkeley: University of California Press.

London, Jonathan, reteller, with Larry Pinola; illustrated by Sylvia Long. 1993. *Fire Race: A Karuk Coyote Tale*. San Francisco: Chronicle Books.

Longfellow, Henry Wadsworth. 1992. *The Song of Hiawatha*. London: J.M. Dent & Sons.

Lopez, Barry Holstun. 1977. *Giving Birth to Thunder, Sleeping with His Daughter: Coyote Builds North America*. New York: Avon Books.

Luckert, Karl W. 1979. *Coyoteway: A Navajo Holyway Healing Ceremonial*. Tucson: University of Arizona Press; and Flagstaff: Museum of Northern Arizona Press.

Malotki, Ekkehart, editor. 1985. *Gullible Coyote/Una'ihu: A Bilingual Collection of Hopi Coyote Stories*. Tucson: University of Arizona Press.

Malotki, Ekkehart and Michael Lomatuway'ma, editors. 1984. *Hopi Coyote Tales/ Istutuwutsi*. Lincoln: University of Nebraska Press.

Matthews, Cornelius. 1877. *The Enchanted Moccasins and Other Legends of the Americans (sic) Indians*. New York: G.P. Putnam's Sons.

Maud, Ralph, editor. 1993. *The Porcupine Hunter and Other Stories: The Original Tsimshian Texts of Henry W. Tate*. Vancouver, BC: Talonbooks.

Mayo, Gretchen Will, reteller and illustrator. 1993. *Meet Tricky Coyote! Native American Trickster Tales*. New York: Walker and Company.

Monroe, Jean Guard and Ray A. Williamson, retellers. 1987. *They Dance in the Sky: Native American Star Myths*. Boston: Houghton Mifflin Company.

Morgan, William, collector. 1988. *Navajo Coyote Tales*. Santa Fe, NM: Ancient City Press.

Radin, Paul. 1972. *The Trickster: A Study in American Indian Mythology*. Introduction by Stanley Diamond. New York: Schocken Books.

Ramsey, Jarold, editor. 1977. *Coyote Was Going There: Indian Literature of the Oregon Country*. Seattle: University of Washington Press.

Ramsey, Jarold. 1983. *Reading the Fire: Essays in the Traditional Indian Literatures of the Far West*. Lincoln: University of Nebraska Press.

Reid, Dorothy M. 1963. *Tales of Nanabozho*. Toronto: Oxford University Press.

Ricketts, Mac Linscott. 1966. "The North American Trickster." *History of Religions* 5 (Winter): 327-50.

Roessel, Robert A., Jr. and Dillon Platero, editors. 1991. *Coyote Stories of the Navajo People*. Chinle, AZ: Rough Rock Press.

Root, Phyllis; illustrated by Sandra Speidel. 1993. *Coyote and the Magic Words*. New York: Lothrop, Lee & Shepard Books.

Rothenberg, Jerome and Diane Rothenberg, editors. 1983. *Symposium of the Whole: A Range of Discourse Toward an Ethnopoetics*. Berkeley: University of California Press.

Snyder, Gary. 1975. "The Incredible Survival of Coyote." *Western American Literature* 9 (Winter): 255-72.

Swann, Brian, editor. 1983. *Smoothing the Ground: Essays on Native American Oral Literature*. Berkeley: University of California Press.

Swann, Brian and Arnold Krupat, editors. 1987. *Recovering the Word: Essays on Native American Literature*. Berkeley: University of California Press.

Taylor, Harriet Peck, reteller and illustrator. 1993. *Coyote Places the Stars*. New York: Bradbury Press

Tedlock, Dennis, translator. 1978. *Finding the Center: Narrative Poetry of the Zuni Indians*. Lincoln: University of Nebraska Press.

Thompson, Stith, editor. 1929. *Tales of the North American Indians*. Bloomington: Indiana University Press.

Thompson, Stith. 1977. *The Folktale*. Berkeley: University of California Press.

Toelken, J. Barre. 1969. "The 'Pretty Language' of Yellowman: Genre, Mode, and Texture in Navajo Coyote Narratives." *Genre* 2 (September): 211-35.

———. 1987. "Life and Death in the Navajo Coyote Tales." In *Recovering the Word: Essays on Native American Literature*, edited by Brian Swann and Arnold Krupat. Berkeley: University of California Press.

Trejo, Judy. 1979. "Coyote Tales: A Paiute Commentary." In *Readings in American Folklore*, edited by Jan Harold Brunvand. New York: W.W. Norton.

Vizenor, Gerald. 1988. *The Trickster of Liberty: Tribal Heirs to a Wild Baronage*. Minneapolis: University of Minnesota Press.

Williams, Mentor L., editor. 1991. *Schoolcraft's Indian Legends*. East Lansing, MI: Michigan State University Press.

CHAPTER
4
▼▼▼

Cultures in Conflict:
Native Experiences in Children's
Novels

NATIVE THEMES AND NARRATIVE TECHNIQUES IN NOVELS
ABOUT AND BY NATIVE PEOPLES

Most traditional Native culture groups told some stories that were very long. However, these groups did not approach characters, actions, and conflicts in the same way that non-Native creators of novels did. Very few Native Americans had written novels before Kiowa writer N. Scott Momaday won the Pulitzer Prize in 1968 for *House Made of Dawn*. This was partly because they perceived reality differently than did Europeans, for whom, for over two centuries, the novel had been the dominant literary vehicle for expressing their view of reality. Since 1968, many Native writers—the most notable being Momaday, James Welch, Leslie Silko, Gerald Vizenor, Michael Dorris, and Louise Erdrich—have used the genre to interpret historical and contemporary Native life. An understanding of how they have done so and how their novels are different in form and focus from those of non-Native writers will provide a basis for evaluating children's novels by both Native and non-Native writers.

Unlike the shared, communal experience of hearing a traditional story, the reading of a novel is a private, solitary experience. As Walter J. Ong has written, "Oral communication unites people in groups. Writing and reading are solitary activities that throw the psyche back on itself" (Ong 1982, 69). Not surprisingly, within three centuries after the invention of print, the dominant type of written literature was the novel. Able to sit by themselves with a book, individuals could read stories about other individuals struggling to define their unique identities in relation to and frequently in conflict with their social, physical, and spiritual surroundings. In the twentieth century, alienation, isolation, and separation from others has been a dominant theme of novelists, many of whom view this situation as being the basic condition of human life. In discussing this aspect of the novel, Louis Owens, a Chocktaw-Cherokee novelist and critic, has stated: "The privileging of the individual necessary for the conception of the modern novel . . . is a more radical departure for American Indian cultures than for the western world as a whole" (Owens 1992, 10).

In discussing the differences between Native and "main stream" novelists, Owens finds that the novel, as an embodiment of a view that emphasized individuality rather than collectivity, was a form foreign to the group focus of Native life and the oral literature that reflected it in both content and method of presentation. The challenge for contemporary Native writers has been to discover ways of transforming this foreign genre so that it can accurately portray both traditional and modern physical, social, and spiritual dimensions of Native life. Native peoples told the types of stories they did and the way they did not only because they did not possess systems of writing, but also because both the genres and their method of presentation were an integral part of their communally focused way of life. Could these realities be embodied in novelistic form?

In order to recapture the dynamic, interactive quality of the traditional storytelling situation, Native writers employed devices designed to make their readers cocreators of their novels' meanings. A notable feature was the breakup of a chronological ordering of events. Momaday, in *House Made of Dawn*; Leslie Silko, in *Ceremony*; and Michael Dorris, in *A Yellow Raft in Blue Water*, expect their readers to perceive the implicit connections between apparently unconnected, nonchronologically sequenced chapters or sections. There is a parallel between what readers have to do—understand the unity of a work of fiction—and what traditional story characters and traditional peoples themselves had to do—discover the harmony and balance inherent in the world in which they lived.

A second major technique Native novelists used also related to a feature of traditional stories. The statement of Papago Maria Chona, noted earlier, that "The story is very short . . . because we understand so much" (Ramsey 1983, 186), is paradoxically applicable to Native novels. Because the traditional stories dealt with familiar materials, tellers could expect their listeners to supply the unstated details: tellers and listeners were united through their shared communal knowledge and experiences. Owens notes that "The emphasis in such storytelling falls . . . not upon the creative role of the storyteller but upon the communal nature of the stories, with the 'outcome' of each story already being known to the audience" (Owens 1992, 10). When Erdrich gives the surname Nanapush to one of the characters in *The Bingo Palace*, an Ojibway reader would immediately recall the personality and adventures of the trickster Nanabozho and relate these to the novel. Similarly, *House Made of Dawn*, the title of Momaday's best-known novel, would evoke not only the Navajo Night Chant, but the sacred beliefs about healing it embodied. Of course, such a technique creates difficulties for uninformed non-Native readers, but as Owens argues, "Indian writers today have come to expect, even demand, that readers learn something about the mythology and literary (oral) history of Native Americans" (Owens 1992, 29).

The incorporation of references to traditional beliefs and allusions to traditional myths and legends is also a significant component of a dominant theme in modern Native literature, the rediscovery and repossession of the cultural and spiritual concepts that provided the basis of traditional Native life. Since the beginning of European invasion in the late fifteenth century, many Native nations have been either destroyed or deprived of their birthrights. Tribes have been exterminated, languages obliterated, traditional lands expropriated, and religious customs ruthlessly crushed. The Sacred Hoop, as Laguna Pueblo author Paula Gunn Allen has termed the holistic world view and lifestyle (Allen 1975, 113), was shattered. *Ceremony*, the title of Leslie Silko's first novel, indicates an essential element of her novel: the sacred traditions that her psychologically shattered hero seeks to recover. In *Ceremony*, Tayo, like Abel, the hero of *House Made of Dawn*, succeeds in the arduous task of reintegrating himself with his people's ancient, but still vital, values.

These and several other novels by Native authors explore the theme of what William Bevis calls "Homing In" (Bevis 1987, 580). Individuals who feel apart from both their own people and white Americans and who have been all but destroyed psychologically and spiritually, return to their ancestral lands to begin the process of becoming part of a community instead of isolated, rootless misfits. Tayo, Abel, Set (in Momaday's *The Ancient Child*), and Will (in Thomas King's *Medicine River*) are examples of such individuals. Important to the success of their quests is the rediscovery of stories. As Silko writes, "It's stories that make this into a community. There have to be stories. That's how you know; that's how you belong; that's how you know you belong" (Katz 1980, 190). Acutely aware of the historical and contemporary events and forces that have weakened and nearly destroyed traditional cultures, Native authors adapt the form of the novel to recreate and reinterpret the past and present lives of their peoples.

In breaking novelistic conventions and using mythical allusions and mythic structures in their works, Native American novelists are adapting some of the more innovative techniques of such modern novelists as William Faulkner and James Joyce. In contrast, most writers of children's novels do not employ these, preferring instead to focus on single individuals whose development toward adult integration into their societies is presented in linear fashion.

Although many children's novelists have presented the complexity of their characters and the difficulty of the inner and outer struggles they undergo, their approach is a conservative one. The protagonists' quests are not to challenge, rebel against, or reject the adult world toward which they are moving but to seek a way of affirming their individual integrity and dignity in relationship with, rather than in opposition to, the society in which they will become members. Just as their stories are about the socialization process, reading them is part of the socialization processes of young readers.

It is against this background summary about the nature of adult novels from the "Native American Literary Renaissance" of the last quarter century and the form and purpose of children's novels by non-Native writers that children's novels about traditional and contemporary Native experiences can be examined. The major questions to be asked are not "Are the books accurate?" or "Are they free of stereotypes?" but "How well do they embody the cultural realities they depict?" and "To what extent do their methods of presentation relate to the novelistic techniques of Native writers?" The works of two non-Native authors, Scott O'Dell and Jean Craighead George, will be examined first, and then two novels by Native writers, Michael Dorris' *Morning Girl* and Beatrice Culleton's *In Search of April Raintree*.

INVASION AND THE SEARCH FOR HOME IN THE NOVELS OF SCOTT O'DELL

One of the foremost American creators of historical fiction for children, Scott O'Dell wrote many novels about the lives of traditional Native young people in conflict with Aleutian, Spanish, and Anglo-American invaders. *Island of the Blue Dolphins* (1960), winner of the Newbery Medal; *Zia* (1976), its sequel; and *Sing Down the Moon* (1970), a Newbery Honor Book, are among the best-known. In each, he writes with sensitivity about the difficult lives of his heroines as they face the destruction of their ages-old ways of life, and he recreates with meticulous accuracy the physical and cultural dimensions of these lives. However, as his own comments, those of critics, and the shape and content of the novels themselves reveal, there may be limitations to his portrayals of Native life. Although his novels are superbly crafted, readers must ask, "Are they presentations of the ways the people's lives were, or are they embodiments of the author's own views of the way human nature is for all people?"

Island of the Blue Dolphins, the first and most highly acclaimed of O'Dell's two dozen children's books, is the first-person account of the 18 years spent by Karana on the off-shore California island that had long been the home of her people. It is based on the brief accounts of an actual woman who had lived alone on San Nicolas Island between 1835 and 1853. A totally integrated member of her family, the central character sees her father and most of the male members of her tribe killed by otter-hunting Aleuts. As the depleted tribe sails from its home, Karana discovers that her brother has been inadvertently left on shore and jumps overboard to join him. However, after he is killed by a pack of wild dogs, she is alone and begins the long and arduous process of learning to survive psychologically and physically. As O'Dell stated in his Newbery Acceptance Speech, "She learned first that we each must be an island secure unto ourselves. Then, that we must 'transgress our limits,' in reverence for all life" (O'Dell 1965, 104). The process involves finding food and shelter, learning to combat her loneliness, establishing a rapport with the creatures around her, and establishing a friendship with Tutok, an Aleut girl who accompanies a ship to the island several years into Karana's solitary stay. At first filled with a desire to kill the leader of the dog pack, she later tames the dog and comes to love him. Later, she makes a decision to kill no animals because "Without them the earth would be an unhappy place" (O'Dell [1960] 1971, 156). Most significant, she tells Tutok her secret name, giving, with trust and friendship, the word that would give the girl power over her. Finally, when she leaves the island, she has regrets but thinks, "There is no sound like this [the human voice] in all the world" (O'Dell [1960] 1971, 178). She has completed a maturation process in which hatred, fear, and loneliness have been replaced by love and sociality.

Island of the Blue Dolphins rightly deserves both the popular and critical acclaim it has received and its reputation as a twentieth-century children's classic. O'Dell skillfully integrates accounts of Karana's day-to-day activities with the highlights of her adventures. Thus, the narrative pace is never allowed to slacken, while, at the same time, the reader is given a sense of the routine nature of most of her days. These "how-to" sections are rendered interesting not only because they are placed between the action segments but also because of the vividness of O'Dell's presentation. He succeeds so well because of his deep knowledge of the area. A native of the California coast, he has dried abalone, hunted for devil fish, and learned to handle off-shore tides. But most important is the skill of his portrayal of Karana's character. O'Dell wisely chooses the first-person point of view. While the heroine's life is interesting, her attitude toward it is more so. He depicts the nature of her responses toward her daily survival activities, inanimate objects, animals, and other people from a female perspective. *Island of the Blue Dolphins* may be the most successful presentation by a male children's writer of a major female character.

However, given its many virtues, how fully does the novel embody a Native response to the invasion of an alien people? In 1992, critic Susan Naramore Maher argued that the author does succeed: "One of O'Dell's ideological projects was to turn the adventure genre—as expressed in the popular western—on its head, to uncover the morally repugnant consequences of cultural domination. In his alternative counterwesterns, O'Dell gave voice to the oppressed, to those who lost their lands and their cultures" (Maher 1992, 216). In contrast to the wandering male cowboy, the heroines of O'Dell's novels have a strong sense of home. Karana's life and adventures suggest viable alternatives to the rapacious imperialism of the captain who leads the slaughter of the sea otters. Because no one understood her language, the events and meaning of her experience as a woman and member of a Native culture remained unarticulated until O'Dell gave it a voice.

This interpretation bears a closer relationship to the fashions of literary theory and criticism of the early 1990s than to the novel itself or to O'Dell's own statements about it. While the effects of imperialistic invasion on the tiny Ghalas-at tribe are crucial, the voice that O'Dell creates gives us very little sense of the nonmaterial aspects of the culture that governs Karana's life. She is sensitive to her tribe's female fashions, marks her face in the manner of an unmarried woman, worries about the violation of tribal taboos against women making and using weapons, and fears that revealing her secret name will give another control over her. Although the tribe has been extinct and its language lost for nearly a century and a half and no detailed study of it exists, there were no doubt similarities between its culture and those cultures of such nearby groups as the Chumash and Gabrielino. And like them, the Ghalas-at would have lived in a world filled with spirit powers who would have influenced their lives and whose exploits would have been the subject of a rich mythology. Living in relationship to these powers would have been a central, if not the central, element of the people's material and spiritual lives.

This element is precisely what one misses in the voice that O'Dell creates and the voice that Maher describes. Three examples will illustrate the absence: Karana's relationship with the animals, her visit to Black Cave where she sees what appears to be some kind of ancestral shrine, and her violation of the weapon-making taboo. Karana's creating a family of the wild dog Rontu and later his son, two fledgling birds, and an otter is motivated by her loneliness. Her refusal to kill two fighting sea lions, the dog who killed her brother, and, finally, all living beings is presented by O'Dell as a symbol of her reintegration process. These actions would have, no doubt, appeared unusual to her people, for whom hunting was the main source of food and materials. She does not see the animals as possessing spirits, as did Native people all along the Pacific Coast, but treats them as pets, in the manner of European children. Moreover, as shall be discussed later, her changing attitudes to them are related to ideas the author himself held.

Karana discovers Black Cave, about which she had never heard anyone speak, by accident. Exploring it out of curiosity, she sees a group of human-sized reed figures clothed with gull feathers. In their midst is a human skeleton, in a seated position, holding a pelican bone flute. Karana realizes that it is one of her ancestors, but refuses to look at it again. Trapped by the rising tide, she spends the night in the cave as far from the figures as possible, and, at first light, flees to the outside looking only toward the daylight. On the way home, she tells her dog, "never in all our days [will we] go there again" (O'Dell [1960] 1971, 129). She does not return, nor does she refer to the incident. Maher states that in the cave "Karana absorbs the long history of her people" (Maher 1992, 220) and that the experience "lends her strength to brave her greatest foe: the hunters" (Maher 1992, 220). The episode could have depicted a moment of crucial insight in which Karana is ennobled by the living, timeless spiritual forces of her culture. However, as O'Dell develops it, it does not do this. It seems more likely that Karana has faced her past and found that, to survive, she must never dwell on it, for to do so would be to become engulfed in and entrapped by an inner darkness as great as that surrounding the figures in the cave.

As she prepares weapons, designed primarily to execute her vow of revenge against the wild dogs, Karana worries about the prohibition against women making weapons. Will such actions fulfill her people's warnings about wind storms, earth quakes, or tidal waves caused by angered spirits? She does make weapons with which she kills many wild dogs and a large number of cormorants, from whose feathers she plans to make a cape. A tidal wave and earthquake do occur but only after she has given up killing animals, and, when it does, she does not remember her earlier fears about angering the gods. In fact, surviving the natural disasters, she is relieved that they have not been as great as they would have been "if those who make the world shake had really been angry with us" (O'Dell [1960] 1971, 170).

If O'Dell does not create the voice of a specific Native "Other," what voice does he create? Peter Roop, in a discussion of the author's use of historical materials notes, "He uses history, and with honest accuracy, to tell a story which welled up from deep within inside himself. . . . Because of O'Dell's style, historical concern, and evocative story, the reader receives a valuable book based on history yet essentially outside of history, a story of growth, development, and the enrichment of a human life" (Roop 1987, 173). O'Dell, as his own comments also reveal, is creating both personal and universal voices. "The fundamental human is about the same as he was a couple of thousand years ago. . . . Human needs for love, affection, understanding, a chance to succeed at something, are about the same" (Wintle and Fisher 1975, 172). O'Dell also recalled that the story grew out of his anger at the ruthless slaughter of animals occurring not far from his own southern California home. "I wanted to say to children and to all those who will listen that we have a chance to come into a new relationship to the things around us" (O'Dell 1965, 104). Finally, he remembered how, as a boy, he had both loved exploring the lands and seas around his San Diego home and, with friends, had cruelly killed small animals. These memories found their way into the book. *Island of the Blue Dolphins* used imaginatively reconstructed history to create a story that expiated remembered guilt, emphasized a powerful modern ecological message, and portrayed what the author considered universal needs and longings of human beings.

Reviewing *Sarah Bishop*, a later O'Dell novel about a white girl who survives on her own, Zena Sutherland wrote: "the primary appeal of the book may be the way in which Sarah, like the heroine of *Island of the Blue Dolphins*, like Robinson Crusoe, makes a comfortable life in the isolation of the wilderness" (Stine and Marowski 1984, 276). Both books, she implies, are linked to the British literary tradition of the survival story and embody ideas that, in the view of Euro-American writers, may be universal.

Sing Down the Moon, published in 1970, bears similarities to *Island of the Blue Dolphins*. It is the first-person narrative of a young woman whose homeland is invaded by rapacious aliens. However, there is a significant difference in the works. Perhaps because in the latter story O'Dell was dealing with a people whose traditional life had been carefully researched and with an historical incident, the 1864 "Long Walk" of the Navajo, he is able to present a great deal more about the values and beliefs of his heroine. O'Dell stated that "I'm not interested in the Navajos particularly" (Wintle and Fisher 1975, 172), and that he took what was a ready-made situation because of its dramatic possibilities. Critic Perry Nodelman has emphasized the novel's universality, saying that, although it "convincingly describes an alien culture . . . it is also about ourselves. The story is very strange and very familiar—both at the same time" (Nodelman 1984, 98). However, despite both of these statements, what makes it different from *Island of the Blue Dolphins* is that it comes closer to presenting the voice and world view of the Navajo "Other."

The heroine is Bright Morning, who does not give anyone her name (and never gives her secret name) until nearly the end of the book. She is a participant in the Long Walk, the climactic event of the 1863-1868 war between the Navajo people and the American government. "By the beginning of 1863," historian Raymond Friday Locke wrote, "the Navajos were a defeated people: poor, hungry and demoralized by the New Mexican slave raids" (Locke 1989, 349). For at least three centuries, the Dinéh (meaning the People), as they called themselves, had lived as herders in Dinéhtah, the lands that were sacred because they were also the homes of their gods. They had evolved a rich, complex ceremonial life that was designed to maintain a balance and harmony with the land and spirits that ensured their physical and spiritual health. American forces, believing the land to be rich in precious metals, killed Navajo livestock, burned cornfields and orchards, and destroyed hogans, spiritual, as well as physical, homes, and then, during the winter, forced 8,000 people to march to Bosque Redondo, New Mexico, 300 miles to the east. Hundreds of the aged, ill, and infirm perished along the way; the remainder found themselves placed on an arid land next to their frequent enemies the Apaches. Here they were forced to till infertile land, eat foreign foods, and build inadequate shelters that in no way resembled their physically and spiritually protective hogans. When, at last, in 1868, they were permitted to return to their homelands, their joy was so great that, according to one Navajo, "we felt like talking to the ground, we loved it so" (Brown 1972, 35). O'Dell's success in *Sing Down the Moon* lies in the fact that he is able to communicate the people's love of the land, and the physical, cultural, and spiritual alienation they experienced during the removal.

Like Karana, Bright Morning goes through a maturation process during the course of her two periods of captivity, the first as a slave in the Anglo household in a town four days' ride south of her home in Canyon de Chelly, the second as one of the disposessed Navajo journeying to and then living at Bosque Redondo. On the one hand, O'Dell's portrayal of this process is less detailed than the portrayal of Karana's growth in *Island of the Blue Dolphin*; on the other, it is more culture specific. Karana, without tribal support, evolved in her attitude to the natural world in a manner parallel to that of the author. However, Bright Morning becomes very much a Navajo woman. One reviewer of *Sing Down the Moon* perceptively remarked that "If Bright Morning gave her story to an anthropologist, she would tell it the way Scott O'Dell does" (Stine and Marowski 1984, 269). Indeed, the achievement of the novel can be judged precisely according to the extent that O'Dell moves away from portraying a unique, individual heroine to a more generalized Native heroine, one who resembles the women who, in telling their stories to anthropologists, presented themselves as members of a group and defined themselves in terms of that group. In the novel, Bright Morning becomes less of a good Navajo woman when she forgets the group ethos that should govern her life.

The importance of seeing oneself as a member of a group is evident early in the novel, before Bright Morning and her friend are captured by Spanish slavers. She recalls how, a year earlier, when she was 13, she had placed personal concerns ahead of her role within the family, abandoning the sheep in her charge to run home during a spring blizzard. She also notes that an open expression of personal joy is offensive not only to the people but also to the gods, who had killed her brother for such behavior by striking him with lightning. However, moments before the two Spaniards ride up, she ignores her friends' questions about the ominous appearance of American soldiers in her village and, anticipating owning her own flock of sheep, "jumped up and began to dance" (O'Dell [1970] 1992, 20). Her capture must certainly be a result of her selfish focus, her disregard of Running Bird's concern about a community matter. She has displeased the gods and becomes an involuntary exile from her homeland.

In a town and a house so unlike the scattered hogans of Dinéhtah, living where her gods are replaced by Christ, who is represented in an Easter pageant by the Spaniard who had abducted her, she learns the value of her community and lands and makes the determined vow to return. Her attitude is a contrast to that of Rosita, another Navajo, who has never heard of Canyon de Chelly, who has taken a Spanish name, who thinks the Christian God superior to the Navajo ones, and who is content in her new life. Concerned only about herself, Rosita has turned her back on her heritage. After Bright Morning has engineered her escape with the aid of a Nez Percé girl and made her dangerous way back home, she happily notices the wind: "A dawn wind blew. . . . It was a Navaho wind" (O'Dell [1970],1992 62). She is responding both to the physical sensation and to the spiritual powers her people knew the wind possessed.

After this return, the heroine does not undergo any major character growth. Instead, she actualizes the qualities of character she had developed during her captivity and escape. The most important traits she reveals are her nurturing qualities and her love of Canyon de Chelly. After Tall Boy, whom she will later marry, has been injured attempting to rescue her, he can no longer perform his male role as warrior and hunter and, like most of the Navajo men during the internment at Bosque Redondo, becomes dispirited. After the marriage, she recognizes what he does not, the spiritually revitaliz- ing qualities of their homeland, and, in effect, brings him back to life by gently and firmly but subtly leading the escape home to the canyon. They arrive in the spring with their newborn child. She raises her face to the newly falling rain, and, in an echo of her thoughts during the first return, she affirms: "It was Navaho rain" (O'Dell [1970] 1992 134).

This apparently simple statement is very complex and reveals the culture- specific nature of the novel's conclusion. On one level, it contrasts an element of her familiar homeland with the alien world of Bosque Redondo. As a spring rain, it also suggests the beginning of a new cycle of plant life and, thus, suggests a contrast to the state of the land after the American soldiers had scorched it and to the aridity of the land around Bosque Redondo. Most likely, it is not just a Navajo rain, but what the people themselves would have called a she-rain, the gentle rain that, unlike the male rain of violent thunderstorms, had nurturing, creative, restorative powers. Like this rain, Bright Morning has created new life, her son, and has brought her husband back to spiritual life. Finally, it should be noted that the rain falls upon the newly returned family members because they are in a state of harmony and balance, among themselves and with the spiritual and physical qualities of the land. The gods, who had not accompanied them on their Long Walk, as evidenced by the failure of the sacred chants to save so many dying people, have welcomed their return with the gift of rain. It is like the gentle rain that falls on the restored Abel at the end of Momaday's *House Made of Dawn*.

Bright Morning's acquisition of a strong sense of her membership in her Navajo community is seen in her narration of events and description of the various settings. These implicitly reveal how fully she embraces the Navajo belief in the sacredness of Canyon de Chelly and the extent of her people's sense of loss and alienation as they watch its destruction and then move to the distant reservation. Scott O'Dell is not only historically accurate in his account of the invasion of the canyon and the setting and way of life in the prison camp; he is, in presenting these in the voice of Bright Morning, culturally accurate as well. As part of the exposition, O'Dell must set the opening scene: the hogans, river, peach orchards, and sheep meadows. As the heroine describes these, the peach trees are a "miracle" (O'Dell [1970] 1992, 2); the hogans, places of warmth and safety; the sounds of the river swollen with melted snow, "wonderful" (O'Dell [1970] 1992, 2); and the sight of the grazing sheep is a source of happiness. A sense of plenty is implied in the account of preparations for her womanhood ceremony. However, all these sensations are quickly destroyed by the soldiers, and she can only view the events from the mesa, helpless to intervene. Her feelings of loss of and alienation from a once living landscape are emphasized: "gray ashes" (O'Dell [1970] 1992, 83), "bare stumps" (O'Dell [1970] 1992, 83), and red stained earth replace hogans, peach trees, and planted fields. Shortly after the invasion, the first deaths of the novel, those of the old chief and a young child, occur. Deprived of the physical resources of the canyon and removed from its spiritual powers, the people's vitality is sapped.

As it is viewed by Bright Morning, Bosque Redondo is the complete opposite of Canyon de Chelly. In the novel's opening paragraph, joyously describing the river as it moved through the canyon, she had noted how it made "a big loop past our village" (O'Dell [1970] 1992, 2). At the end of the Long Walk, after a spring that comes overnight, like the one she depicted in the first chapter, she sees their destination. "It was in a bend of a big looping river, flat bottomland covered with brush" (O'Dell [1970] 1992, 100). This one similarity makes her aware of the things that are missing: the blue snow-melted water, the canyon walls, and the peach trees.

Bright Morning does not complain about how much she misses her home-land or even mention it until after she is married and has decided to return. Such would have been a breach of Navajo etiquette and decorum, a self-pity that would weaken the communal bonds. But in her account of their lives at Bosque Redondo, she uses terms that implicitly compare the place negatively with Canyon de Chelly. The shelters the people create of brush and discarded materials are not physically and spiritually embracing hogans. Instead of living by themselves unmolested, they are bothered by aggressively hostile

Apaches, also exiles. They must plant unfamiliar crops using new types of implements and, in a land with less water than their own, must build irrigation systems, which prove inadequate. When she describes the drought-induced crop failure, she must be remembering how, the year before, her mother had noticed the dryness of the earth and told her to plant seeds very deep, which she had done and with successful results. With no corn to grind, sheep to sheer, wool to weave, or game to hunt, the people are deprived of the daily activities that kept them busy and productive and in vital contact with the land. The men become lethargic; their gods seem to have abandoned them, and they are prey to evil spirits. "There were ghosts and witches everywhere and many people sickened and died" (O'Dell [1970] 1992, 105).

Seeing the physical and spiritual effects of this flat, gray, arid landscape on her people, the newly married Bright Morning realizes that her baby must not be born here and, with great difficulty, persuades Tall Boy to escape. Even so, she must constantly remind him that "the canyon is our home" (O'Dell [1970] 1992, 125). Only on the sacred lands of Dinéhtah will her husband find new life and her son grow into a full life. Like the physical and spiritual powers of the female spring rain, O'Dell's heroine has the insight and wisdom to understand fully the power of Canyon de Chelly. In bringing her family back to its home, she is the first of her nation to take the step that will lead to a renaissance of physical, cultural, and spiritual life that continues to this day. O'Dell's ability to perceive the truths behind the fact of this chapter of Navajo history and to communicate the cultural realities through the voice of his Navajo narrator may well make this book his most authentic portrayal of a traditional Native lifestyle and world view.

Even so, as several Native readers of the novel have noted, O'Dell's presentation of the male figures, particularly Bright Morning's husband, Tall Boy, is less than positive. Dispirited because of his injury and the fate of his people, he is almost completely dependent on his spouse. While no doubt many Navajo men were devastated by these historical events, the extended presentation of Tall Boy's behavior and attitude ignores the sense of equality and cooperation that characterized Navajo marriages, especially in these tragic times.

Although both *Island of the Blue Dolphins* and *Sing Down the Moon* deal with the invasion of Native lands, the major focus of the two novels is not on the impact of invasion. In the former, O'Dell is more interested in portraying the heroine's changing response to her natural environment; in the latter, his interest is in examining the power of Canyon de Chelly on the lives of Bright Morning, her family, and her people generally. *Zia*, a sequel to *Island of the Blue Dolphins*, examines in extensive detail the politics of colonization and the effect it has on Native peoples. Karana's significance in this novel is different from that of the first book, and she is of secondary importance to the title heroine. And the ultimate impact of the invasion is different from that of the invasion in *Sing Down the Moon*.

Zia, the niece of Karana, has come, with her brother Mando, from the mountain home of their adopted tribe, the Cupeño, to the coastal mission town of Santa Barbara. From here, she hopes to sail to San Nicolas Island, the Island of the Blue Dolphins, to bring back her aunt, who, along with herself and her brother, are the last members of their tribe. Zia is seeking to recover her heritage, her past. However, she fails in her attempt to reach the island, and, when she meets her aunt, neither can understand the other's language. At the conclusion of the novel, Karana has died, Mando has left the mission hoping to sign on with a Yankee whaling vessel, and Zia returns alone to the mountains to rejoin the tribe that itself had recently been displaced by newly arrived Anglos.

Most of the novel is set in Santa Barbara in 1853, the year of Karana's rescue and the third year of California's statehood. Mexican, Spanish, Anglo, and Native cultures clash. The religious orders are in conflict with the severely weakened Mexican military authority; both seek to control the various Native groups in the area, but are themselves virtually powerless before the new American regime. There is little agreement between the old Native peoples and the dissident young Natives who rebel against virtual enslavement by secular and ecclesiastical authorities. In her quest to find her past, Zia is caught in the middle of the present conflicts, struggles that will determine the future of the new state, and must finally retreat from this meeting place of culture clash, this crossroads where the new orders meet and crush the old.

Zia had come to Santa Barbara after a priest had visited her tribe, promising plenty of food and little work and stating, "we will teach you to speak Spanish and introduce you to our God, who will bless you and look over you" (O'Dell [1976] 1978, 18). The promise of an easier physical life hides the religious objectives of conquerors. Although she has her own reasons for going, she does fall under the influence of Spanish and Christian culture, quickly learning a new language, discussing with her brother school lessons about European explorers and discovers, and frequently praying to the Virgin Mary. This European culture is not just displacing Native ones, it is also displacing people from their traditional lands, stealing from them, and punishing the indigenous peoples for attempting to reclaim what is theirs. The missionary leaders do not understand the Native peoples' love of their old ways or their failure to willingly espouse Christianity. Zia becomes involved in an uprising led by Stone Hands, an angry young man whose dictatorial attitude towards his followers results in the failure of his revolt. Because she helps several Native women to escape from the mission, she is imprisoned by Captain Cordova who, having lost much of his authority with the coming of the Americans, uses the girl as a pawn in his long-standing feud with the mission. Caught in the mission's quest for souls, the Spaniards' quest for power, and the Anglos' quest for land, the Native people are helpless to do anything but flee. As one reviewer noted, Zia's homecoming in the final chapter will not ultimately be happy. "California is not an island, and one knows historically that there was no escape for the Zias whose way of life was obliterated by the coming of the Spanish" (Stine and Marowski 1984, 273) and, one might add, the Anglo Americans. Unlike Bright Morning, who in the years following her return to her home will see a great recovery of her culture, Zia, whose people had been controlled by the Spanish missionaries, will see them all but obliterated by the new inhabitants of the new state. Like Ishi, a member of the now extinct Yana people, whose story was made famous in the studies of anthropologist Theodora Kroeber, Zia is the last of her tribe.

However, whereas "Ishi lived long enough to leave a record of what the Yana were like" (Kroeber 1973, 210), Zia can leave no record of her island people. Her greatest tragedy is not so much the effects of the present conflicts on her but her loss of a past by which to define herself. When she and her brother attempt to paddle to the island, the tides force them back and they are briefly captured by the crew of a New England whaling boat. The kindly Captain Nidever, who does bring Karana from the Island, does not take Zia on the trip, choosing instead Father Vicente, a good man who, nonetheless, is motivated by his desire to convert Karana to Christianity. When the woman is brought to Santa Barbara, Zia first sees her from the window of the prison to which Captain Cordova has sent her. The powers of the Europeans are the first obstacle between the girl and her past. The greatest obstacle, however, is language. Zia has forgotten the few words of the language her mother had taught her. Significantly, her mother had "died of a disease the gringos brought" (O'Dell [1976] 1978, 85). Indirectly, the Anglos are responsible for the girl not having had the continued language training that would have enabled her to communicate with her aunt and, thus, to keep the language and traditions alive. Quite literally, the gringo disease has destroyed Zia's mother tongue.

Whereas *Island of the Dolphins* portrayed the positive character growth of the isolated Karana and *Sing Down the Moon* concluded with Bright Morning's joyous return to her homelands, *Zia* foregrounds the devastating effects of imperial invasion. Like Zia, readers learn little about what Karana thinks and feels; they do experience the displacement and alienation both feel in a world in which the masters view the different Native groups as, at best, slave labor and, at worst, obstacles standing in the way of their own objectives. O'Dell, writing the novel in the 1970s, at a time when Native cultures had all but been obliterated in southern California, seems to despair.

O'Dell's plots fit the conventional linear coming-of-age pattern found in most children's novels. While there are some flashbacks designed to present background information, O'Dell is mainly concerned with examining how the young heroines will move from their present situations into their futures. At a time when contemporary Native authors were portraying their protagonists discovering elements of their spiritual pasts and seeking to perceive the unities informing these and then living healthy lives within them, he makes few references to the mythological and spiritual systems of his character's lives. In *Island of the Blue Dolphins* and *Zia*, there are scattered allusions to the gods Mukat and Zando. But Zia also prays to the Virgin Mary, and O'Dell seems more interested in the spiritual myopia of the missionaries. In these two novels, his focus is less spiritual than psychological and sociological. Although he alludes to healing songs in *Sing Down the Moon*, he does not draw on the complex ceremonial systems of which these are small parts and which governed all aspects of Navajo life. In this novel, he does deal with the "homing in" theme; but in the other two, he gives greater attention to the destructive social and psychological effects of invasion. In contrast to O'Dell, contemporary non-Native novelist Jean Craighead George describes the integrative social and spiritual forces at work in the lives of modern Alaskan Eskimos.

SELF-DISCOVERY AND CULTURAL RECOVERY IN THE NOVELS OF JEAN CRAIGHEAD GEORGE

Whereas Scott O'Dell's novels portrayed young Native people of earlier times struggling to define themselves as they faced invaders intent on destroying their cultures, those of Jean Craighead George examine the tensions experienced by contemporary Natives attempting to recover their traditions in a world dominated by the mechanical and social forces of white "civilization." In *Julie of the Wolves;* its sequel, *Julie; The Talking Earth;* and *Water Sky*, she combines her scientific knowledge, keen observation of aspects of contemporary Native life, study of Native traditions and spiritual beliefs, and sensitivity toward the problems experienced by young people entering into adulthood. A study of these books in the order in which they were published, along with her autobiography, *Journey Inward*, reveals a shift in George's focus. *Julie of the Wolves*, published in 1972, emphasizes the ecological soundness and validity of the traditional Eskimo ways the heroine discovers, while *Julie*, which appeared in 1994, is concerned with the spiritual basis of these ways. The movement is from a view of the Native peoples as the world's first ecologists to them as "Other," as groups possessing completely different world views that need to be understood on their own terms. The books published between these two mark stages in the author's shift in approach.

Before the publication of *Julie of the Wolves*, winner of the Newbery Award and still her most acclaimed novel, George had established a reputation as a significant writer of nonfiction studies of nature and novels in which young people confront the tensions between the natural and industrialized worlds. For example, *My Side of the Mountain*, published in 1959, while centering on the self-sufficient life spent by Sam Gribly wintering in a hollow tree in the Catskills, has as its background the New York congestion from which the boy has escaped. The young lad comes to the painful realization that he cannot maintain his solitude and self-sufficiency and that he must return home. The forces of civilization encroach on his natural paradise. In *Julie of the Wolves*, the conflict between nature and civilization—a major theme in American literature since the late seventeenth century—is the major focus of the book.

The novel was written after the author's 1970 trip to Alaska to do research for an article on wolves. There she not only gained more detailed knowledge of the physical and social lives of the animals, but also witnessed the destruction of the environment by people from the south and met an Eskimo family who practised both the old and new ways. The sight of a young Eskimo girl walking on the tundra beyond the town of Barrow provided the impetus for her story, as George wondered where the child might be going and how she might feel about a life balanced between childhood and adulthood and between traditional and modern ways. When the book appeared, it contained the themes and character types of her earlier novels, influenced by her new awareness of the landscape, wolves, and people of the Arctic. It also made use of one of the best-known genres of children's adventure fiction, the survival story.

Popular since the middle of the eighteenth century, when children's adaptations of Daniel Defoe's *Robinson Crusoe* (1719) first appeared, the Robinsonade, as the form came to be known, reflected the cultural values of writers and their intended audiences. In order to survive physically and psychologically, the heroes had to rely on the material and spiritual traditions of their cultures. Return home marked reunion with their culture group, a kind of completed initiation. Given the popularity of the survival story, it is not surprising that the North American Arctic should be used as the setting for many Robinsonades. Its harsh weather, dangerous animals, and large, desolate, uninhabited areas are ideally suited to the genre. Readers familiar with the form, especially with such novels as Armstrong Sperry's *Call It Courage*, Scott O'Dell's *Island of the Blue Dolphins*, and Gary Paulsen's *Hatchet*, will quickly recognize the conventions as they appear in *Julie of the Wolves*: the apparently hostile and desolate location, the limited means for survival, the use of memory and ingenuity to survive, and the return to a family or cultural group. However, they will also notice differences: the heroine's departure from her village is voluntary; wild animals, instead of being threats, help her to survive; the culture group to which she returns is the greatest danger to her; and her return is not joyous. The differences arise because the society from which she departs and to which she returns is not unified, being composed of people caught or, perhaps, stranded midway between ages-old ways of living and the very recently arrived economic, technical, and social forces of mainstream American life. Moreover, within herself she experiences the tug of the two forces and, at different times, holds different attitudes toward each of them. In *Julie of the Wolves*, George builds on and then breaks readers' expectations about a literary form in order to tell a story about the breakup of a traditional pattern of life and the sequential shattering of her heroine's expectations.

Miyax Kapugen, whose white, or gussak, name is Julie Edwards, flees Barrow, site of one of the oldest known North American settlements, but now a town of quonset huts and TV dinners. She is escaping consummation of her arranged marriage with 13-year-old Daniel and attempting to reach Point Hope, there to take a ship to San Francisco, to her the epitome of civilization. However, to get to her destination, she must travel across the tundra, where she becomes lost, is befriended by a pack of wolves, and spends the winter. She comes to recognize the value of the old ways she had repudiated while in Barrow only to realize that these are being destroyed by the encroachments of civilization. In the end, she reluctantly rejoins her father, who has taken the white name Charlie Edwards and has espoused the destructive modern ways he had once abhorred.

In describing the thoughts and actions of Julie as she survives on the tundra, George focuses on a theme found in her works from *My Side of the Mountain* to *The Talking Earth*: the belief that the ideal life is one in which human beings revere and live in harmony with the rhythms of the natural world. In this novel, the ideal world is the Arctic tundra where wolves live, and where, in earlier days, Eskimos lived in harmony with nature. The purpose of placing Julie in the middle of this location is to enable her to perceive the values of the old ways of her people. At various stages, her attitudes toward the tundra, the seal camp (where she and her father had once lived according to the old ways), Barrow, and San Francisco change. Just after she has rejected San Francisco and embraced the harmonious, integrated life in nature, bounty hunters (one of whom turns out to be her father) shoot and kill Amaroq, the alpha wolf, from a plane. George has led her heroine to a valuable discovery; but at the same instant, she has allowed the new ways to emerge victorious. At the novel's conclusion, Julie enters her father's village, one like the settlement at Barrow from which she fled. She knows that she must live with her father, who has lost his reverence for the natural world and turned bounty hunter, and she accepts her future realistically and with grim fortitude.

The depiction of character, setting, and events emphasize the ecological theme of young peoples' growing respect for the nonhuman world and understanding of their place in it. However, George sensitively and accurately presents traditional Eskimo beliefs and customs. She shows that the old-time Eskimos were intuitive ecologists, that their customs were conservation methods the success of which has since been scientifically proved. Thinking about the old ways, the heroine muses: "The old Eskimos were scientists too. . . . The people at seal camp had not been as outdated and old-fashioned as she had been led to believe" (George 1972, 121). Later she notes that "The old Eskimo customs are not so foolish—they have purpose" (George 1972, 126).

In addition, George presents aspects of the rich spirituality underlying these customs and practices. For the Eskimo, the world was filled with spirit powers; every animal possessed an "inua," or soul, and this must be respected. Their ecologically sound practices were motivated by religious rather than conservationist beliefs. George uses these beliefs to reveal the profound and negative changes that Julie's father undergoes in the few years separating his life at the seal camp from his life in the village of Kangik.

One of Julie's most vivid memories of her life with her father, Kapugen, concerns his participation in the Bladder Festival at the seal camp. William W. Fitzhugh and Susan A. Kaplan have described the significance of this event.

> Bladders were supposed to contain the shades of *inuas* of animals slain by hunters. Throughout the year each man had preserved the bladders of his game and when the time for the long festival approached he sang a song, inflated each bladder, and hung it in the *qasgiq*. The festival amused and pleased the shades of the animals, and the bladders were returned to the sea through a hole in the ice. The shades of the animals swam far out to sea where they entered the bodies of unborn animals of their kind. Thus they became reincarnated, rendering game plentiful the following year. If the shades were pleased with the manner in which they had been treated by a hunter, they would not be afraid when they met him again and they would permit him to approach and kill them without any trouble. (Fitzhugh and Kaplin 1982, 206)

Kapugen is a central character in the festival, with his partner Naka, and he inflates the bladders, dropping them into the sea in front of his admiring daughter and an approving female shaman. When Julie meets Naka several years later, he has become a chronic and violent alcoholic; when she is reunited with her father, he has abandoned his beliefs. Not only had her father permitted shooting from planes, a violation of all game-hunting ethics, he left the body of the dead wolf on the ground, paying no homage to its *inua* and not even bothering to claim it for bounty. He has abandoned his spirituality; he has become the same as the formerly deplored white people.

This change is further symbolized by an important event near the conclusion of the novel. While on the tundra, Julie had rescued a lost plover, whom she had named Tornait. The name, learned from her father, means "Spirit of the Birds." After she rushes out of her father's house, the bird catches a chill and dies. The excessive warmth of the place, equipped with the latest modern conveniences, has been the cause of its death. Kapugen is, in fact, responsible for the destruction of the "Spirit of the Birds." Because the spirit is dead within him, he now kills it in others.

Although George recognizes the value and validity of traditional customs and beliefs, the conclusion of the novel seems to be one of despair, a lament for the passing of a wonderful, spiritual, holistic approach to life. After the girl sings that "the hour of the wolf and the Eskimo is over," the author ends the book with the sentence: "Julie pointed her boots toward Kapugen" (George 1972, 170). She has assumed her modern name. However, the use of her father's Eskimo name, coupled with her realization, a few hours earlier, that "Kapugen, after all, was dead to her" (George 1972, 169) emphasizes the fact that she, in going to her father's house, is entering a life without the spirituality that had made her earlier time with him so important. In many ways, *Julie of the Wolves* is like those novels dealing with earlier invasions of white people. The Arctic, one of the last places where people lived as a part of, not apart from, the natural world, has been destroyed. Or, to use a white term, modern people have crossed the last frontier and destroyed the unspoiled land beyond it.

Both *Journey Inward* and *The Talking Earth*, published in 1982 and 1983, respectively, mark a shift in the author's treatment of Native people's spiritual relationships to the lands on which and with which they live. Billie Moon, the central character of *The Talking Earth*, is a young Seminole girl living at the edge of the Florida Everglades. Like Julie just before she had fled from Barrow, the girl is skeptical of her people's religious beliefs. Having spent time at Kennedy Space Center, Billie scoffs at her very conservative culture's notions about talking animal gods, a great serpent, and a race of little people. As a wise elder informs her, "We believe that each person is part of the Great Spirit who is the wind and the rain and the sun and the earth, and the air above the earth. . . . we do agree that you should be punished for being a doubter" (George 1983, 3). She chooses her punishment: spending time alone in the Everglades, not returning until she has proof of the existence of these supernatural beings. After 12 weeks, she comes home having fulfilled her quest. However, the answers she finds do not result from her having had any encounters with supernatural forces or beings. Instead, through careful observation of the physical and animal world around her, she discovers that her ancestral homeland is, indeed, "a talking earth." She learns how to understand its language by interpreting atmospheric conditions and the gestures and sounds of animals and by discovering the uses of old artifacts and dwellings she comes across. Bulldozers driven by white men are encroaching on the Everglades and destroying traces of the old life. Nonetheless, Billie Moon has reclaimed her people's faith and returns to her village filled with hopes that elements of it can be preserved and used well. Like *Julie of the Wolves*, *The Talking Earth* links traditional beliefs to the "facts" of modern ecology. Unlike *Julie of the Wolves*, it expresses confidence in the survival of those beliefs.

Journey Inward combines the author's memories of her 1970 trip to Alaska and her retrospective understanding of it. In her meeting with biologists stationed at the Arctic Research Laboratory in Barrow, she learned about and observed many of the wolf habits she incorporated into *Julie of the Wolves*. More important, she learned from both scientists and Eskimo friends the parallels between wolf and old Eskimo societies. Naturalist Gordon Haber explained to her that "The Eskimo and the wolf, both hunters, seemed to have evolved the same social arrangement: the alpha male was the hunting decision maker, the alpha female the family decision maker, and their jobs were as one. The Eskimo family and the wolf pack were a single operation" (George 1982, 204). At the home of Julia Sebeva, a traditional shaman, and her husband, who still whaled and hunted in the old ways, she observed this division of responsibilities. Although she does not mention it in her autobiography, George no doubt heard from them the mythological explanation for the parallels between the species, a legend she mentions in both *Water Sky* and *Julie*. At a time when the world was upside down, there were two wolf pups who, after Raven had turned it right side up, tumbled out as the first human man and woman. To the traditional Eskimo people, wolves were thus literally, not figuratively, related to the people.

From the Sebevas, she also learned about the spiritual basis of traditional hunting. As a shaman, Julia's role was to release the souls of the animals to the ocean to be reborn, thus providing new animals to be hunted again. George notes that for these people, as for their ancestors, the whale's spirit "seemed to have passed into them . . . [and that the whale] constituted not only food but religion, culture and history" (George 1982, 182). She also met Charlie Edwardson, the political leader of the north Alaska Eskimo, from whom she learned that "The Eskimo is the scientific man of the Arctic" (George 1983, 198). From these two people, she received not only the names for the two principal characters of *Julie of the Wolves* and *Julie*, but also the understanding of the spiritual basis of Eskimo life that would profoundly influence the themes of *Water Sky* and *Julie*. Each of these books was written after the author had made several more trips to Alaska and had been accepted into the inner circles of many Eskimo families.

Water Sky is the story of Lincoln Noah Stonewright, member of a prosperous Boston family, who travels to Barrow, Alaska, in search of Jack James, his uncle and closest friend, who has not been heard from for nearly two years. Lincoln, who is one-sixteenth Eskimo himself, becomes an accepted member of a traditional whaling camp and learns of the old ways from Vincent Ogolak, the ill and aging leader who holds "his head high, like the leader of a wolf pack or the president of a people" (George 1987, 32). At first skeptical of the old man's spiritual views about hunting and a supporter of white scientists' theories about diminishing numbers of whales, Lincoln becomes a believer in the Eskimo ways, participates in a hunt, falls in love with a young Eskimo woman, and wishes to become a member of the people. However, he finally realizes the gulf between the two cultures and, having found his uncle safe and well, prepares to return to Boston.

The focus of the book is on the nature and purpose of the whale hunt and its relationship to the Eskimo who are caught between their traditional beliefs and the science of the taniks, or white people. They feel secure in their beliefs, knowledge, customs, and practices and know long before the scientists do that the whales are increasing in numbers and that, for them, the quota system imposes unnecessary restrictions. Not only are there more whales, but the hunters have never harvested more than they could use or share with others. Only practices of European origin have caused shortages. They also know that the whale will choose the hunter to whom he should offer his body, as indeed happens, and that the "whale and the Eskimo are one" (George 1987, 40). The activities of hunting and rendering are acts of sharing, the whale giving his body, the people working together, the edible parts of the whale becoming parts of the people. The entire process symbolizes the holistic view of the Eskimo: the whale dies to give life to the people, who, in turn, give his spirit new life by returning the skull to the sea. A successful hunt is physically rewarding, spiritually ennobling, and culturally unifying. The people drop their quarrels in a cooperative venture. Every whale hunt is an affirmation of the physical, social, and religious life of the people. Even Roy, a recovering drug addict and the only Eskimo who uses only a tanik name, is a healthier person after he travels to the whale camp and participates in the hunt.

It is appropriate that the novel should focus on Lincoln's point of view, for like many white readers, he is skeptical of the beliefs of his new friends and amazed at their confidence in them. However, he is delighted when events prove them correct and wishes to be a member of the group. This, however, is impossible, for, in spite of his love of, sympathy for, and growing understanding about the people and their ways, he is and will remain an outsider, separated by cultural differences that, if anything, have increased since the time when his great-great-grandfather, a whaling Captain, had married an Eskimo woman. Before the whale hunt, he realizes that no matter how great his wish to be one of them, "he would never be more than a visitor from the outside. He did not know the ancient languages" (George 1987, 147). These are more than spoken words, they are deeply engrained intellectual, social, and religious ways of responding—often without words—to the tangible aspects of their environment. Shortly before the killing of the whale, he refuses the job of harpooner, correctly stating, "I think like a tanik" (George 1987, 162). The final revelation comes to Lincoln in the concluding pages of the novel, when he and Little Owl, whom he loves, are briefly stranded on an ice flow. Both a helicopter and an umiak (a large Eskimo boat) arrive to save them. Standing beside the boat, she calls to him to "come back to your people with me" (George 1987, 205). He responds by urging her to climb the ladder to the helicopter: "It's good. It has everything you need—dry clothing, food, medicine" (George 1987, 205). She then speaks her own language, shutting him out, and he realizes that "he would never understand the beautiful people of the ice" (George 1987, 208).

The author does not condemn her tanik hero, who has learned so much about himself and these very different people. However, she honestly presents the inescapable fact of cultural differences. The Eskimos are recovering their traditions, finding fulfillment in "homing in." Lincoln, too, is going home, but to a very different cultural home. "Otherness," cultural difference, is an essential aspect of the human race. Groups and individuals can respect and become better people as a result of their friendships with each other. As Little Owl tells Lincoln, "it is very important that I learn what the taniks know. I am now learning the great knowledge of our elders" (George 1987, 128). But, cultural groups must finally know and be themselves.

Although the events of *Julie* begin only a day after the conclusion of *Julie and the Wolves*, the sequel was published 22 years after the first book. Not surprisingly, it is very closely linked to its predecessor in character, event, and theme and contains many phrases that are explicit echoes and several situations that are implicit echoes of *Julie and the Wolves*. However, it is not just more of the same as the sequels to some well-known books are. It portrays an important new phase in the title hero's coming-of-age, and it reveals the author's new perspectives on and deepening awareness of the relationship of contemporary Eskimo people to their traditions and to the physical and spiritual dimensions of their land. Julie, her father, and the author progress not only to the next chronological stage of the events but also to a fuller understanding of the link between that stage, past and future, animal and human lives, and natural and supernatural worlds.

Although Julie is quickly reunited with a father whom, in spite of his failings, she loves deeply, she has entered a social and natural setting that is deeply fractured. The village of Kangik is not so prosperous as it initially appears: the activities of the modern corporation are not sufficient to sustain the people, and because the caribou on which they still depend have not returned for two years, many people are leaving for larger Alaskan towns and cities. Kapugen is slowly developing a domesticated herd of muskox, a once wild animal that his own people hunted to the verge of extinction after they had received guns from white traders. However, with the shortage of caribou, the muskox are prey to Julie's wolves. Kapugen had shot Amaroq to protect the herd for his people, and Julie knows that he would shoot the wolves again, painful as that would be for him. The heroine's conflict is both simple and profound. She understands her father's need to help his people; she also wishes to help her wolves, to save them as their leader had once saved her. A solution is far more complex than the problem.

The problem has deeper causes than the failure of the caribou herds to return. The people in Kangik still work together: their communal values are seen at the smelt fishing camp and during the festival celebrating a successful whale hunt. These, significantly, are customs and practices from traditional times. The muskox, as they always did, still function as a herd, protecting each other. And, it is implied, the wolf pack now led by Kapu, Amaroq's son, still works together. But without the caribou, the once closely integrated biosphere of the northern slopes of Alaska is broken. None of the different groups of living beings is existing in an harmonious relationship with the others. The most important human element in such a world is notably absent. The deep spirituality, the people's reverence for the souls of their relatives, the animals, is not mentioned in Part I of the novel. Only Julie, who twice early in the novel fingers the carving possessing the soul of the slain Amaroq, seems to retain this spirituality. But even so, she keeps her totem hidden in her pocket, not showing it to other people.

Yet there are some signs of hope in the novel's first section, hope for a regeneration of the different worlds on which the health of the land depends. Julie forgives her father for shooting the wolf, understanding that he must work for the good of his people, and she overcomes her hostility to Ellen, his Minnesota-born wife, coming to love and respect her. There is also new life in the land. Together, she and Ellen assist at the birth of a muskox calf, and Ellen is pregnant. But at the conclusion of Part I, the conflict reaches crisis proportions. A hungry grizzly bear breaks the fencing of the muskox corral, and while Peter, her father's partner, is driving it off, Kapu's pack kills one of the calves. To prevent her father from shooting the wolves, Julie must find them and lead them far from danger.

Having gained Kapugen's promise that he will not hunt the wolves for two weeks, Julie sets out. She is successful, finding Kapu, his mate, and their puppy, Amy; establishing herself as a member of the pack; and leading them to a moose filled valley where she is instrumental in their joining with another pack to form a larger, more efficient hunting unit. Her actions not only lead to an immediate, practical solution to the problem of the wolves attacking her father's herd, but they also mark a significant step in her helping to reintegrate the broken world of the Arctic landscape. As she departs from the village, she takes her totem out of her pocket for the first time, allowing its spiritual potency to act on the world around her. Arriving in the pack's territory, she, in effect, becomes one of its members reestablishing the link between the animal and human worlds her father had long ago celebrated. Discovering Kapu's female pup, she befriends it until they are "as close as sisters" (George 1994, 134). Significantly, she gives it an *atiq*, a namesake, that of her pen pal Amy, linking it to the human world as she has linked herself to the animal world. When she realizes that her wolves will not enter the game-rich valley because it marks a "no-man's land" between two packs, she acts as a mediator, the agent creating cooperation and unity between two groups.

Significantly, many of her observations and actions are based on her memories of her people's traditional wisdom and belief. When Kapu refuses to eat a duck caught by a falcon, she remembers the saying that the wolf does without for the rest of his pack and for "the whole environment" (George 1994, 141). Approaching Silver, the female wolf, she walks in the manner of the traditional dancer acting out the story of the mythic wolves from whom the people had originated. This is the first time a wolf dance has been performed in the novel. In *Julie of the Wolves*, Kapugen, at the seal camp, had performed a dance celebrating the cooperative spirit of wolves. However, in the festival earlier in this novel, Peter had imitated many animals but not wolves. Julie's actions are a step toward reestablishing the unified world that had been so vital an aspect of her life so long ago at the seal camp on Nunivak Island. Finally, watching the cooperation of the newly formed pack chasing a moose, she remembers an elder's saying: "We are all here for each other; the Eskimo, the mammals, the river, the ice, the sun, plants, birds, and fish" (George 1994, 156). She has initiated steps toward the re-establishment of this state of interrelationship.

Two major steps remain to be taken. Her father must be helped to recover his spiritual approach to life, and she must complete her journey to woman-hood, as an adult female contributing to the life of the community. The two will be linked. In her autobiography, George had noted the woman's primary role in the religious life of the family. By leading her father back to his spirituality, Julie will be fulfilling this role. And, as the closing lines of Part II indicate, she will be moving closer to achieving an adult male-female rela-tionship with Peter. In words that emphatically echo the conclusion of *Julie of the Wolves*, Julie, to her own amazement, "pointed them [her boots] home-ward, toward . . . Peter Sugluk" (George 1994, 159).

The major conflict has not yet been resolved. Julie realizes that, should the caribou not return, the wolves will again come to prey on the herd and Kapugen will kill them. He has based his attitude on what he calls the

Minnesota law, the belief of white people that when wolves kill their livestock the predators can be shot. Although he agrees with his daughter that this is a violation of the old ways, he states, "Industry is under another law" (George, 1994, 171). "That is how it is in our modern world" (George 1994, 171). However, there are signs that he is beginning to regain his spiritual orientation, for he has named his newborn son Amaroq. He tells his daughter of his admiration for the wolf and his belief that the soul of the pack leader has entered into his son along with the name. Later, he recounts to his wife the legend of the origin of people from wolves, explaining: "That is why we are so much like them" (George 1994, 184). Yet he also tells her that the only hope for his people is for them to adopt modern ways. His daughter realizes that "his heart had frozen solidly around [the Minnesota law]" (George 1994, 185). Julie, however, has hope; it is expressed in a new version of the song to Amaroq she had sung at the end of *Julie of the Wolves*. Looking at her half-brother, she says that because of his birth "The wolf and Eskimo are one again" (George 1994, 181).

This reunion does occur. Watching a female walrus free its trapped baby, Kapugen rediscovers the old truth of the relationship between all creatures. He also refuses to allow another hunter to kill more walrus than the people need, even though additional tusks would bring a great deal of money. And, he ceremonially gives a walrus heart to the sea, offering thanks to its spirit and liberating it so that it will be reborn. The wolves do return, and Kapugen sets out to kill them. However, he rejects the Minnesota law and sets his herd free, returning them to the wilderness that is their natural home. He once again listens to the voices of the land, hearing in the wolves' howls the announcement that the caribou are returning. The balance of the land has been restored, and he is a part of it. His daughter has led him back. The renaissance of Eskimo life is at hand.

Julie has also resolved her conflict between her love and respect for her father and for the wolves whom he so resembles. She is now ready to enter the next phase of her life. It will include study at university with Peter, a return to her homeland where she can help children retain the richness of their traditions while at the same time learning the best that the white world can offer, and a marriage with Peter that will truly be a cooperation in the old ways. The dream she had had in *Julie of the Wolves* of being with such a partner will be fulfilled: "They would raise children, who would live with the rhythms of the beasts and the land" (George 1972, 167).

Of the novels considered so far, Jean Craighead George's *Julie* most fully embodies the "homing in" theme. Moreover, although its plot is arranged in a conventionally linear fashion, it employs the allusive quality characteristic of novels by Native writers. It can be read by those unfamiliar with its predecessor, for the author has included all the necessary factual background. However, only those familiar with the incidents, phrases, and songs of *Julie of the Wolves* will respond fully to the richness of the many implied echoes in *Julie*. The section titles, "Kapugen, the Hunter," "Amy, the Wolf Pup," "Miyax, the Young Woman," echo "Amaroq, the Wolf," "Miyax, the Girl," and "Kapugen, the Hunter," from the first book. But in their new order, they reverse the pattern of breakup of the first book and outline the movement toward regeneration and wholeness. The new songs to Amaroq, the return of the walrus spirits to the sea, the rejoining of a wolf pack to save rather than to be saved, all contribute, through their parallels and contrasts, to the portrayal of the creation of a brave new world that is also a glorious return to a crucially vital old one.

DISCOVERY AND RECOVERY IN CHILDREN'S NOVELS BY NATIVE WRITERS

As Scott O'Dell did in his books, Michael Dorris, in *Morning Girl*, portrays his young protagonists encountering newly arrived Europeans. Like Jean George, Beatrice Culleton, in *In Search of April Raintree*, portrays her heroine recovering her cultural heritage. However, there are significant differences arising from the fact that both Dorris and Culleton are members of Native cultures. Viewing historical and contemporary events from their Modoc and Métis backgrounds, respectively, they understand the events of the novels in relation to their own cultures' traditional world views and with a cynicism and irony born of having had to define themselves and their peoples in opposition to the perceptions of the dominant and dominating white culture. Both novelists use the first-person point of view, giving voices to members of cultures long rendered silent because of controls exercised by the ruling majority (Fee 1990, 168). In *Morning Girl*, Dorris presents a brother and sister's responses to events in their lives just before the arrival of Christopher Columbus in 1492. Culleton's *In Search of April Raintree* is the coming-of-age novel of a Canadian Métis who faces her inner prejudices and those of modern Canadian society in general.

Until page 69 of *Morning Girl*, readers appear to be listening to the thoughts of a typical Caribbean boy and girl reacting to their own growing pains, their family and the rest of their village, and the natural world around them. Morning Girl, so named because of her love of getting up before the rest of her family, is the more social of the siblings. She frequently thinks of gifts for her parents and brother, looks forward to having a new sister, acts in a motherly way toward her brother, is ashamed for uttering "unsisterly words" (Dorris 1992, 67), and is anxious to know what her face looks like to other people. When, at the novel's conclusion, strangers arrive, she eagerly greets them, rushes home to summon the other villagers, and anticipates a festive, social welcome. By contrast, Star Boy is happiest alone, in the night, studying the stars. He frequently quarrels with his friends and family and often stays out all night by himself. There are hints that he has the potential to be some kind of shaman. He imagines himself experiencing the world as a rock and, during a hurricane, has a conversation with the spirit of his long-dead grandfather. Brother and sister are different from each other, but they complement each other, just as each member in the village is unique but forms an integral part of the social unit. Though the events and emotions the boy and girl experience are special to each of them, they are represented as being fairly typical for their people.

Until page 69, then, *Morning Girl* appears to be a simple, clearly and crisply written account of what it was probably like to be a young member of this Caribbean settlement in some unspecified precontact time. Up to this point, a reader could not be blamed for thinking: "Interesting, yes; but exciting, no! Not much of a story." However, the final six pages provide a specific historical context for the preceding events, a context that causes the reader to reconsider the significance of the earlier parts of the narrative. Morning Girl's description of a canoe of strangers she sees coming toward shore makes it obvious that they are European. They are fully clothed, have beards, wear metal helmets, and their "canoe" is a rowboat or ship's launch. Just who they are is made explicit in the first and last lines of the "Epilogue," a journal entry dated "October 11, 1492" (Dorris 1992, 73) and signed "Christopher Columbus" (Dorris 1992, 74). Morning Girl has been the first person to witness the arrival of Europeans in the Caribbean, Christopher Columbus' "discovery of the New World."

With this knowledge, the rereader of the short, apparently simple text discovers a great number of new meanings. Dorris' story is short because he and other Native people's understand so much about the impact of Columbus's arrival. Published in 1992, the quadracentennial of the famous journey, this novel, along with *The Crown of Columbus* (an adult novel cowritten by Dorris with his wife Louise Erdrich) and many other writings by Native peoples, presents an alternate view of the historical event widely celebrated by so many Americans. For Native Americans, Columbus Day does not honor a wonderful new beginning, but a tragic end. If it was a beginning, it was the beginning of the destruction of centuries' old ways of life. The words of Morning Girl and Star Boy show life as it is to them and as their people always expect it will be. The silent text, what is not stated, is ironic and filled with ominous foreshadowings. Without direct statement, Dorris presents readers with a revisionist interpretation of the first major event in the history of European-Native relations.

The lives of Morning Girl's people, their adaptability to the rhythmic patterns of the seasons, including the devastation of a hurricane, suggest a pattern that has existed for centuries and that none of them have any idea will soon end. Just as her mother and uncle quarreled and her grandfather rescued her father, so she and Star Boy quarrel, and he is saved by his grandfather's spirit during the storm. After the hurricane passes, the people celebrate their deliverance and begin rebuilding as they have done after previous natural disasters. However, with a knowledge that this is the autumn of 1492 and an awareness of the major and destructive changes that Columbus' arrival brought for America's indigenous peoples, readers retrospectively understand that this is not just another typical October but the final typical October. The ingenuousness of the child narrators and the unspoiled purity of the lives they recount are rendered poignant because of the unstated fact that this is the last time these types of events will occur and be experienced in this way.

However, there are events that, in retrospect, seem to foreshadow the disastrous events that follow Columbus' arrival. Just before the storm, Star Boy notices that "there was a worry on . . . [father's] face I had only seen there once before—the time when the bad visitors, their bodies painted white for death, were spotted in three big rafts to the south of the nearest island" (Dorris 1992, 38). Later, the white explorers from Columbus' three ships will bring their own forms of death—physical and cultural—to the people. The day before the Europeans' arrival, Star Boy quarrels with his friend and each member of his family, and Morning Girl displeases her mother and father by speaking unkindly about her brother. The closely knit family experiences tensions on the eve of an experience that will lead to a shattering of the larger cultural unit of which they are members.

There is an even more ominous undercurrent. In the epilogue, Columbus writes that "it seems to me that they have no religion" (Dorris 1992, 74) and notes his plans to take six of the islanders back to Spain so that they can be clothed, can "learn to speak" (Dorris 1992, 74), and can be converted to Christianity—in a word, be "civilized." As the novel reveals, in their environment, they do not need clothing, they do speak a language, and they do have spiritual experiences. They are neither heathen savages nor nature's children. But by including these remarks of Columbus, Dorris not only reveals the invaders' ignorance about the nature of the people they are soon to conquer but also implicitly raises the question, "Could Morning Girl or Star Boy be one of the half-dozen about to be abducted?" Three times during the novel Star Boy spends the night alone, away from his village. One time, his mother states that she does not think he would go from home without saying goodbye. Later, his father remarks, "nothing can replace a son" (Dorris 1992, 28). Each of these incidents appears to be an ominous hint that Star Boy may be taken. If so, having him as one of the narrators of the story is highly ironic. He may be sensitively describing his attempts to understand himself in relation to his people just before he is to be parted from them forever.

Finally, read in the light of Columbus' remarks about the people and his intentions (and by implicit extension those of Europeans generally), Morning Girl's response to the arrivals is ironic. When she sees that the visitors do not wear hostile paint markings, she assumes that they are friendly and that, in spite of their odd clothing and behavior, they will get along with her people. She anticipates "a memorable day, a day full and new" (Dorris 1992, 71). She is not the hostile savage, the primitive and unregenerate heathen so many Europeans expected they would encounter. In fact, as her story has revealed, she is kind and social and is anxious to meet them, and she is a member of a highly functional social organization. Dorris, through Morning Girl's voice, presents a vastly different view of the initial contacts between the two cultures from that presented by European writers of children's adventure novels. He also gives the meeting an ironic twist by implying that the girl's openhearted welcome of the Spaniards is the unwitting first step in the destruction of her culture, a destruction that may well include the loss of her brother.

Dorris, then, presents a simple, short text with a complex, invisible subtext. Beneath the simple narrative and description is a devastating portrayal of the beginning of the end of a culture. At a time when Columbus was being celebrated, the author used his Native point of view to reveal a situation vastly different from the one commonly accepted. It is one that can be perceived only by those readers who can interpret not only what the words say directly but what they silently imply.

Beatrice Culleton, a Canadian Métis of European-Native background, uses events from her own life to portray a young woman's rejection and recovery of her heritage. The author was raised in foster homes and two of her sisters committed suicide. She grew up with little knowledge of Métis history. The picture of "the drunken, poverty-stricken, irresponsible person remained like a truth with me until I began to write *In Search of April Raintree*" (Culleton 1989, 120). The title hero spends her school years in foster homes, and she, too, harbors a stereotypical view of her people, whom she wishes to deny. Her sister Cheryl represents another side of the author: through studying and writing, she tries to discover and recover her Métis heritage.

As the title suggests, the novel is the study of a search for identity, a coming-of-age story in which the heroine comes to live up to the sense of new beginnings inherent in her spring-time name. However, even though the narrator refers to herself as a Cinderella and the man to whom she is briefly married as Prince Charming, it is not the rags-to-riches story of European folktales, the escape from a dreary life in one place to a wonderful new one in another. Instead, it is a "Homing In Novel," typical of so many novels written by Native authors. April, whose narrative begins when she is a five-year-old in the Canadian city of Winnipeg, returns there at the novel's conclusion, a sadder and wiser person who believes that "there would be a tomorrow. And it would be better" (Culleton 1983, 228).

Culleton portrays April's life up to the time of the breakup of her marriage in ways that parallel the fairytale of the poor girl who marries the prince, the Harlequin-type story of a glorious romance leading to wealth and happiness, and the saga of the growth to maturity of a hardworking, disadvantaged individual who overcomes obstacles through determination and courage and achieves success. In drawing parallels to these popular story types, the author is showing the falseness of her heroine's expectations and the shallowness of her character. Ashamed of her Métis background, April envies white children, dreams of a beautiful home, rejects her sister's attempts to interest her in their people's past, and tries to pass as a white person. At one point, she portrays herself as a literal orphan, telling schoolmates that she lost her parents in an airplane crash; and she does not want her friends to meet her sister, who looks more Native than she does. She makes attempts to find her alcoholic parents, from whom she and her sister had been taken when she was five, but when she fails in the search she is relieved: "That part of my life was now finished for good" (Culleton 1983, 100). Shortly after, she marries a wealthy businessman and moves to his family estate in Toronto. She has escaped from her heritage and seems to have achieved the kind of life portrayed in popular literature written by white people. However, unlike the heroines of fairytales and romance novels, she has not become successful through hard work or virtuous actions. She has denied much and has succeeded only because of luck and good looks. The first half of the novel can thus be seen as a parody of the popular narratives, a criticism of the values they espouse, and a condemnation of April for having embraced these values.

The second half of the novel traces April's fall from her ill-deserved "good fortune." Her husband has married her to displease his domineering mother, who despises April for being Métis, and he is having an affair with his mother's tacit approval. April returns to Winnipeg to discover that her sister, a Native rights advocate and brilliant student, has dropped out of university and developed a severe drinking problem. April is brutally raped by white men who mistake her for her sister, on whom they seek revenge. At their trial, she learns that her sister had become a prostitute. Shortly after, Cheryl commits suicide as her mother had done years earlier. April cannot escape from her past or from the heritage she denied. The rape, literally a case of mistaken identity, proves this. In spite of her non-Native appearance, the men, who think that she is Cheryl, refer to her as a "squaw" (Culleton 1983, 140) and "savage" (Culleton 1983, 142). She is forcibly subjected to the violation and degradation that, in one form or another, are inflicted on large numbers of her people.

Gradually these painful confrontations with the Native part of herself that she had attempted to deny lead her to accept and later to honor it. She suggests that she and her sister attend a Pow Wow, and at it she experiences "stirrings of pride" (Culleton 1983, 166). At the Native Friendship Centre she meets a respected elder who sees in her "something that was deserving of her respect" (Culleton 1983, 175). And to her friend Roger, she haltingly admits that she is Métis. Her greatest breakthrough occurs on the novel's final page when she meets her sister's young son, Henry Liberty Raintree. His middle name is symbolic of the new freedom April finds in joyously accepting her birthright. Together, the woman and child will form a new family, a new beginning repairing the shattering of family units that had occurred through-out the novel. She has completed her search; she has found herself in finding her roots, her past, and in hoping for a future for her nephew and "For my people" (Culleton 1983, 228). Like the central characters in Scott Momaday's *House Made of Dawn* and *The Ancient Child*, she has replaced denial with acceptance and has returned home. And, as in *House Made of Dawn* and *Sing Down the Moon*, a gentle morning rain falls, symbolizing the new life ahead.

Dorris and Culleton both deal with themes presented by non-Native writers. However, they present inside views, writing as members of Native cultures that had been "discovered" and nearly destroyed by Europeans and that are now rediscovering their own pasts and using a recovered pride to give impetus to new beginnings. As the existence of these and other children's books by Native American authors indicate, an important part of the Native Renaissance is literary. Native writers are helping Native readers use the power of story to recover a past, define a present, and envision a future.

NOVELS PORTRAYING NATIVE EXPERIENCES

Baker, Betty. *Walk the World's Rim.* New York: Harper and Row, 1965.
This novel, set in the sixteenth century, focuses on the relationship between Chakoh, the son of the chief of the Avavare people of the coast of what is now Texas, and Esteban, an African slave, an actual person who played an important role in the Spaniards' incursions into the Southwest. The boy, who deeply admires the slave, joins a small group travelling overland to Mexico City. Along the way, they meet a buffalo hunting tribe and the agrarian Pimas. From Mexico City, they proceed north to the Pueblo City of Cíbola, rumored to be the site of fabulous wealth, where Esteban is killed and Chakoh barely escapes. At the novel's conclusion, Chakoh decides to return to his people. Under the slave's tutelage, Chakoh learns a great deal about the people they encounter and about growing up. However, he is not aware that his teacher is a slave, a member of a group he despises, and, when he discovers the truth, he must come to terms with both his disgust and guilt. In addition to giving a good picture of the various types of culture groups, the novel powerfully addresses the themes of slavery and

freedom, truth and lying, responsibility and selfishness. Only when Chakoh has resolved the conflicts relating to these opposites is he ready to return to his people. In her portrayal of Esteban's character, Baker has provided one of the earlier positive depictions of an African slave in children's literature. Students in the upper elementary grades can discuss the meanings of such abstract terms as freedom, truth, and responsibility and can compare their definitions with those Chakoh seems to hold. They should notice what he learns and how he grows through his encounters with different cultures.

Blos, Joan W. *Brothers of the Heart*. New York: Charles Scribner's Sons, 1985.
Set in Michigan in the late 1830s, this story about the Perkins, a pioneering family, concentrates on the lame son, Shem. Fiercely independent as he approaches young manhood, he quarrels with his father, runs away to Detroit, gains employment as a clerk in a fur trading company, and joins a trading party that is to spend a winter in the north. Left alone in a small cabin because he cannot travel in the deepening snow, he befriends Mary Goodhue, an aging Ottawa woman who has been left to die by her people. During the course of the winter, the two become very close as Shem hunts and maintains the house and Mary teaches him the ways of her people. A healer, she has been a widow for many years, ever since her husband had willingly given up his life in payment for his accidental slaying of another man. Under Mary's guidance, Shem learns to snowshoe, acquiring a mobility he had never before experienced and, with this skill, a sense of confidence and self-worth. The old woman tells him that she believes "you and he [her dead husband] are brothers . . . of the heart. In your manhood he will live" (123). In the springtime, he buries Mary according to traditional ways and, with the lore and language she has given him, makes his way back to his family. This story of a young man's initiation into adulthood is unusual in that his mentor is not only a person from another culture but a very old woman as well. Her Native traditions, stressing justice, respect, and a sense of relationship with other elements of the creation, are what he needs to develop the psychological strength to survive his physical limitations and the violent, ruthlessly selfish attitudes of many of the white pioneers and woodsmen. Students in junior high school can compare Shem's relationship with the non-Native adults in his life to his friendship with Mary and can consider why the encounter with her was vital for his physical survival and for his maturing into a person able to play an important role in his society.

Cooper, Amy Jo. "Hack's Choice," in *Dream Quest*. Toronto: Annick Press, 1987.
This short novel, set in northern Ontario, deals with a contemporary Ojibway boy receiving the sacred vision that will guide his life. When his Uncle Coleman, a former professional hockey player, returns to Spirit River, Hack is flattered by the attentions the man showers on him and ignores his mother's warnings that the association is not a good one. This proves true, as Coleman uses the boy's

hero worship in an attempt to possess and then sell the family's sacred medicine bundle. Bernard Mide, an old man whose name suggests a link with the Great Medicine Society of the Ojibway, becomes young Hack's mentor and explains to him the significance of the objects in the bundle and helps him to understand his dreams. The old man, who is a storyteller, makes reference to his people's trickster figure who, he says, takes the shape of a crow that "Flies between both worlds all the time; doesn't really live in either" (84). Significantly, Coleman's last name is Blackbird, and the man is also a rootless schemer who is to be avoided. Bernard says that stories are like baseball, "you've got to try and see what's hidden" (84). Using this quote as a starting point, upper elementary students can search for the deeper, "hidden" meanings of the story. What, for example, is the difference between what Coleman says and what he means? Why does Hack face a crow four times in the story before it disappears and he can accept his manito (spirit helper), the eagle? Bernard says to readers that he compiles this story by using reports from both Hack and his friend Rabbit. After each chapter, students can discuss whom they think provided the information in the chapter to Bernard and how he has interpreted and, perhaps, changed it.

Craig, John. *No Word for Goodbye.* Toronto: Peter Martin Associates, 1969.
The most acclaimed novel of Canadian author John Craig describes the summer that 15-year-old Ken Warren spends with his parents at their lake cabin in northern Ontario. Early in July, he meets Paul Onaman, an Ojibway teenager with whom he develops a close friendship and from whom he learns about the dignity and hardship of the lives of Native peoples. Ken hopes to overcome the injustices suffered by the Onamans. On one level, he is successful, helping to solve the mystery of a series of break-ins that the prejudiced cottagers and villagers blame on the Ojibway. On another, he fails. A large land development corporation claims the Ojibway land, and, when Ken returns to the lake in October for a visit with Paul, he discovers that Paul's people have had to move much farther north. He cannot help them, and he learns the truth that there is no word for goodbye. However, although Ken has not been able to help his friends, he has developed a greater understanding of and sympathy for a people he had, until then, been basically unaware of. Thus, the summer marks an important stage in his growth to maturity. Students in junior high school can discuss the series of opposites that create many of the conflicts in this book: summer and winter residents; friendship and enmity; ignorance and knowledge; faith and suspicion; rural and city life. How is Ken caught between these, and how does his friendship with Paul help him in his attempts to resolve the conflicts? In this story of an encounter between two young people of different cultures, does author Craig offer hope for a future free of tensions and animosities?

Culleton, Beatrice. *Spirit of the White Bison.* Winnipeg, Canada: Pemmican Publications, 1985.
Written by a Canadian Métis, this autobiography of a white female bison is, in many ways, a symbolic history of the interrelated lives and parallel fates of the buffalo and the Native peoples of the northern plains in the nineteenth century.

Born at a time when her "people" numbered in the millions, the narrator understood that Native hunters needed the buffalo but that they killed with reverence and respect. However, the decimation of the herds by white hunters "was not a quiet, accidental extermination. The horror was that the killings were deliberate, planned military actions. Destroy the livelihood of the Indians and win a war" (3). During her long life, the white bison sees the arrival of more and more hunters, the building of the railroad, and the disastrous effects of European civilization and disease on the Native people. At the story's conclusion, the bison and her Native friend, Lone Wolf, are killed by soldiers, but then buried side by side by a kindly hunter. Their deaths symbolize the end of a way of life that has been needlessly and foolishly destroyed. However, there is some hope. The bison's spirit says, in the concluding lines, "My spirit would return again in the future to walk with those who were gentle but strong" (61). This note of optimism, also seen in Culleton's *In Search of April Raintree*, is characteristic of much contemporary Native writing. Students in the middle and upper elementary grades can study this book in relation to the hunting cultures of the northern plains. Although it is written from the point of view of an animal, which elements of it reflect the values and beliefs of the hunting people? In rereading the book, the students can make a list of each time the bison and Lone Wolf meet. How do these meetings reveal the changing conditions for both human beings and buffalo?

Gregory, Kristiana. *The Legend of Jimmy Spoon.* San Diego: Harcourt Brace Jovanovich, 1990.

Based on the actual accounts of Elijah Nicholas Wilson, who lived among the Shoshoni during the middle of the nineteenth century, this novel is the story of a 12-year-old boy who runs away from his Salt Lake City home because his father will not allow him to have a horse. Jimmy Spoon follows two Shoshoni boys who have promised him one and lives with their people for over two years. He participates in the daily and seasonal activities, sometimes revealing his foolishness, especially when he criticizes many customs, but gradually coming to understand and respect the people. He realizes that his role is to be a new son to Old Mother, who had lost sons and daughters, and, as he perceives her sadness, he feels guilty over having deserted his own family. When news comes that people from Salt Lake City are going to war against the Shoshoni in an effort to bring him home, he is forced to choose between his new life and his old, between Shoshoni and white ways. Although the book is a coming-of-age novel, it is most interesting as a picture of the life of these northern nomadic hunters and as a study of Jimmy's frequently ethnocentric responses to traditional customs and beliefs. Although spirituality is not dealt with in detail, it is seen as informing every aspect of Shoshoni life. As Jimmy realizes, remembering the once-a-week worship at home, "*Every thing they [the Shoshoni] do is connected to their religion. Every day they worship and praise the Great Spirit*" (104). His insights are not always as clear and complete as this one. In fact, much of his difficulty during the story comes from his failure to adapt to Shoshoni ways of thinking and doing. Upper elementary students can make a list of typical Shoshoni activities, beliefs, and customs. They can then notice Jimmy's reactions to these and discuss what his reactions reveal about white attitudes and beliefs to Native peoples.

Haig-Brown, Roderick. *The Whale People.* Toronto: Collins, 1962.
This winner of the Canadian children's book-of-the-year award is about the growth to maturity of a young precontact Nootka boy from Canada's west coast. Son of the great whale chief Nit-gass, Atlin's eventual succession to chieftanship is in no doubt. The question that arises is "Will he be worthy of the title he will eventually assume?" Like his father, he is ambitious and impatient. But the training must be deliberate, following traditional rituals which are grounded on the common sense understanding that lack of adequate foundations can be disastrous. With the death of his father on a whale hunt, Atlin becomes whale chief. However, he must earn the reality as well as the title, undergoing four arduous traditional tests. In *The Whale People*, there is little of the inner conflict found in many novels about young people growing up. Instead, the focus is on presenting the logical and ritual stages of the creation of a whale chief. Haig-Brown's ability to present the dignity of this ritual movement, along with his loving and knowledgeable treatment of the west coast, makes the book the Canadian classic it is. Junior high students can study the first 11 chapters, noticing how Atlin's response to his training reveals both his potentials and his present limitations and character weaknesses. What are the purposes of the four tests he completes after becoming chief? Students can compare the relation-ships between the people, the sea, and the whales in this novel with the relationships between the people, the plains, and the buffalo as seen in the picture books of Paul Goble.

Hale, Janet Campbell. *The Owl's Song.* New York: Doubleday, 1974.
Hale, a member of the Coeur d'Alene tribe of Idaho, recounts the coming-of-age story of Billy White Hawk, an Interior Salish of the same region, who spends a year attending school at a coastal city. His father is an alcoholic, and his mother, dead; his best friend has committed suicide; and the old ways—dancing, vision quests, receiving a name—are all but forgotten by his people. Billy realizes he must leave the reservation. His year living with his sister, herself a controlled alcoholic, is, in a way, a kind of vision quest. On his own most of the time, he is badgered by his guidance counselor and bullied by his African-American "Big Brother" and his gang. Only Mr. Barrows, the art teacher, offers support, encouraging Billy to develop his talents. Yet even he fails the boy, not backing him up when he is accused of troublemaking. Billy has a number of dreams that both reflect his inner struggles and indicate the stages of his quest to perceive the manito, or spirit being, who will give him his special name. Although the year is, in a way, a failure, it is important in that it enables the hero to understand himself more fully and to make the decision to return home to Idaho where he receives his vision. Students in the upper junior high grades will find it useful to study Billy's dreams in the order in which they occur. What do

the dreams reveal about Billy's inner state, and how does he change between dreams? By examining Hale's depiction of the three major settings—Billy's home, his sister's apartment, and the school—students can see how these are used to portray the three lifestyle options available to Billy. What is the significance of the name of the school, Lincoln Junior High, and its motto, "And the Truth Shall Make You Free," in relation to Billy's quest?

Hill, Kirkpatrick. *Toughboy and Sister.* New York: Margaret K. McElderry Books, 1990.
After the death of their mother, 11-year-old Toughboy and 9-year-old Sister, Athabaskans from Alaska, accompany their father to their summer fishing camp. However, after he dies from a drunken binge, the children must learn how to survive on their own. Having depended on their parents for everything, they have little knowledge of how to cope. Even replacing dead batteries in a radio is a challenge. Through trial and error and by remembering how their mother and father had done things, they come through. The children learn not only in order to survive, but also so that they can prove their self-sufficiency to rescuers and thus not be separated from each other when they return home. They learn to make bread, cut wood, wash their clothes, and catch fish. They also develop the skills necessary for emotional survival: Toughboy sings rousing songs to cheer Sister up; she tells him the story of Dorothy and the Wizard of Oz. Their greatest test comes when a bear, whose tracks they had noticed when they first arrived at camp, attempts to break into the cabin. Using an oversized rifle, Toughboy kills the invader. At the novel's conclusion, their rescuer, an old woman from their village, is so impressed with their achievements that she invites both to live with her. With the exception of the bear's attempt to enter the cabin, there is little high adventure. The focus of the story is on the courage of the two children living alone in the wilderness and their character development during the summer. In *Winter Camp*, a sequel, the old woman teaches the two about the old ways and tells them stories of their people. Children in the middle elementary grades can make a list of the problems the children face, the solutions they develop, and the qualities of character each reveals in confronting problems.

Hobbs, Will. *Bearstone.* New York: Atheneum, 1989.
Sent for the summer to a southwestern Colorado farm, Cloyd, a troubled Ute-Navajo teenager, searches for a father, a home, and a sense of both his Ute past and himself. In the opening chapter, he sees his Navajo father for the first time. The man has been brain dead for six months following an automobile accident, and the boy wonders, "How could this . . . wrinkled, shrunken shell of a human being be his father" (3). At the conclusion, he willingly leaves his group home to return to the farm to care for Walter Landis, the aging white man who had given him a home and emotional support all summer. He has, in many ways "come home," for Walter has become a father to him and the farm is close to the mountains from which his tribe was forced decades ago by advancing white settlers. The journey home has been a difficult one for Cloyd. In a fit of anger

after hunters kill a bear, a sacred animal to his people, the youth destroys Walter's cherished peach orchard, an act that echoes, in reverse, the nine-teenth-century white destruction of the Navajo peach trees in Canyon de Chelly. He frequently thinks of running away and is often surly in his behavior to the kindly, sympathetic old man. After he has climbed his people's sacred mountain and rescued Walter from a cave-in at his mine, Cloyd has a surer sense of his identity and destiny. Early in the novel, he had found an ancient stone fetish of a bear and had named himself "Lone Bear." In ways, he is like the solitary grizzlies, once believed extinct in the area, but still struggling to survive. When he asks forgiveness from the soul of a slain bear, he is affirming its continuance and his own. In a sequel, *Beardance*, Cloyd learns more about his past as he and Walter discover orphaned bear cubs in the mountains. Students in junior high can chart Cloyd's changing attitudes toward Walter and his farm and can discuss how these indicate stages of his growth to maturity. They can gather all the references to bears in the novel and then see how bears are symbolic of traditional Ute values.

Houston, James. *Frozen Fire: A Tale of Courage.* New York: Margaret K. McElderry Books, 1977.

The first of this Canadian author's children's books to be set in the contempo-rary Arctic, this story combines elements of the adventure-survival novel and the modern problem novel. Matthew, who is accompanying his prospector father on one of his frequent moves, arrives in a remote northern village feeling homeless and alienated. However, when he befriends Kayak, who has learned many of the old Inuit (Eskimo) ways from his grandfather, and the two of them search for Mr. Morgan, who is missing in a storm, Matthew discovers both inner strength of character and the meaning of home and camaraderie. Significantly, his learning experiences really begin after the snowmobile that he and Kayak are using in the search breaks down. Together, the boys must draw on Kayak's lore, Matthew's knowledge of how to transmit Morse code by flashing the snowmo-bile mirror, and the guidance of an old man who has rejected the modern world. The developing friendship between the boys and Matthew's growing love for and understanding of the land and its people are traced in two sequels: *Black Gold* and *Ice Swords*. Students in upper elementary and junior high grades can make lists of the physical and mental aspects of traditional Inuit (Eskimo) life and the modern world and can discuss the relative values of each of these ways to the boys' well-being. They can also notice that the first two chapters contain details that foreshadow later events.

Houston, James. *River Runners: A Tale of Hardship and Bravery.* New York: Margaret K. McElderry Books, 1979.

Set in Northern Quebec, this novel presents another aspect of Houston's examination of the relationships and conflicts between cultures. The son of an international banker, Andrew Stewart is sent north to work for a year at a fur trading post. After being left on the ice by the supply ship, he feels physically and emotionally alone, totally incapable of fending for himself. However, Pashak, a

Naskapi, befriends him, teaches him how to fish, how to hunt with a bow and arrow and rifle, and how to snowshoe and canoe. These skills become essential when the young men spend a long, severe winter at a distant outpost. Andrew learns the positive and negative elements of Naskapi culture as he hears the ancient stories from Pashak's people and observes a deceitful shaman and as he and the Naskapi desperately stave off starvation. At the end of the novel, Andrew, looking at the springtime landscape, believes that he has found a home and decides to establish a more permanent base at the outpost, near his Naskapi friends. Shortly after he has left the trading post, he notices that his watch has stopped: "he had lost white man's time. It would be a long while before he found it again" (49). Students in upper elementary and junior high can discuss the symbolic significance of this statement, responding to such questions as, "What elements of white civilization did Andrew bring north? How useful were these? What does he replace them with? What valuable lessons does he learn from the traditional stories he hears?"

Houston, James. *The White Archer: An Eskimo Legend*. New York: Harcourt, Brace, World, 1967.
A legend-like short novel based on events that occurred before the white man came among the Inuit (Eskimo), this book, like Houston's other books, is a coming-of-age story. When Indians seeking revenge on three men visiting his family slay his parents and kidnap his sister, Kungo feels a "terrible anger [start] to grow within him" (22). Adopted by a blind old hunter who teaches him hunting skills and tries to impart his wisdom, the young man hopes to use the falcon bow his mentor gives him to avenge the slaughter of his family. Kungo travels alone to the distant home of the Indians. To them he seems to be a ghostly, invisible presence, dressed as he is in white furs. When he discovers his sister living with these people, he experiences a revelation that changes both his attitude and course of action. In addition to reflecting Houston's knowledge of traditional Canadian Inuit life (depicted in the author's illustrations, as well as the text), *The White Archer* embodies the patterns of the legendary hero's life as these are outlined in Joseph Campbell's *The Hero with a Thousand Faces*: orphaned childhood; long period of training with a wise, old teacher; acquisition of a special weapon and distinctive costume; perilous journey leading to an important confrontation; and return home a changed being. A sequel, *The Falcon Bow*, tells of Kungo's adventures after the reunion. Students in the middle elementary grades can notice that although Kungo's change of attitude may seem abrupt, it has been prepared for by Ittok's teachings. Upper elementary and junior high students can compare the stages of Kungo's development as hero with those of King Arthur as a boy and Superman and Luke Skywalker in the 1970s motion pictures.

Hudson, Jan. *Sweetgrass*. New York: G.P. Putnam's, 1989.
Winner of several major Canadian children's literature awards, this coming-of-age novel of a Blackfoot girl is set in western Canada in the earlier nineteenth century. When she sees friends getting married around her, Sweetgrass is

impatient for her turn and hopes that her father will accept Eagle Sun, should that young man ask to marry her. However, she must learn that in her society personal wishes are secondary to the laws and customs that serve to unify the tribe and that she must understand the nature of and then accept her woman's role. During the year that follows, one of her friends marries unhappily and later dies, the village is attacked by an enemy tribe, her father briefly experiences the devastating effects of whiskey, and, during the depths of winter, the family is attacked by smallpox, another "gift" of the soon to be encountered white people. Sweetgrass reveals her new maturity as she cares for the family: burying the tiny baby who succumbs to the disease, nursing her brothers and step-mother, and hunting for medicine and food. Her father announces that she has become a woman, and, early in the summer, as she watches Eagle Sun enter camp, she envisions a happy future. Hudson accurately reports the daily life of the Blackfoot and mixes accounts of this with the major events of the novel, those that show the heroine dealing with the conflicts she must resolve to become a mature, contributing woman in her society. Upper elementary and junior high students, after completing a reading of the novel, can compare the opening and closing chapters, noticing the differences in Sweetgrass' character and situation. They can then notice how each of the 13 chapters, which parallel the 13 moons of the Blackfoot year, marks an important stage in her character growth. After researching the significance of sweetgrass to the people of the northern plains, they can discuss the appropriateness of the heroine's name.

Kortum, Jeanie. *Ghost Vision*. New York: Pantheon, 1983.
This is the story of a contemporary Greenland Eskimo boy's discovery of his shamanic vocation. Travelling with his father to a summer tent camp, Panipaq experiences a series of visions that he cannot understand. At the camp, he is unable to shoot his first seal or catch hawks with the other children, and he displeases his father when he suggests that they leave small meat offerings to thank the spirits for their success in hunting. Later, he meets old Inuk, a shaman who explains the meanings of the visions and tells the boy that he too will be a holy man. Travelling out of his body, Panipaq goes to the bottom of the sea where he meets Neqivik (Sedna), the mother of the sea mammals, and atones for his father's misdeeds. However, when he reports his experiences to the awestruck members of the camp, his father angrily decides to take him home, ignoring the warnings of impending storms. Panipiq falls through the broken ice, is rescued by Neqivik, and is able to reconcile his father to his shamanic powers and the old ways, before returning to his home, his mother, and a new baby brother. In this coming-of-age novel, Kortum deals with a boy learning to accept powers that will separate him from and, perhaps, make him feared by his peers and with the conflict between doubt of and belief in the traditional ways as symbolized by the father and son, respectively. Junior high students can compile a list of the visions Panipaq experiences and the explanations of them and can discuss why these are important elements of his maturation process. The

portrayal of Neqivik in this novel can be compared to those of Sedna in *Sedna* (McDermott) and *Song of Sedna* (San Souci). Which of these two portrayals does the one in *Ghost Vision* most closely resemble, and how accurate is the novel in relation to traditional Eskimo belief?

Le Sueur, Meridel. *Sparrow Hawk.* Stevens Point, WI: Holy Cow! Press, 1987.

Set in western Illinois during the 1830s, this story tells of the coming-of-age of the title hero at the time of the Sauk leader Black Hawk's last stand against invading whites. Member of a proud people whose city, Saukenuk, is one of the largest Native centers in the Midwest, Sparrow Hawk hopes that the new species of corn that he and his white friend Huck are developing will provide food and commerce for the original inhabitants and new settlers alike and that peace will prevail. However, he discovers that there are enemies within and without. Keokuk courts the white people and is prepared to move west with the promise of honors from them. His son and many other young men are easily seduced by the whiskey provided by soldiers and squatters. The soldiers themselves are brutal; greedy people dispossess the Sauk of their mines and their lands; and President Andrew Jackson has no sympathy for Native peoples. Inspired by the noble example of Black Hawk, Sparrow Hawk is willing to fight honorably for his people's lands but loyally follows his leader on a northern flight that, except for betrayal by other Native tribes, would have led to freedom. This story is a tribute to corn, a gift of father sky and mother earth, that should bring people together. However, the attitude to corn as a great good is not held by all; many view it mainly as a source for whiskey, a destructive killer. Junior high school students can focus on the friendship between Huck and Sparrow Hawk. In what ways are their personalities and their situations similar? Students can also notice the sacred power of song, examining the importance of each of the songs Sparrow Hawk sings, and can discuss the symbolic meanings of corn.

Lipsyte, Robert. *The Brave.* New York: HarperCollins, 1991.

Sonny Bear, a promising young boxer, is contemptuous of his small-town opponents and dismisses his uncle Jake's "dumb Indian talk" (13). Half white, half Moscondaga (the name of a fictional Iroquois band), he must fight to control the monster within him, a force Jake considers to be a hawk inside his breast that will destroy him if it is not freed to provide guidance. Jake explains that Sonny is the last person in whose veins flow the flood of the Running Brave Society, an ancient group that used its strength and skills to provide leadership and to seek peace. To become a successful fighter, to release the hawk, and to become a Brave, Sonny must make a long and difficult journey. This literally takes him to New York, where he becomes unwittingly involved with drug-running street people, and, briefly, to prison. However, under the guidance of Uncle Jake and a kind but tough drug cop, he undergoes the arduous training to make him a potential championship boxer and a true Brave. Most important, he must learn discipline to confront and defeat his impulsive nature, his enemies on the street, and his opponents in the ring. Lipsyte is not always completely successful in his portrayal of contemporary Native issues, but he does understand both the boxing scene and the troubled lives of teenagers. His depiction of Sonny Bear's struggle to define his future in relation to his past is convincing. Students in later junior high school can discuss the major episodes of the novel in relation to Jake's two statements: "No man ever got to be a Running Brave without taking a dangerous journey" (19), and "Find the Hawk inside you and let it loose and follow it" (20). They can list, in the order they occur, the references to "the monster" and can see how these reveal Sonny's changing attitudes toward himself in relation to the people around him.

Mayhar, Ardath. *Medicine Walk.* New York: Atheneum, 1985.
When his father dies of a heart attack while crash landing his small airplane, 12-year-old Burr Henderson finds himself alone in the middle of the Arizona desert. With little food and water, the only things he has to help him are memories of his determined father and the words of wisdom that he had heard Nachito, the Apache foreman of the Henderson's ranch, teaching his grandson. Both his father and Nachito had emphasized self-control, and the latter had said: "If you listen to the land, respect her and her gifts, you will be able to overcome anything" (11). Remembering Nachito's wisdom, he is able to hold precious water in his mouth for a long time, calm an angered rattlesnake, catch a fish barehanded, and live by the rhythms of the day and night rather than by his watch. At one point, he realizes that just like his Apache friend Charlie, he, a white boy, is on a medicine walk, a traditional rite of passage in which a young man proved he had learned survival skills, found his guardian spirit, and earned a new name. Although at times Burr calls out in despair that he is not an Apache and therefore can't make it, he does. Only when he stumbles into the desert retreat of an Apache anthropologist does he learn that he has succeeded, with the aid of the wisdom of Nachito, the wise old helper, and a cougar, his totem spirit. The anthropologist wonders if many Apache youths could have done as well as he, an outsider, did. Mayhar, in this book, has skilfully combined elements of the survival novel, knowledge of the southwest desert landscape, and respect for the spiritual traditions of the Apache people. Middle and upper elementary students can keep a log of Burr's major activities and thoughts for each day. How do these reveal that, each day, he is closer to achieving his goal of survival? The wisdom of Nachito can be examined. How is his traditional lore of value to Burr, the white boy? Notice the references to the cougar. In what way is it Burr's totemic spirit? How does his new name indicate the nature of his relationship to the cougar?

Momaday, Natachee Scott; illustrated by Don Perceval. *Owl in the Cedar Tree.* Lincoln: University of Nebraska Press, 1992.
In her short children's novel *Owl in the Cedar Tree*, Natachee Scott Momaday, mother of Kiowa author-painter N. Scott Momaday, presents a familiar theme of recent Native American literature: the conflict within a young person

between the old ways and modern life. Haske, a Navajo boy living with his family in a traditional hogan, wants to be an artist and to own Night Wind, the horse belonging to the white trading post proprietor. At the story's conclusion, he achieves both goals but not before facing profound conflicts. The boy admires his great-grandfather, who had been part of the victorious Navaho side in a battle with enemy raiders and who does not approve of the white man's ways, telling the boy that if he is to become a sandpainter, "you will have to give up the white man's school. You cannot follow the two trails at the same time" (69). The boy's father is unhappy with this advice, viewing the Old One's beliefs as superstition, and advocates progress. His mother offers a solution of balance: "keep the best of the old ways while learning the best of the new ways" (84). Haske discovers that his talent for painting, facilitated by the white school teacher, will enable him to depict scenes from the Old Ways, preserving the memories his great-grandfather cherished. One of the paintings wins a prize that he uses to buy the horse. The story is told sensitively and knowledgeably, giving readers a sympathetic picture of Navajo life half way through the twentieth century. Students in the middle and upper elementary grades can make lists of aspects of the old and new ways and then arrange the secondary characters in a list placing them closer to the old or new. Finally, they can decide whether Haske is closer to the old or new at the end of each chapter.

Paulsen, Gary. *Dogsong.* Scarsdale, NY: Bradbury Press, 1985.

Living in a present-day Alaskan village, 14-year-old Russel Susskit is dissatisfied with modern ways and seeks advice from Oogruk, who still follows traditional Eskimo customs. The old man gives him his sled and dog team and, before he dies, tells Russel about the old ways, an important element of which is song. Russel sets out north, determined that "I *will* get a song, I will be a song" (29). Songs, like respect from a dog team, must be earned, and, during his long and difficult journey to manhood, Russel acquires both. Travelling with his dogs, hunting in the traditional ways, he learns how to live with the land spiritually as well as physically. He shoots game, pays increasing attention to his dogs, rescues a pregnant girl who is nearly frozen to death on the tundra, kills a polar bear, and takes the girl to a northern village for medical help. He also discovers an ancient stone lamp that, along with a series of dreams, links him spiritually to people of several centuries earlier. In his dream, he sees a family starving to death while the man is away hunting, recognizes their lamp as the one he has found, and sees parallels between himself and the girl, on the one hand, and the hunter and his wife on the other. In a world increasingly dominated by snowmachines, white traders, and Christianity, Russel discovers a past that, like the lamp, has been long buried. However, just as the lamp had been in the land all along, waiting to be found and to give light and heat, so, too, the traditions remained on the land and, when discovered by Russel, illuminate and give new meaning to his life. Students in junior high can begin detailed study by noting Oogruk's statement: "It isn't the destination that counts. It is the journey. That is what life is" (119).

What are the major events in the journey that began when Russel left his own house, and how do these help him to mature and to discover his song? Students should pay careful attention to the dreams. What does Russel learn from each of them, and how does this help him in his journey? Students can discuss the significance of songs in the novel and suggest reasons why Russel's song is the appropriate one for him.

Paulsen, Gary. *Canyons.* New York: Delacorte Press, 1990.

A loner who runs "to be with himself" (9), 14-year-old Brennan Cole finds a skull while on a camping trip with his mother and her friend. Driven by a mysterious compulsion to keep it and learn about it, Brennan discovers that it is the remains of Coyote Runs, a 14-year-old Apache boy who, in 1864, had been brutally shot by American soldiers. In a series of chapters written from the point of view of the Apache, Paulsen presents the youth's desire to become a man, his vision quest atop a mesa at the canyon near present-day El Paso, Texas, where Brennan found the skull, his first horse raid into Mexico, and his vain attempt to escape the soldiers. After gaining possession of the skull and discovering about the Apache, Brennan feels that he has become the slain boy and that he must return the skull to the mesa toward which Coyote Runs had been fleeing. When he does this, both become free: the slain youth's soul travels into the skies, and Brennan can come to terms with the people in his life. The book is developed around a series of parallels, the most important being the lives and personalities of the two boys. Although Brennan feels at times that he has become Coyote Runs, he is much different. Not only are they separated by over a century of time, their cultures, and their "fates," they have different personalities and goals. Coyote Runs wants very much to become an adult member of his tribe, has close friendships, and, at times, a sense of self-confidence that is excessive. Brennan, on the other hand, is happiest on his own, his closest friend is a teacher he doesn't really know, and he lacks confidence. The adults in Brennan's life, especially Stoney Romero, for whom he works; Homesley, his teacher; and Bill, his mother's friend, are very different and are incomplete, partial versions of the father he never had. Students in the later junior high grades can begin their study by noticing the basic differences in the personalities of Brennan and Coyote Runs. Given the differences, why is Brennan so drawn to the Apache and so determined to take the skull to the canyon area? They can discuss the stages by which he comes to learn about Coyote Runs' life and death. Why is it significant that Brennan comes to understand more than just the facts that he gains from Homesley, the pathologist, and the archivist?

Robinson, Margaret A. *A Woman of Her Tribe.* New York: Charles Scribner's Sons, 1990.

When 15-year-old Annette leaves her Nootka village on Canada's west coast to join her white mother in a large city, she finds herself torn between two cultures. At her school, she is self-conscious and isolated as a member of a very small cultural minority. However, when she returns to her village at Christmas, she feels different from her long-time friends. Luckily, she is blessed with two wise-women teachers who help her to discover her own destiny. Miss Doud, her anthropology teacher, encourages her students to explore their cultural heritage and tells them that learning involves struggle, hard work, and pain. Her grandmother, one of the few villagers to still believe in the old ways, instructs her about the equally difficult female coming-of-age rituals of the Nootka. At the end of the Christmas vacation, she has passed the arduous tests and is a woman of her tribe. But does this mean she must renounce her mother's way of life and the schooling it offers? Which life should she choose? "One of these lives she had witnessed for fifteen years. The other was new and led to an unknown future" (127). Her grandmother wisely leaves the choice up to her, and she decides to draw on the best of both worlds and achieve a balance of the old and new. The novel is skilfully organized around a series of contrasts that embody the conflicts Annette experiences: her small village and the city, the ancient oral teachings and modern book oriented schools, Nootka and white cultures, Granmaw and Miss Doud, Native and clock time, to name but five. Students in the later junior high grades can examine these contrasts, noting how they relate to the tensions in the heroine's life. Does the novel present any hope that these can be reconciled and that Annette can achieve a happy, fulfilled life?

Rogers, Jean. *Goodbye, My Island.* New York: Greenwillow Books, 1983.
This short novel is the story of 12-year-old Esther Atoolik's last winter on King Island, the generations-old home of a dwindling group of western Alaskan Eskimo families. Most of the book describes the seasonal activities of the people: the return home after a summer in Nome where they sold carvings to tourists; church and school events; baseball games on the ice; hunting seal, walrus, and whales; Christmas and other festivals; the arrival of a plane that drops mail and needed supplies. As Esther explains, "Everyone knows just what to do. We have done this every year for as long as anyone can remember" (13). It is a coopera-tive effort. "We are all working together so that we will be safe and comfortable" (15). Underlying the girl's joy in her life on King Island is a note of sadness. In the opening chapter, it is noted that every year fewer people are returning from Nome, and, when the families arrive back on the island, they are informed that the co-op store and the school must be closed at the end of the winter. The next summer, she thinks, "I . . . am sad in spite of the good things I can see ahead. I do not want to go and never come back again" (79). King Island, whose traditional life is lovingly and sensitively portrayed by the author, is caught between two worlds and, regrettably, survival can only be achieved by leaving the old for the new. Students in the middle elementary grades can keep a calendar of the basic activities of the King Island year. They can also notice how, during each of the seasons, the influence of modern civilization can be seen. Which of these influences are positive and which are negative? Like Esther, students can keep a short weekly log about key events at home or school.

Rumbaut, Hendle. *Dove Dream.* Boston: Houghton Mifflin Co., 1994.

While her parents sort out their marital problems, Dovey goes to spend the summer with her Aunt Anna in rural Kansas. The 12-year-old half Chickasaw girl delights in her free-spirited relative, who treats her as an equal. However, the greatest influence on the girl is Winona, her dead grandmother, whose wisdom still reaches her in dreams and visions, in letters discovered in Anna's house, and in the memories of the stories Dovey heard as a little girl. Early in the novel, she thinks that her own life "seemed lost between past and present, the reservation and the city, pride and shame" (21). However, the summer is one of reconciliation and reunification. Her sickly mother and alcoholic father redis-cover their love for each other; Anna, who becomes pregnant, will marry her friend Troy; and, in the novel's concluding chapter, Choctaw, Chickasaw, and whites joyously congregate at a huge family reunion. For Dovey, the central event of the summer is a vision quest. Without food and water, she spends two nights alone beside a creek, where a vision of her grandmother tells her that the old woman and many other spirits watch over the girl. She will never lose her heritage. Skinny and flat-chested at the beginning, she experiences her first menstrual cycle on the novel's closing page. While this book contains implicitly sexual scenes, the author, part Chikasaw herself, makes these a very appropriate element of the novel's themes of love, rebirth, and reaffirmation. Upper elemen-tary students can trace these themes and can examine the roles of the two strong females, the aunt and the grandmother, in Dovey's coming-of-age. They should particularly notice the significance of the grandmother's stories and letters.

Sharpe, Susan. *Spirit Quest.* New York: Bradbury Press, 1991.

About to spend a month's vacation with his marine-scientist mother and artist father near the Quileute village on Washington's rugged coast, 11-year-old Aaron Singer "felt as if he needed some room to grow on his own" (4) and wonders if the local Native people "still believe their mythology" (6). At the end of the month, he has grown and discovered that many still do believe and that, in a way, he does as well. His entré into the Native world comes through a friendship with Robert Greene, a Quileute his own age. Together they explore the beaches and forests and discuss their vastly different backgrounds. Aaron becomes fascinated with the spiritual aspects of Native life after hearing a Native storyteller recount Raven legends, and he, with Robert, decides to go on a spirit quest like that of traditional Native people. However, the quest does not go according to custom: the two are accompanied by Robert's older brother, and only Aaron spends the night alone—accidentally, as it were. When the two find a bald eagle trapped in a fish net, Robert goes for help, while Aaron cares for the bird during a long, storm filled night. He has had a kind of vision, understanding and caring for another creature, a bird related to the mythological thunderbird, and, although he returns to Seattle happy, he understands the essential differ-ence between himself and his Quileute friend: "He realized that Robert belonged to LaPush [his village], more than he would ever belong to anyplace" (122). It is a summer of growth, a growth that includes recognition of and respect for cultural differences. Robert refers to Raven as the Transformer, because that mythological being altered the shapes and natures of living creatures. Students in the upper elementary grades can ask, "To what extent has Aaron fallen under Raven's power; that is, been changed?" At one point, Aaron thinks that a whale is his spirit guardian. But, after collecting references to eagles and their mythological counterparts, the thunderbirds, students can consider if the guardian spirit might be the eagle, and if so, why it would be a valuable helper for Aaron.

Sneve, Virginia Driving Hawk. *High Elk's Treasure*. New York: Holiday House, 1972.

A descendant of High Elk, who was present at the Battle of the Little Big Horn and who had begun breeding a famous line of horses, Joe High Elk, an eighth grader, loses one of the family's horses during a spring thunderstorm. Taking shelter in a cave sacred to his ancestor, the youth discovers a bundle wrapped in raw hide and takes it home, where his traditionalist grandmother recounts a legend that High Elk had buried something that was not to be uncovered until a century after the battle. By the end of the novel, the lost horse is rescued from horse thieves; a distant relative is reunited with the family; the secret of the bundle is revealed; and a colt is born to the last mare in the line begun by High Elk. Lakota author Sneve has carefully integrated a family's history and contemporary Native life to emphasize the continuity of her people's traditions. The return of Howard High Elk, the contents of the bundle, the continuance of the horse breed, and the presence of a grandmother who will only speak Lakota link past and present together to ensure that Joe High Elk, the story's central character, will have a meaningful future rooted in still vital traditions. Students in the middle and upper elementary grades can make a list of these links to the past and discuss why they are so important for Joe.

Speare, Elizabeth George. *The Sign of the Beaver*. Boston: Houghton Mifflin Co., 1983.

In the later eighteenth century, 13-year-old Matt must spend the summer and fall alone in a Maine woods cabin while his father travels to Massachusetts to bring back his wife and daughter. When a white woodsman steals his gun, the boy fears he will face a long and difficult time procuring food. However, a friendship with Attean, a member of an unnamed Indian tribe, helps to change things. Matt will teach him reading in exchange for food. Matt gains much more, as Attean teaches him a great deal of woodlore. The book used for reading instruction, Daniel Defoe's classic survival story, *Robinson Crusoe*, is ironic for, as Matt realizes, he is most frequently in the subservient position of Friday, Crusoe's servant. Often the white boy is angry and frustrated with the Native boy, judging him ethnocentrically. The end result of their encounter is a close friendship and a parting forever, as the tribe moves westward to escape the invasion of European settlers. Speare gives a vivid and accurate portrayal of settler and Native life in this period, and her account of the coming-of-age of the two boys, particularly as they overcome their initial disdain for each other, is convincing. Yet the book is flawed in its presentation of Native peoples. Not only is Attean's nation, presumably Penobscot, not named, but his people are designated by the generic term "Indian." Descriptions of the village dwellings as "ramshackle and flimsy" (85) and the description of women "jabbering like bluejays" (85) are but two examples of language that degrades the Native peoples. Students in junior high grades can study the novel, particularly Chapter 17, for examples of negative stereotyping. Students in the upper elementary grades, after having the stereotypes pointed out, can examine the stages of Matt's maturing, noticing how his increasing understanding of the woods and the Native people mark important stages in his development.

Wallin, Luke. *Ceremony of the Panther.* New York: Bradbury Press, 1987.
Sixteen-year-old John Raincrow, a member of the Miccosukee tribe from the Florida Everglades, feels animosity toward his father. Often under the influence of alcohol and drugs supplied by his friend Max, he is angered that his father, who is a shaman following traditional ways, supports his family by wrestling alligators for tourists. After the two have an angry confrontation, the teenager is sent to his grandmother's home on an island deep in the Everglades—to dry out; to be away from Max, who has adopted the worst of the white ways; and to learn from his grandmother the traditional relationship among the people, the land and its creatures, and the Sky Spirits. The underlying cause of John's unhappiness gradually becomes apparent here: he is unsure of his desire and ability to become a medicine man, as his father wishes. While father and son go through the ritual preparations for the slaying of a panther necessary for use in a ceremony to cure his grandmother's serious illness, John begins to understand and appreciate the spiritual basis of his traditional life, and both he and his father develop a strong respect for each other. His father is arrested for the killing of a panther, an endangered species. However, the killing took place on Native land, outside federal jurisdiction. John recognizes both his responsibility to his father and grandmother and the need for him to follow his own destiny. Junior high students can trace the stages by which John comes to understand his traditions and himself, noting the customs of traditional life that help him to come to his realization. They can discuss the prefatory and follow-up ceremonies relating to hunting and compare these to the beliefs on the hunting cultures of the north central woodlands (seen in inverted form in many Ojibway tales of Nanabozho) and the northwest coast (embodied in tales retold by Christie Harris).

Wisler, G. Clifton. *The Wolf's Tooth.* New York: E.P. Dutton, 1987.
This novel of an encounter and friendship between a white and Native boy possesses most of the characteristics of the story type but with important differences. In the middle of the nineteenth century, 13-year-old Elias Walsh

reluctantly accompanies his parents to the Brazos Valley, Texas, school where his father will teach the small group of Native children. There he meets Thomas Three Feathers, a Tonkawa his own age. After an awkward beginning and several misunderstandings about each other's cultures, the two become fast friends, killing marauding wolves, the tooth from one of which becomes Elias's amulet, joining a buffalo hunt, and finally, just before they depart from each other, becoming brothers. However, the story has tragic undertones for, during the harsh winter, many of the Native people, having been given insufficient provisions, starve; the government decides to close the school; and the Native peoples are relocated to make room for white settlers. Thomas has been scarred literally and psychologically by whites and feels a deep sense of loneliness that his friendship with Elias cannot overcome. Caught between two worlds, he finally chooses to be with his people, even though he realizes: "My people . . . fade like the evening sun. We won't rise again with dawn, I fear" (117). Sensitive in relating the plight of Native peoples, the novel does have some white biasses. The Comanches, a hunting culture, are seen as inferior to the Native planters around the tiny settlement; yet, even these agrarians can be made better through white schools and by wearing civilized clothing. The portrayal of the wolves as aggressive attackers of human beings and Thomas' statement that "they come to prey on the dead" (75) seem both naturalistically and ethnologically incorrect. Students in upper elementary and junior high grades might wish to compare the descriptions of and attitudes toward wolves in this book and Jean Craighead George's *Julie of the Wolves*. They can also discuss the political motivations behind the closing of the school and the relocations of the Native peoples. In what ways have Elias and Thomas learned from each other, and who has learned the most?

Wosmek, Frances. *A Brown Bird Singing*. New York: Lothrop, Lee & Shepard, 1986.

This is the account of Anego, a Chippewa (Ojibway) girl who has been adopted into a white family in northern Minnesota early in the twentieth century. Happy and secure in her life, she becomes worried when news is heard of her father, who had been her adoptive father's best friend. Will she have to leave the people she loves? In her fear, she is unable to hear the brown bird whose singing gives her peace and courage. When her father does arrive, Anego flees into the woods, hoping to hide long enough so that she will not have to go to the reservation with him. She becomes lost and is found by her father, who explains that she may choose to live where she wishes; he only wants the best for her in times when the traditional Chippewa ways are being rapidly destroyed. She can again hear her brown bird singing. Much of the novel presents the seasonal and daily activities of a fifth grader of that time and place: school festivals, Christmas, the birth of a baby brother, the loss of a pet, and, symbolic of the new ways, the purchase of an automobile. Underlying this presentation is the insecurity felt by Anego, a girl living between two cultures. In reading the novel, middle elementary students can make a list of all the references to the brown bird and then discuss its meaning in relation to the conflicts the heroine experiences. They can consider the tug between the two worlds and the loneliness and insecurity it creates for Anego. In what way will she be able to enjoy and learn from the best that each of these worlds has to offer?

REFERENCES

Allen, Paula Gunn. 1975. "The Sacred Hoop: A Contemporary Indian Perspective on American Indian Literature." In *Literature of the American Indians: Views and Interpretations*, edited by Abraham Chapman. New York: New American Library.

Bevis, William. 1987. "Native American Novels: Homing In." In *Recovering the Word Essays on Native American Literature*, edited by Brian Swann and Arnold Krupat. Berkeley: University of California Press, 1987.

Brown, Dee. 1972. *Bury My Heart at Wounded Knee: An Indian History of the American West*. New York: Bantam Books.

Culleton, Beatrice. 1983. *In Search of April Raintree*. Winnipeg, Canada: Pemmican Publications.

———. 1989. "Native Peoples." In *Writers on Writing*, edited by David Booth. Markham, Canada: Overlea House.

Dorris, Michael. 1987. *A Yellow Raft in Blue Water*. New York: Henry Holt.

———. 1992. *Morning Girl*. New York: Hyperion Books.

Dorris, Michael and Louise Erdrich. 1991. *The Crown of Columbus*. New York: Harper Collins.

Erdrich, Louise. 1994. *The Bingo Palace*. New York: Harper Collins.

Fee, Margery. 1990. "Upsetting Fake Ideals: Jeanette Armstrong's 'Slash' and Beatrice Culleton's 'April Raintree.'" In *Native Writers and Canadian Writing*, edited by W.H. New. Vancouver, Canada: University of British Columbia Press.

Fitzhugh, William W. and Susan A. Kaplin. 1982. *Inua: The Spirit World of the Bering Sea Eskimo*. Washington: Smithsonian Institution Press.

George, Jean Craighead. 1959. *My Side of the Mountain*. New York: E.P. Dutton.

———. 1972. *Julie of the Wolves*. New York: Harper and Row.

———. 1982. *Journey Inward*. New York: E.P. Dutton.

———. 1983. *The Talking Earth*. New York: Harper and Row.

———. 1987. *Water Sky*. New York: Harper and Row.

————. 1994. *Julie*. New York: Harper Collins.

Katz, Jane B., editor. 1980. *This Song Remembers: Self-Portraits of Native Americans in the Arts*. Boston: Houghton Mifflin Co.

King, Thomas. 1989. *Medicine River*. Toronto: Penguin Books Canada.

Kroeber, Theodora. 1973. *Ishi: Last of His Tribe*. New York: Bantam Books.

Locke, Raymond Friday. 1989. *The Book of the Navajo*. 4th edition. Los Angeles: Mankind Publishing Company.

Maher, Susan Naramore. 1992. "Encountering Others: The Meeting of Cultures in Scott O'Dell's *Island of the Blue Dolphins* and *Sing Down the Moon*." *Children's Literature in Education* 23: 215-27.

Momaday, N. Scott. 1968. *House Made of Dawn*. New York: Harper and Row.

————. 1989. *The Ancient Child*. New York: Doubleday.

Nodelman, Perry. 1984. "A Second Look: *Sing Down the Moon*." *Horn Book* 60 (February): 94-98.

O'Dell, Scott. 1965. "Newbery Award Acceptance." In *Newbery and Caldecott Medal Books: 1956-1965*, edited by Lee Kingman. Boston: Horn Book.

————. 1971. (Originally published 1960.) *Island of the Blue Dolphins*. New York: Dell.

————. 1978. (Originally published 1976.) *Zia*. New York: Dell.

————. 1992. (Originally published 1970.) *Sing Down the Moon*. New York: Dell.

Ong, Walter J. 1982. *Orality and Literacy: The Technologizing of the Word*. London: Routledge.

Owens, Louis. 1992. *Other Destinies: Understanding the American Indian Novel*. Norman: University of Oklahoma Press.

Paulsen, Gary. 1987. *Hatchet*. New York: Bradbury Press.

Ramsey, Jarold. 1983. *Reading the Fire: Essays in the Traditional Indian Literatures of the Far West*. Lincoln: University of Nebraska Press.

Roop, Peter. 1987. "Scott O'Dell: Using History to Tell His Story." *Children's Literature Association Quarterly* 12 (Winter): 172-75.

Silko, Leslie Marmon. 1977. *Ceremony*. New York: Viking Press.

Sperry, Armstrong. 1940. *Call It Courage*. New York: Macmillan.

Stine, Jean C. and Daniel G. Marowski, editors. 1984. *Contemporary Literary Criticism*. Volume 30. Detroit: Gale Research Company.

Wintle, Justin and Emma Fisher. 1975. *The Pied Pipers: Interviews with the Influential Creators of Children's Literature*. New York: Paddington Press.

EPILOGUE

▼▼▼

Writing Between Two Worlds: The Inuit Stories of Michael Kusugak

W hen Gerald McDermott first visited Zuni Pueblo, the people were surprised that it was his first trip to the Southwest. They told him that they had been using *Arrow to the Sun* in schools for many years to introduce their children to their narrative and spiritual history. McDermott had engaged in extensive research before creating his picture book; however, much of it involved reading the academic studies of non-Native scholars who, many years earlier, had recorded their observations of rapidly vanishing traditions. During the first half of the twentieth century, many of the beliefs and tales that had existed for generations were, to use an often repeated saying, "one generation from extinction." In fact, the stories were virtually endangered species, artificially preserved in anthropological journals and museum publications. With the exception of conservative centers like Taos Pueblo, remote woodlands in the Canadian north, or undeveloped regions like the Arctic archipelago, there were few places where elders remembered the stories and children were interested in hearing them. Reservation schools all but stamped out Native languages and introduced children to Bible stories and secular tales in the European tradition. Just after World War II, radio programs, motion pictures, and comic books, all widely available, virtually displaced oral storytelling as the major sources of narrative entertainment. During the 1950s, television became more accessible in rural areas, including reservations, further displacing the oral traditions.

It is not surprising, then, that McDermott's book was a major educational resource. In many instances, materials developed through study of the academic research conducted by non-Natives were the most readily available links to the traditional past. In the Southwest during the middle of the twentieth century, a large number of the books created for Native children came from the pen of Ann Nolan Clark, a white employee of the education division of the Bureau of Indian Affairs. During the 1970s, an aging Lakota woman who had gone to hear English-born Paul Goble speak, expressed surprise that this reteller and illustrator of northern plains myths and legends was not Native. How, she wondered, could an outsider know and understand so much about her people's traditions? The situation was more typical than she realized.

However, the Native tradition of storytelling, while seriously weakened, was not dead. Certainly most children's adaptations were written, not always accurately, respectfully, or sympathetically, by non-Natives; and western novels, motion pictures, and television programs supplied Native and non-Native audiences with erroneous views of Native history. Yet, some elders continued to pass on their stories, as is indicated by the publication since mid-century of a number of scholarly transcriptions of orally presented tales. And, since 1909, when Lakota author and physician Arthur Eastman published *Wigwam Evenings*, there have been Native novelists and adapters of traditional stories. However, such authors as Eastman, Mourning Dove, Pauline Johnson, and D'Arcy McNickle were generally considered untypical of Native peoples. To many non-Natives, they were curiosities rising above their Native limitations, individuals worthy of praise because they were successful in a European activity—writing books.

When N. Scott Momaday won the Pulitzer Prize for his 1968 novel, *House Made of Dawn*, attitudes toward Native writers and the contemporary and historical lives and traditions they celebrated in their books changed considerably. The non-Native reading public became aware of both individual talents and literary traditions they had not realized existed. Aspiring Native writers were encouraged because they now had a role model and a larger, more accepting audience. The awakening of interest in the new Native writing and the rebirth, in print form, of traditional stories were parts of the general social climate of the 1960s, in which members of the white majority became sensitive to the importance of minority cultures and their arts and traditions and members of minority cultures experienced a sense of pride in their heritages and of self-worth in their own accomplishments.

Momaday's novel was followed over the next two decades by the novels of Gerald Vizenor, James Welch, Leslie Silko, Linda Hogan, Paula Gunn Allen, Michael Dorris, Louise Erdrich, and Thomas King. Many poets, including Louise Erdrich, Wendy Rose, Duane Niatum, Ray Young Bear, and Joseph Bruchac published in important literary magazines. Vizenor and Bruchac created written versions of traditional tales they had heard from grandparents and other tribal elders. These works were published not only by smaller presses but also by the major American publishing houses. University presses responded to the new interest by reprinting long unavailable editions of anthropologists' collections of tales and by publishing works of literary criticism by such Native scholars as Vizenor, Kenneth Lincoln, and Louis Owens. In some cases, publishers may have been capitalizing on fashionable trends. Be that as it may, Native writers had access to much larger markets, and Native and non-Native readers had the opportunity to encounter not only the best of contemporary Native writing but also important scholarly materials from and dealing with the past. There was, to use the title of Lincoln's book, a Native American Renaissance (Lincoln 1983,).

In the field of children's literature, this Renaissance has taken place in two areas: educational and trade publishing. *Coyote Stories of the Navajo People* (Roessel 1991) and *The Mishomis Book* (Benton-Benai 1988), both discussed in Chapter 3, are the works of educators attempting to develop culturally appropriate reading materials for Native schools. *Arikara Coyote Tales*, edited by Douglas R. Parks, is just one example of a growing number of bilingual collections of traditional tales in which the goal is not just to introduce children to their narrative heritage, but also to help them learn their Native languages by proceeding from versions in the more familiar English, to, in this case, the less familiar Lakota. As they take charge of their own educational systems, many culture groups are developing curriculum guides in which specific units of instruction are based on traditional tales. One such example is *'Ulkatchot'en: The People of Ulkatcho*, published by Ulkatcho Indian Band of northern British Columbia, Canada. As they were generations ago, stories are being used to provide the foundations on which a variety of educational programs and experiences are erected. Unlike their parents and grandparents, who were forced to attend distant residential schools where they were instructed in what was to them a foreign language and learned the stories, history, and values of a foreign culture, contemporary Native students have available to them a rapidly increasing number of trade books that contain their own literature, much of it written by Native peoples. Joseph Bruchac, Michael Dorris, Shonto Begay, Basil Johnston, Virginia Driving Hawk Sneve, and C. J. Taylor are just a few of the Native authors and illustrators who are presenting traditional stories to younger members of their own culture, as well as to a larger reading public.

Evidence of the influence of this Native literary renaissance on young Native peoples is seen in publications of writing by Native school children. Arlene B. Hirschfelder and Beverly R. Singer have edited *Rising Voices: Writings of Young Native Americans*, and, in Canada, Georgia Elston edited *Giving: Ojibwa Stories and Legends from the Children of Curve Lake*. These are just two examples of students reclaiming their literary traditions and writing pieces in which they define themselves as they relate to the natural and cultural worlds around them.

Native authors creating books for young people face complex tasks. Heirs of oral traditions, they must communicate in a print medium. Knowledgeable about their cultures' histories and traditions, they must write for young audiences, including members of their own cultures, who know little, if anything, about this past. Creators of written narratives, they must make their printed products of interest to audiences whose major source of narrative is visual, through television, motion pictures, videos, and electronic games. And because of the small numbers of potential buyers within their own cultures, they must create books that, without compromising cultural values and historical accuracy, appeal to the much larger non-Native market. They attempt to bridge a gap between two worlds and to maintain a delicate balance between the story expectations of two culturally different groups of readers.

The difficult position of the Native author is exemplified in the life and writing of Canadian Inuit (Eskimo) storyteller Michael Kusugak, whose books have achieved wide popularity among Canadian elementary school children. The four and a half decades of his life include experiences that could symbolize the various stages of Native history since precontact times. During his first seven years, Kusugak and his family lived a traditional nomadic, hunting life. He spoke no English and spent many hours listening to his grandmother retelling the old myths and legends. When the Canadian government began developing the north in the 1950s, the family moved to Rankin Inlet where his father sought work. Michael was precipitated into the modern world and, at age seven, was sent to a residential school. The next year he hid when the plane arrived to take him back to the school. Later he completed his high school education in the south and earned a degree in English Literature at the University of Saskatchewan. For the last 15 years he has worked in a variety of government jobs and has published four children's books: A Promise Is a Promise (1988, with noted Canadian children's author Robert Munsch), Baseball Bats for Christmas (1990), Hide and Sneak (1992), and Northern Lights: The Soccer Trails (1993). He travels frequently across Canada, telling his stories to school children and addressing educational conferences. As he remarked in conversation, his life is like an anthropological survey of Native life in North America: from a precontact style of life in a hunting culture, to residential schools, to a return to his homeland to seek to link his people's traditional and modern lifestyles.

His love of stories comes from his familiarity with the traditions of oral Eskimo literature and written English literature. From his grandmother, he learned to create narratives that put images in listeners' heads. From fourteenth-century British author Geoffrey Chaucer, he learned how to recreate in a written text the flow of words of the oral storyteller. Having learned these techniques, he set about saving from oblivion the stories his ancestors had kept alive for centuries. However, he had to find a way of gaining and then holding the interest of his young, video educated audience. "I was thinking that if I could popularize the stories in picture book form, kids would read them. Children in southern Canada liked the stories when I visited the schools. I realized that if I could hook the southern kids, then our kids, who like what these southern kids like, who watch southern TV all the time, would follow along. It was a kind of backdoor approach to reintroducing my people to their own stories" (Stott 1993). Kusugak recognizes that southern audiences are more important than just being a means of hooking his own people. "I had to attract a large southern audience if I were going to be able to support myself by writing. I would have to create characters with whom they could identify to a degree. They had to be modern children and to experience the kinds of feelings all children have. But I am Inuit, and I write about the subjects I know about. I write about children who encountered the types of things I encountered when I was a child. In my stories, I try to bridge the gap between the northern and southern child" (Stott 1993).

Each of Kusugak's stories is about a modern Inuit child. One is based on his own experiences in the mid 1950s; the others are about contemporary girls. Three of them include traditional spiritual beliefs or encounters with supernatural beings from the old tales and myths. In *Baseball Bats for Christmas*, Avaarluk, a seven-year-old asthmatic boy, like the author, recounts how, at Christmas 1955, a bush pilot left them six evergreen trees, much to the mystification of the tiny village. Only after the boy receives a rubber ball for Christmas, do the children decide that the trees have been given to them so that they will have wood with which to fashion baseball bats. This short episode is more than an autobiographical reminiscence; it is a humorous account of the differences between the two cultures that only then were beginning to interrelate in the far north. *Northern Lights: The Soccer Trails* is a testimony to the continuing validity of the belief that the shifting patterns of the northern lights mark the movements of the spirits of dead loved ones playing soccer in the sky. After her mother dies, Kataujaq feels very lonely. However, one winter night, while the villagers play ball on the ice, her grandmother points to the northern lights above and explains that the spirit of Kataujaq's mother is playing there. The girl no longer feels lonely. Her people's old beliefs, communicated by her grandmother, sustain her.

Kusugak's best-known books, *A Promise Is a Promise* and *Hide and Sneak*, narrate the adventures of Allashua as she is captured by, but then escapes from, two supernatural beings who had always been threats to little children. In the first book, the girl breaks her promise not to go near the dangerous spring sea ice where, her parents warn her, the Qallupilluit trap solitary children. She has seen Santa Claus, fairy godmothers, and the Tooth Fairy on the television, and so she believes in them. But she does not believe in the existence of Qallupilluit and sings mocking songs. However, they are real and she is captured. Selfishly, she gains her freedom by promising to bring her brothers and sisters to them. The conflict is only resolved through her mother's cleverness. On one level, the story is a modern example of the traditional Inuit type of story designed to teach appropriate behavior. On a deeper level, it is the story of a girl who learns that television programs from a non-Inuit culture do not tell the whole story, that the old beliefs are also true.

In *Hide and Sneak*, Allashua is much older and is able to escape from another supernatural being on her own. The Ijiraq is a creature who likes to lure children away by pretending to help them play hide and seak. Because the heroine is not very good at the game, she is an easy victim. Once again, she uses non-Inuit folklore to justify ignoring her mother's warnings: "Elves don't hide you forever; dwarves don't hide you forever; leprechauns don't hide you forever" (Kusugak 1992, n.p.). Trapped, she relies on one of her people's old customs to engineer an escape: she ridicules the creature and stares at him, using mockery as a means of shaming him into proper behavior. When he disappears in the tundra, she uses an inuksugaq, an old stone statue, to guide her home, just as her people have always done. Because she has relied on her people's practices, she has escaped from one of their more dangerous supernatural beings. Readers from southern Canada will recognize in Allashua a familiar story character: the lost little girl who uses her cleverness to save herself. Inuit children will see in her a little girl who saves herself by remembering and responding to the elements of her culture that her mother had taught her but that she had earlier ignored.

Written between two worlds, the stories of Michael Kusugak may well be harbingers of a new tradition in children's literature about Native peoples. Created by Native writers knowledgeable about their cultures' traditional and contemporary lives, books in this tradition will appeal to Native and non-Native readers alike, reaffirming traditions and values for the former and introducing and encouraging respect for these in the latter. The Native Renaissance in children's literature, as it continues to develop and expand, will be influential in producing truly knowledgeable, sympathetic, and humane young readers in all cultures.

REFERENCES

Benton-Benai, Edward. 1988. *The Mishomis Book: The Voice of the Ojibway.* St. Paul, MN: Red School House.

Birchwater, Sage; illustrated by Ronald Cahoose. 1991. *'Ulkatchot'en: The People of Ulkatcho.* Anahim Lake, Canada: Ulkatcho Indian Band.

Eastman, Charles A. (Ohiyesa) and Elaine Goodale Eastman, retellers. 1990. *Wigwam Evenings: Sioux Folk Tales Retold*. Lincoln: University of Nebraska Press. (First published in 1909.)

Elston, Georgia, editor. 1985. *Giving: Ojibwa Stories and Legends from the Children of Curve Lake*. Lakeview, Canada: Waapoone Publishing.

Hirschfelder, Arlene B. and Beverly R. Singer, editors. 1992. *Rising Voices: Writings of Young Native Americans*. New York: Charles Scribner's Sons.

Kusugak, Michael and Robert Munsch; illustrated by Vladyana Krykorka. 1988. *A Promise Is a Promise*. Toronto: Annick Press.

Kusugak, Michael. 1990. *Baseball Bats for Christmas*. Illustrated by Vladyana Krykorka. Toronto: Annick Press.

———. 1992. *Hide and Sneak*. Illustrated by Vladyana Krykorka. Toronto: Annick Press.

———. 1993. *Northern Lights: The Soccer Trails*. Illustrated by Vladyana Krykurka. Toronto: Annick Press.

Lincoln, Kenneth. 1983. *Native American Renaissance*. Berkeley: University of California Press.

Momaday, N. Scott. 1968. *House Made of Dawn*. New York: Harper and Row.

Parks, Douglas R., editor; illustrated by David J. Ripley. 1984. *Arikara Coyote Tales: A Bilingual Reader/Naa'iikawis Sahnis*. Roseglen, ND: White Shield School District.

Roessel, Robert A., Jr. and Dillon Platero, editors. 1991. *Coyote Stories of the Navajo People*. Chinle, AZ: Rough Rock Press.

Stott, Jon C. Interview with Michael Kusugak, Edmonton, November 26, 1993.

APPENDIX

▼▼▼

Incorporating Native
Stories in the
Language Arts Program

PHILOSOPHY AND OBJECTIVES

As the study of literature becomes more and more a central element of language arts, reading, and social studies curriculums, it becomes essential that stories are chosen not only to meet the learning goals of the various programs, but also to reflect the multicultural makeup of school populations. Although representations of Native North American peoples have been a part of popular culture since the arrival of the first European settlers, accurate presentations of their history, cultures, and traditional stories have not always been available. As the annotated reading lists that conclude Chapters 2, 3, and 4 reveal, this situation has changed considerably during the last quarter of a century. There are now plentiful resources for integrating stories about traditional and contemporary Native peoples into the various areas of elementary school instruction.

It has been said that in order to understand a culture, it is necessary to understand the stories the members of that culture tell each other. By using picture books, adaptations of traditional tales, and novels in language arts and reading programs, as well as in other areas across the curriculum, teachers can assist students in better understanding the North American continent's first settlers. The following suggestions for thematic units, author and illustrator studies, and novel study based on stories about Native Americans are designed to help fulfill that and a variety of other objectives.

The general aims underlying each of the following study units are as follows:

1. **To introduce students to a variety of story types from the various Native culture groups of the United States and Canada.** In reading examples of these story types, students will have a clearer idea of the ways in which Native stories differ generally from those of Europe and

the rest of the world and of the ways in which stories from specific Native culture groups differ from those of other groups. Reading and comparing the stories, students will better understand the social and spiritual beliefs of the specific Native groups who are the subjects of or who originally told the stories.

2. **To help students develop the skills necessary for a fuller understanding of literature in general.** Like other stories students read, these contain conflicts leading to resolution; portray character growth; use setting to develop mood, theme, and conflict; and create ironic situations. In addition, picture books use color, design, and detail within and between pages to communicate character, action, setting, conflict, and theme.

3. **To extend the study of these stories generally into the language arts curriculum.** Picture books containing very few words provide students with opportunities to create their own texts. Students in the older grades can keep journals, make their own dictionaries of words important in individual stories, write book reviews, and create sequels. Developing readers will find reading Native stories from their own geographical area more interesting than reading generalized stories from basal readers.

4. **To extend discussion of the content of the stories and novels into other areas of the curriculum.** Students can study the use of traditional Native design patterns in picture books and use similar design patterns to create illustrations for stories from unillustrated collections of folktales. Before or after reading a story from a specific culture area, they can study the kind of dwelling in which it might have been told and can discuss why the house design and materials used to build it were appropriate to the terrain and climate, and the ways in which the specific groups viewed their dwellings as homes with social and spiritual values. Stories can be acted out, and, if collections of Native music are available, students can listen to tapes or disks of music from the culture associated with the story being read.

No specific grade levels have been assigned to the following unit outlines. However, they have been arranged in an order beginning with a unit of stories most easily accessible in the early elementary grades to one containing stories more accessible in the upper elementary or junior high grades. Teachers in later grades may wish to use some of the earlier units with their students, dealing with some of the less obvious, more complex elements of plot, theme, and character development, as well as subtleties of cultural beliefs revealed in the stories. The description of each unit begins with a brief introductory overview, followed by a list of titles to be considered, objectives for the unit, and suggestions for presentation and classroom activities.

These units are intended to be descriptive rather than prescriptive. They are based on materials developed in elementary and junior high schools in

Edmonton, Alberta, and Munising, Michigan, and have been in a process of revision and adaptation over several years. They suggest ways in which students can be encouraged to get closer to the Native stories they read, can relate the materials to other areas of their studies, and can relate them to their lives as inhabitants of an increasingly multicultural world. Teachers will no doubt want to ignore certain activities, modify others, and develop their own. However, it is hoped that these units will provide some starting points for a full and rewarding engagement with the rich heritages of Native cultures and stories.

ARCTIC FOOD ON ICE

Introduction: For the people of the Arctic, the sea was extremely important and dangerous. From the ocean, they harvested the shellfish, fish, and mammals (from seals to whales) that provided food, fuel, and clothing. However, the animals they hunted could be dangerous, the water could be churned into storms, and the ice, particularly during the spring, could be very hazardous. Going to the sea or to the ice to find materials they needed to live, they faced the possibility of dying. Each of these stories stresses the importance of the sea and lakes to the Eskimo people and the positive or negative character traits the central characters exhibit during their adventures. Listening to these tales in an igloo or sod hut, traditional Eskimo children would be entertained; moreover, they would learn about proper or improper behavior and its importance for their safety and for the well-being of their people.

Texts: *The Eye of the Needle,* by Teri Sloat (Dutton); *Nessa's Fish,* by Nancy Luenn, illustrated by Neil Waldman (Atheneum); *Very Last First Time,* by Jan Andrews, illustrated by Ian Wallace (Atheneum); *A Promise Is a Promise,* by Robert Munsch and Michael Kusugak, illustrated by Vladyana Krykorka (Annick Press).

Objectives:
1. To examine the dangers of the traditional practice of searching for food on the spring ice.
2. To see how the characters reveal their personalities while searching for food.
3. To examine how the pictures contribute to the telling of the stories.

The Eye of the Needle (Alaskan Eskimo). In this story, Amik is given an adult responsibility for the first time in his life. Students can provide answers to these questions. How well does he fulfill his responsibility? What lessons from the story would traditional listeners have been able to apply to their own lives? Looking at the pictures, they can predict what the next fish he swallows will be. This is a cumulative story like "Henny Penny," in which there is more (in the boy's stomach!) after each event. Students could retell the story in the manner of "Henny Penny" or "The Old Lady Who Swallowed a Fly." They can notice the different words used for swallowing and suggest others. Have the students link the appropriate "glump" (which changes in sound, length, and size as he swallows bigger fish) to the fish swallowed.

Nessa's Fish (Alaskan Eskimo). Students can discuss Nessa's actions in relation to each of the animals. Is there any reason for the order in which she encounters the animals? Notice that they are more difficult to drive away. Discuss the qualities of character she reveals and how her fishing trip is different from Amik's? Compare the characters of Nessa and Amik. Students can retell the story for their own area, replacing the animals with three that are found near the places where they live.

A Promise Is a Promise (Canadian Inuit). After reading the story, students can discuss Allashua's character. What lessons has she learned in the story? How can her actions be used to teach Inuit children important safety lessons? Discuss the conflict that arises after Allashua is captured by the Qallupilluit and after she makes her promise to them. Notice that the conflict arises because she has broken her promise and that in making a new one she creates more problems. How can she save her brothers and sisters and still not break her promise to the Qallupilluit? Students can trace, step by step, the way in which the mother solves the problem. Have the students discuss the mother's secret reasons for acting toward and saying what she does to the Quallupilluit.

Very Last First Time (Canadian Inuit). Note that the traditional method of going beneath the sea ice at low tide to gather mussels is still practiced in some Arctic communities. After reading the story, have the children compare the kitchen at the beginning and the end. How are Eva's emotions different at the end? What is the significance of the change in the dominant color of the illustrations from yellow to purple and back again? Yellow is associated with the familiar world, and purple, the unfamiliar and dangerous one. Have the students discuss why they think that the drawings expand to cover both pages when Eva goes under the ice. Perhaps her range of experience is expanding. They should notice the figures in the pictures that are not mentioned in the words and offer their interpretations of what these may mean in relation to the girl's under-ice adventure. Have students discuss possible meanings for the title and then talk or write about something they did on their own for the "very last first time."

AUTHOR STUDY: ELIZABETH CLEAVER'S COLLAGES

Introduction: Canadian author-illustrator Elizabeth Cleaver has created several illustrated versions of Canadian Native tales by making collages of materials appropriate to the stories and the locations in which the stories were told. She also includes graphic styles appropriate for the different cultures. Although the texts of the stories are simple, the illustrations of these three well-known Native legends give added emotional depth to the conflicts.

Texts: *How Summer Came to Canada*, by William Toye, illustrated by Elizabeth Cleaver (Oxford); *The Mountain Goats of Temlaham*, by William Toye, illustrated by Elizabeth Cleaver (Oxford); *The Fire Stealer*, by William Toye, illustrated by Elizabeth Cleaver (Oxford).

Objectives:
1. To discuss the relationship between the three main characters and their natural worlds in legends from Atlantic, central, and Pacific Canada.
2. To notice how Cleaver uses color, design, and collage (pasting objects onto the surface of the picture) to communicate theme, conflict, and mood.
3. To use Cleaver's techniques of illustration to provide an illustrated version of a traditional Native story from the geographical area of the reader.

How Summer Came to Canada (Micmac). Have the students notice the changing colors on the title page and later discuss how these relate to the theme of seasonal change. Why does Glooskap have green leaves in his hair? Why do the winter scenes include green coloring? What might this foreshadow? What do the colors depicting the dream and the travel on the back of the whale foreshadow? How do the colors and flowers on the trip north foreshadow the coming of summer? The children can discuss the characters of Giant Winter, Glooskap, and the Queen of Summer.

The Mountain Goats of Temlaham (Tshimshan). Students can notice how the colors are natural at the beginning, after the boy releases the goat, and at the end. These reflect the happy emotions and the harmony between animals and people. What do the darker colors in the lodge indicate? Students should notice that there are relatively gentle flowing lines at the beginning and the end of the book and more jagged, sharper lines when the people mistreat the goats and the goats take their revenge. What do the changes in line patterns reveal about the mood of the story? How do Raven Feather's actions contrast with those of the other people, and how do they influence his life? The children can discuss the themes of respect for and kindness to animals as these relate to the hunt and the fate of the people.

The Fire Stealer (Ojibway). Students can begin by noticing the dominant color of the cover and endpapers and discuss its appropriateness. What do the browns of the materials used in the collages suggest about the weather and how the people feel? What is the difference in the pictures of the landscape after Nanabozho seizes the fire. Why is so much birch bark used to create the collages? It is found in the Lake Superior region of the story, and the Ojibway use the bark in many ways. The teacher can introduce the term *pourquoi story*, a tale that explains how things originated (why we have fire, bright autumn leaves, etc.). Discuss this story and the preceding two as pourquoi stories explaining natural phenomena for the people who told them. Introduce the term *conflict*. A conflict starts when something is or goes wrong at the beginning of a story and is not fixed or resolved until the end. What are the conflicts in this story and the preceding two? How do the pictures reveal the conflict through their use of color, design, and details?

Nanabozho and the Windego. This original story is based on a number of Ojibway legends. It was created recently for a group of Michigan students who had just studied the above stories. The idea was to link it with the story of Nanabozho in *The Fire Stealer* and then to have students illustrate it in the manner of an Elizabeth Cleaver story. It also includes a series of brief questions designed to have the children participate in the telling of the story. During a first reading, the students doodled on a large piece of paper, using different colored crayons and creating different line patterns to indicate the mood at different points of the story. They were then given a copy of the story in which a series of blank lines followed each question. They then provided their own answers, thus contributing to the depiction of theme, conflict, and character. Finally, they illustrated one of the scenes, some of them creating collages, but all of them using color and line patterns in the manner of Cleaver's illustrations. This story can be used for this unit, or teachers can create a story based on one of the legends from their own culture area.

Nanabozho and the Windego: An Ojibway Story from Lake Superior
Based on an Ojibway legend and adapted by Jon C. Stott

Have you ever noticed how quickly the weather changes near the Gitchie Gummie (Lake Superior)? It can be a beautiful day, and all of a sudden it turns cold and miserable. Or sometimes it can be rainy and windy, and then in a few minutes the sun will be shining. It wasn't always this way. But here's what happened to make the weather change so quickly.

It was a beautiful day in the moon of the Maple Syrup (late April). Nanabozho was walking along the shores of the Gitchie Gummie. All around him he saw signs of spring.

Can you think of some of the things he noticed?

But even while he was enjoying all of these wonderful things, the weather began to change. The wind started to blow from the north off of the Gitchie Gummie, clouds began to build up, and it began to rain. From far out on the lake came a strange noise like someone howling and moaning at the same time.

Suddenly, Nanabozho was alert. His heart started to beat quickly, and he felt afraid. Wind, clouds, rain—and now this eerie sound. It could only mean one thing. The windego was coming. Everyone was terrified of the evil windego, even Nanabozho. He could freeze you to death, or he could turn your heart to ice so that you could never feel love for anyone.

Nanabozho turned and started to run, southward, away from the Gitchie Gummie into the woods. He was going so fast and he was so frightened that he kept slipping on the brown leaves that lay on the forest floor and tripping over the branches that had broken during the winter. And as he ran, he could feel the wind blowing harder. The cold started to bite his skin, and the rain started to turn into sleet. Behind him, the moaning sounds of the windego were getting louder. The monster was coming nearer and nearer.

What do you think Nanabozho was thinking as he ran away?

While he sped along, Nanabozho began to notice the creatures in the forest: the robins, squirrels, deer, and ducks. They had just started to get ready for spring and summer. Some of the birds had flown back from the south and some of the animals had ended their long winter sleeps. Soon their babies would be born. What would happen to them if the windego settled down in the area and brought winter back into the land? The animals seemed surprised to see Nanabozho running along so quickly. Why was their hero running away from the windego? They called out to him.

What did the creatures of the forest say to Nanabozho?

Nanabozho realized that he couldn't keep running away. His friends needed him; he had to help them so that the summer would come and their children could grow. He had to defeat the windego. But how? The monster was very strong, much stronger than Nanabozho. Nanabozho kept on running, but he slowed down and started to think of a plan.

The sleet had turned to snow. It was a blizzard. Nanabozho stumbled as his feet hit a patch of slippery leaves. He fell forward onto the ground and lay still. He did not move, and the thick snowflakes quickly covered his body.

Has Nanabozho been knocked unconscious? Will the windego catch him and freeze him to death or freeze his heart so that he will never think of his friends again? What do you think will happen?

The windego had created the blizzard, and it was so fierce that even he could hardly see the trees in front of him as he chased through the forest after Nanabozho. As he passed a snow covered mound, his body lurched forward, and he fell so heavily to the ground that his breath was knocked out of him. His loud moans turned into gasps as he tried to get his breath back. Suddenly, he felt a strong hand close around his ankle, and then, moments later, two knees pressed on his shoulder blades as someone kneeled on his back.

What has happened to the windego? Has he just slipped on some leaves or tripped on a tree trunk hidden under the snow?

"I have you now, you windego," said Nanabozho. "I knew that you would catch me if I kept running, and I knew that I had to help my friends. I will make a bargain with you. You may come to live in this land with me every year after all the birds have flown south and the leaves have fallen off the trees. But when it is time for the birds to come back, the young animals to be born, and the flowers to grow, you must leave and go north across the Gitchie Gummie."

The windego nodded his head in agreement; but there was something about the look on his face that made Nanabozho suspicious. "If you try to come back in the spring or summer, I will have to fight you and drive you back across the lake."

The windego left, moaning his long, sad howl as he crossed the shining waters of the Gitchie Gummie. The sun shone; the birds and animals thanked Nanabozho. Spring had begun.

Ever since that time, the windego has come to live in Nanabozho's land during the winter. And, just as Nanabozho thought, the windego tries to sneak back during the summer. And every time he comes across the water, the weather suddenly changes, becoming cold and rainy and windy. Nanabozho must fight him and drive him back to the north. Sometimes it is a short fight, and the warmth and sunshine quickly return. Sometimes it is a long fight, and the summer days and nights are cold and rainy and windy. But always Nanabozho is on guard, helping his animal friends, making it possible for them to build their homes, have their babies, and train their young to grow up.

AS THE CROW FLIES: POURQUOI LEGENDS FROM ACROSS THE CONTINENT

Introduction: Many Native pourquoi legends explain how animals, birds, and other living beings received their distinctive features. Set in a time before the world assumed its present characteristics, when animals and people could talk together, these stories frequently reflect the moral values of the people telling them. Often a superior individual, a culture hero or supreme being, gives the various characters their recognizable markings or habits as reward or punishment for their deeds. Seeing the animals, birds, or plants and noticing their unique traits, people will remember the stories and the moral lessons associated with them. Members of the crow family, including the raven, are found across most of North America. Studying legends about how these birds acquired their black color, students will be able to see how each culture group provides a different explanation and reveals different moral and cultural values.

Texts: *Rainbow Crow*, by Nancy Van Laan, illustrated by Beatriz Vidal (Knopf); "Why Crows Are Black," in *Medicine Boy and Other Cree Tales*, by Eleanor Brass, illustrated by Henry Nanooch (Glenbow Museum); *Crow Chief*, by Paul Goble (Orchard Books); *How Raven Brought Light to People*, by Ann Dixon, illustrated by James Watts (Margaret K. McElderry Books); *Raven*, by Gerald McDermott (Harcourt Brace Jovanovich); *Raven's Light*, by Susan Hand Shetterly, illustrated by Robert Shetterly (Atheneum).

Objectives:
1. To examine different cultural interpretations of a common natural phenomenon: the blackness of the crow.
2. To discuss story conflict and its relation to character. The actions of the crow and its final fate are a result of its attitudes and motivation.
3. To create adjectives (crow words) to describe character.
4. To compare different illustrated versions of the same story, noticing how differing visual approaches and changes in actions and other details alter the meaning of the story. The focus here will be on the northwest coast story of Raven stealing the light.

Rainbow Crow (Lenape). Before reading this story to the children, have them briefly look at the front and back endpapers, noticing the changes to the crow. Have the students predict what the story will be about. After a first reading, review the predictions. Introduce/reintroduce the term *conflict* and have the children discuss the conflict in this story. Students can respond to the following questions. How is it resolved? Why is the crow a more suitable messenger to the Great Spirit than the other birds or animals? Compare him with them and discuss the traits he reveals on his trip to the sun. In what way does he gain more than he loses? Why doesn't the Great Spirit stop winter? Notice that he will not alter the course of nature, but he will help the animal people adapt to it. Reintroduce the term *pourquoi story*. What does this story explain the origins of, and, when they saw these things, what moral values would the Lenape people of eastern Pennsylvania remember? Have the students keep a list of adjectives under the term "Crow Words." An adjective is a word that can fit in the blank between these words: "a ——— bird." Students should explain why they chose these adjectives. After each new crow story, they should add two or three more words to their list.

"Why Crows Are Black" (Plains Cree). What qualities of character does Crow reveal in this story? What are the consequences of his weaknesses? Is his punishment too much or too little? Students might wish to discuss the character of Wesuketchuk considering whether his anger at Crow was excessive or not. What would traditional Cree children have learned when they listened to the tale? Compare the bird in the story to Rainbow Crow and add to the list of crow words.

Crow Chief (Lakota). Students should notice the details of the cover and two title pages. Who are the major characters in these illustrations, and what is unusual about Crow? On the basis of the cover and title pages, readers can predict the conflict and its resolution. Discuss with students the significance of the word "chief," noticing that for the plains peoples, a chief had to prove himself worthy of his role, acting always for the good of his group in relation to the natural and supernatural worlds. After reading the story, the children can discuss how suitable Crow is for his role. Outline the steps Falling Star uses to outwit the crow and resolve the conflict facing his people. Notice that Goble's tipi decorations are culturally accurate and appropriate to this story, with the buffalo pictures indicating the importance of these animals to the human beings. Have the students create a decoration for a tipi that would be appropriate for "Why Crows are Black." Discuss with them the moral of the story: the need for balance and harmony between human beings and animals.

How Raven Brought Light to People (Tlingit). Students can compare the amount of light in the title page illustration with that in the final illustration. As they look at individual illustrations, they should notice the movement of light from inside the house to outside. What is the nature of the problem and the role of the problem solver? What steps does he take to solve it? Introduce the term *irony*, which occurs in a story when something takes place that is not what the characters expect. Students can look for the ironies in this story and how Raven causes them. Look at the three doublespreads of the landscape each time Raven has released a light from the boxes. Notice the differences in the pictures and discuss how they are important. Have the students write brief dialogues for the people seen in each of these pictures as they respond to the new lights. Don't forget the "Crow Words." After reading this story, carefully read McDermott's *Raven* and Shetterly's *Raven's Light*, and have the students make a list of all the differences in plot between these stories and *How Raven Brought Light to People*. How do these differences influence the meanings of the stories? Which illustrator is most effective in communicating and expanding on the meanings of the words?

After reading and discussing these crow stories, students can compare the similarities and differences between all of them, discussing the reasons for the blackness of crows, the characters of the birds, and the justice of the final outcome. In addition, they can either write their own pourquoi legends about how Raven or Crow became black, or they can write a pourquoi legend about the physical appearance or habits of a distinctive bird from their own area. These can then be illustrated and read to younger children.

BRAVE HUNTERS: INUIT LEGENDS RETOLD BY JAMES HOUSTON

Introduction: For over 15 years in the 1950s and 1960s, Canadian James Houston lived with the Inuit (Canadian Eskimos), acting as territorial administrator, introducing them to the art of print making, and learning about their traditional beliefs, customs, and stories. In retelling several of their stories for children, he emphasized the danger and beauty of the Arctic landscape and its inhabitants and the courage of the people who risked death in a never-ending quest for food. These three short books emphasize the bravery of children who must leave their homes to find food for their starving families.

Texts: *Wolf Run*, by James Houston (Harcourt, Brace); *Long Claws*, by James Houston (Atheneum); *Tikta'Liktak*, by James Houston (Harcourt, Brace).

Objectives:
1. To see how an author often presents similar themes, character types, and conflicts in many of his stories.
2. To examine in detail the differences in two very similar stories.
3. To study the precariousness of traditional Inuit life, the danger of poor hunting, bad weather, and dangerous animals, all of which could cause starvation or death.
4. To notice how the young heroes in each of the books resolve the conflicts that face them.

Long Claws (Canadian Inuit). Have students use the cover illustration to predict the basic conflict. Who/what are the major characters? Notice how the animals are important during the story. Before reading, discuss with students the basic necessities of food, shelter, and clothing, and have students realize that the Inuit filled these needs by hunting. Then discuss the dangers of hunting in an Arctic winter: failure to find game, blizzards, attacking animals, cold, hunger, and fear. How do these dangers provide interesting and exciting conflicts for stories? After reading a few pages aloud, discuss with the class the major conflict in this story—the danger of starvation. What makes the solution difficult? The father is dead, there are no sled dogs, and only the two children can look for food. Discuss with students the significance of the owl's appearances in the story. Notice the role that each child plays in getting to the food cache. What dilemmas do they face on the way home? Should they keep the caribou or let the grizzly have it? Should they kill the bear or not? Should the girl leave her brother and run home or stay and try to help him? After reading the story, the class can make a large, panoramic picture map of the travels of the brother and sister and discuss the qualities of character they reveal at each point on the map where a major event occurs.

Wolf Run (Canadian Inuit). After reading the first 10 or 15 pages of the story, students can compare the opening with the opening of *Long Claws*. What similarities and differences in setting, conflict, and character are there? Introduce the idea that there are *Families of Stories*, that is, groups of stories that are very similar to each other. These two stories, along with *Tikta'Liktak*, could be considered members of a story family. Introduce the idea of weaving a story. Just as weavers make patterns by introducing different colors of thread/yarn that they bring to the surface or keep hidden and that they combine with other colors, so, too, storytellers introduce themes that sometimes come to the surface and appear in relation to other themes. In *Wolf Run*, three themes are introduced: the idea of magic or spirit power, the importance of the grandmother, and the presence of wolves. Have the students notice these each time they appear. How are these themes important in developing the conflict of the story and in portraying the growth of Punik's character? Point out to students that the three themes are not woven together until nearly the end of the story, at which time the conflicts are resolved and Punik has revealed his courage, learned the importance of spiritual belief, and found food for his family.

Tikta'Liktak (Canadian Inuit). In addition to the theme of starvation, this story introduces the theme of coming-of-age, as the hero "wished most of all to be a good hunter" (11) like his father. If students have read *A Promise Is a Promise* (Kusugak and Munsch), they will understand the dangers of spring ice. Discuss with the class what Tikta'Liktak must do at each stage of his journey to survive both physically and psychologically. Have the students draw a large picture map on which they illustrate key events and indicate whether Tikta' Liktak feels more or less hopeful or depressed. They can draw a small thermometer next to each event and color in the mercury—higher for more hopeful, lower for more depressed. They can then discuss why and how he feels the way they have indicated. How is this story similar to the first two? In what ways is it significantly different?

TRACKING THE TRICKSTER

Introduction: As noted in Chapter 3, trickster stories are told by virtually every Native American culture group. Although sometimes a helper, the trickster is usually a selfish individual who seeks to fulfill his need for glory and food, but who often outwits himself. In many ways, the trickster is an irony-maker, using deceit to get what he wants from his unsuspecting victims. However, the results are not always what he expects, and, then, the ironic results are on himself. Often, he is a creative problem solver, using language cleverly and playing a variety of roles designed to fool others. Although trickster stories have many common characteristics, they also vary from culture group to culture group and even between nations or bands within a culture group. Even individual storytellers make their own subtle changes, sometimes from telling to telling.

Texts: *Muwin and the Magic Hare*, by Susan Hand Shetterly, illustrated by Robert Shetterly (Atheneum); *Great Rabbit and the Long-Tailed Wildcat*, retold by Andy Gregg, illustrated by Cat Bowman Smith (Albert Whitman); "Nanabush and the Ducks" in *Adventures of Nanabush*, by Emerson Coatsworth (Doubleday Canada); *Iktomi and the Ducks*, by Paul Goble (Orchard Books); "How Saynday Ran a Foot Race with Coyote" in *Saynday's People*, by Alice Marriott (University of Nebraska Press).

Objectives:
1. To introduce students to trickster figures from several cultures so that they can see both the general characteristics and cultural differences of the character type.
2. To make a comparison of very similar stories to see how alterations in plot, character, and setting change the meanings. This discussion will reinforce the idea of "Families of Stories."
3. To discuss the ironies in the trickster stories and how ironic situations are created.
4. To discuss the creative problem-solving techniques the trickster uses and how and why these techniques are or are not successful.
5. To discuss the trickster's motivations for his actions and for his character as revealed by his reactions to the outcomes of the events. What moral or social values do these express for the culture telling the story?

Muwin and the Magic Hare (Micmac). After a first reading, students can consider who is the intended victim and who is the real victim. What causes the roles to become reversed by the end of the story? What qualities does the trickster possess that make him successful? Students can list in order the three characters Muwin meets. Why do they play these specific tricks on him? What traditional lessons do the tricks illustrate? Discuss the story's ironies. Students should look carefully at the illustrations for details that Muwin does not notice. They can make up appropriate dialogue tags for Muwin. These should not just be "he said, asked, etc." They should indicate his emotions at the time: e.g., he growled, whined, etc.

Great Rabbit and the Long-Tailed Wildcat (Micmac). Begin reading the story and have the students interrupt when they recognize what story (*Muwin*) it reminds them of. Finish reading the story and introduce (or reintroduce) the idea of *The Family of Stories*, that is, stories that are similar in many ways. Have the students list and then discuss the significance of the similarities and differences between the two stories. Review the story, considering the success of the trick. Is it a morally good or bad trick? Why does the victim deserve to have the trick played on him? Have the students compare the illustrations of the people the wildcat meets with those depicting the people Muwin meets. How do these reveal similarities between the two characters who are tricked?

"Nanabush and the Ducks" (Ojibway). This story, along with the next two, belong to a family known as the "Hoodwinked Dancers Tale." What characteristics does Nanabush reveal early in the story? How does he go about getting a great feast without a lot of work? How is he able to get so many ducks into his lodge? Students should notice that he poses as a friend, lies, and appeals to their weakness—love of dancing. Does he need to kill so many ducks? In doing so, he is violating the Ojibway law that you must kill only what you need. He also violates the law that you should thank the spirits of the animals who have given their lives to feed you. He has worked hard building the lodge, trapping the ducks, and building the fire so that he can have a great feast. Are the results what he expected? Discuss the ironies, first for the ducks and then for Nanabush. What natural phenomena does this pourquoi story explain?

Iktomi and the Ducks (Lakota). After briefly outlining the events of the previous story, have the students look at the cover and title of this story and predict what they think will be similar and what different from "Nanabush and the Ducks." In reading the story, invite students to respond to the questions in the book printed in gray type. How similar is the means Iktomi uses to deceive the ducks to Nanabush's trick? Have the class look for the appearance of the fox in the pictures. Notice that Iktomi doesn't see it. What might the fox be thinking? What does Iktomi's reaction to the trees reveal about his character? Explain to the students that this is what the Lakota call an "ohunkaka" story: not true, but designed to teach lessons. What lessons would Lakota children have learned? Have the students make a list of the things Iktomi says to the ducks. Then have them write next to each item what they think Iktomi is really thinking as he talks to his victims.

"How Saynday Ran a Foot Race with Coyote" (Kiowa). Read the story right through and then have the students discuss the major difference between this story and the last two stories: the use of prairie dogs instead of ducks. What does this reveal about the physical conditions of Kiowa life?

Does this major change make the story that much different from the ones about Iktomi and Nanabush? Does the fact that the prairie dogs are vain make them partly responsible for their deaths? Discuss the major irony of the story, the fact that the trickster is out-tricked. How is Coyote able to make his trick work against so sly a person? Notice that he appeals to Saynday's greed and pride. The man thinks he can easily win and won't have to share. The final irony is that he expects to be able to keep all the soup and ends up with none.

WHERE THE BUFFALO ROAMED: PLAINS INDIAN MYTHOLOGY

Introduction: Until the later part of the nineteenth century, the Native peoples of the northern plains depended upon the buffalo to provide nearly all of their basic needs. In addition to being a source of food, shelter, clothing, and fuel, the buffalo gave the people many of their sacred rituals. The animal was, to use a Lakota word, *wakan*, or sacred. Men hunted the animals, impounding them, driving them over cliffs, stalking them, or killing them from horseback. Women prepared the slain beasts: preserving meat; preparing hides for clothing, tipi covers, and containers; and making instruments and utensils from the bones. Both before and after the hunt, sacred rituals were performed to ensure a good hunt and to thank the souls of the buffalo for offering themselves up to the people. The skull was sacred and was often ceremonially placed out on the prairie so that the soul of the buffalo could return to the earth to be reborn. The destruction of millions of buffalo in the last half of the nineteenth century not only destroyed physical materials the people needed to live, but also facilitated the collapse of cultural and spiritual organizations that had lasted for centuries.

Texts: *Where the Buffaloes Begin*, by Olaf Baker, illustrated by Stephen Gammell (Frederick Warne); "Why the Buffalo Has a Hump" in *Adventures of Nanabush*, by Emerson Coatsworth (Doubleday Canada); *The Great Race*, by Paul Goble (Bradbury Press); *The Secret of the White Buffalo*, C.J. Taylor (Tundra); *Buffalo Dance*, by Nancy Van Laan, illustrated by Beatriz Vidal (Little, Brown); *Buffalo Woman*, by Paul Goble (Bradbury Press); *Crow Chief*, by Paul Goble (Orchard Books); *Iktomi and the Buffalo Skull*, by Paul Goble (Orchard Books); *There Still Are Buffalo*, by Ann Nolan Clark, illustrated by Stephen Tongier (Ancient City Press).

Objectives:
1. To help students gain an understanding of the physical, cultural, and spiritual significance of the buffalo to the people of the northern plains.
2. To trace in detail the introduction, development, and resolution of conflict in a story. Stories begin with "but" and end when there are "no buts about it." Stories "kick but."

3. To study a number of stories by Paul Goble, noticing general characteristics of his style and themes.
4. To examine the role of illustrations in each story, noticing particularly
   how the spiritual qualities in the stories are communicated in the
   pictures.
5. To extend the study of these stories in relation to language arts, art, and
   social studies.

Preliminary Activities: Write the word "Superstore" on the board or a
large piece of paper and leave it where students can see it for a day or two
before beginning the unit. Start the unit by asking the students to describe a
superstore, then show them the picture of a buffalo and explain that 150 years
ago this was the superstore of the Native peoples of the northern plains.
Discuss the various parts of the buffalo and what they were used for and have
the students keep a record of these. Describe the methods of hunting and the
destruction of the herds in the later nineteenth century. *Buffalo Hunt*, by
Russell Freedman (Holiday House) is a very good resource with excellent
nineteenth-century paintings. Conclude the lesson by writing on the board,
but not explaining, the word *wakan*. Begin the next day by explaining that
wakan is a Sioux word meaning sacred or holy and that the buffalo was sacred.
Explain that the stories to be studied make up a mythic, *wakan*, history of the
buffalo.

Where the Buffaloes Begin (Blackfoot). This story explains the mystical,
sacred birth of the buffalo. Discuss the character of Little Wolf before he
makes his trip. What potentially heroic qualities does he exhibit? How is he
different at the end of his quest? Discuss the events that result in his assuming
heroic status. Why is he a legendary hero? Have the students study the
picture of the buffalo arising from the lake, and, then, after brainstorming in
groups, have each person write a paragraph describing the sight as the boy
might have experienced it, including what he saw, heard, and smelled, and
how he felt emotionally. The only requirement is that they should remember
that he would have considered the episode a sacred experience. Give each
student an inexpensive accordian shaped manilla folder. Show the students
pictures of parfleches, the buffalo-skin containers in which the people carried
their personal belongings. Have them decorate their folders in the manner of
parfleche designs. Explain that these folders will be their portfolio/parfleches
in which to keep the writing and art work they do during this unit.

"Why the Buffalo Has a Hump" (Ojibway) and *The Great Race* (Cheyenne). These pourquoi myths explain how the buffalo got its hump and
goatee and why people eat buffalo and not the reverse. After reading both
stories, students can discuss the roles of Nanabush and Magpie in helping
others. Notice that the buffalo had not respected the other beings in creation.

What lessons about balance and harmony would traditional children remember when they saw the buffalo's hump and goatee and the magpie's sheen? Have the students notice that in *The Great Race* there are radiant lines around the creator and the sun. These are visual representations of spiritual power or supernatural presence. They could be called *wakan* lines.

The Secret of the White Buffalo (Lakota). This account of the acquisition of sacred ceremonies emphasizes the importance of the buffalo as spiritual, as well as physical, giver. Discuss with students the problems among the people at the beginning of the story and how these influence the success or lack of success in their hunting. Why is one young man and not the other given the job of taking the buffalo woman's message to the people? How do the people then prove themselves worthy of receiving the secret of the Sacred Pipe ceremony? Discuss the symbol of the pipe and how it represents the unity of the six directions: sky father (eagle feathers), earth mother (red clay and buffalo carving), south, west, north, and east (the different colored ribbons). Discuss the importance of the tipi as a sacred, as well as a domestic, center. Explain that the tipi was built as a circle facing east, the direction of new life.

Buffalo Dance (Blackfoot). Have the students listen for the beginning of the conflict—the unsuccessful hunting. How is the conflict finally resolved? Notice that the buffalo give the worthy people the ceremony that will ensure good hunting. What is the dance designed to illustrate? It shows the respect the people have for the buffalo; they show their repect for the buffalo by imitating them. Students can notice that there are smaller conflicts along the way. Each of these must be successfully resolved before the resolution of the major conflict. Study the illustrations, noticing that the robe with the sacred circle becomes more obvious. The circle of unity is seen in many illustrations. Have students look for these illustrations and discuss their significance. Magpie's sacred role can be compared with his role in *The Great Race*. On the bottom of each page are a series of pictographs. Using these as guides, students can retell the story orally.

Buffalo Woman (Lakota). Before the story is read have students suggest what the relationship between the people and the buffalo on the cover and title page suggest about the possible theme of the story? Study details of the wordless doublespread at the beginning. What do these symbolize about the character of the hunter? Notice that he is observing the sacred rituals: thanking the soul of the buffalo and offering the skull back to nature. After reading the story, students can consider the reason for the marriage at the beginning. Because the man was physically and spiritually a good hunter, his marriage to the buffalo woman symbolized an ideal unity between hunter and hunted. What causes the conflict, and how do the man's actions restore harmony and resolve the conflict? What quality of character does he exhibit through the journey? Introduce the Lakota term *mitakuye oyasin*, "we are all related," and have the students discuss its applicability to this story. Look at the locations of the people in relation to the tipis and discuss how this reflects the extent of their relationship with animals. Which of the tipis are treated as both sacred centers and domestic centers?

Crow Chief (Lakota). Refer to the activities in the unit on "As the Crow Flies." In addition, discuss the imbalance between the buffalo and the people, caused by the crow. When the balance is restored by Falling Star, what are the duties and obligations of the human beings? Have students notice the *wakan* lines around Falling Star, indicating his sacred power. Have the students study the illustrations in relation to those in the other Goble books considered in this unit. Have them write a paragraph describing what there is about the illustrations that make these recognizable as being by Goble.

Iktomi and the Buffalo Skull (Lakota). Review the idea of the sacredness of the buffalo skull and then have students look at the cover and discuss Iktomi's possible character. After reading the story, discuss the lessons traditional Lakota children would have learned from the story. Compare Iktomi's chief's garb with that of Falling Star in *Crow Chief*. How do the differences reflect the differences in their leadership qualities? Have the students write a report on Iktomi, explaining why he should not be considered a candidate for the position of chief in his tribe. The students can compare Goble's style in this book with the style of the sacred stories he has retold.

There Still Are Buffalo (Lakota). This story is a tribute to the survival of the buffalo and the traditions of the Lakota people. After reading the story, students can discuss what this biography tells us about these people, as well as about buffalo. Have them notice the *mitakuye oyasin* theme implicit in the story.

Follow-up Activity: Have each student write a brief paragraph explaining which is his or her favorite buffalo story and why. The class can discuss the lessons that modern people can gain from these traditional stories. Finally, they can create a large, wall-sized line extending from earliest times to the present, with most of the space given to the eighteenth and nineteenth centuries. They can indicate physical facts on the top of the timeline (the changing of hunting methods with the arrival of horses, etc.) and spiritual or mythical facts on the bottom (the mysterious birth of buffalo, the great race, the arrival of the white buffalo woman, etc.). The timeline can be illustrated with pictures based on those in the books studied.

DEVELOPING A NOVEL STUDY UNIT: *JULIE OF THE WOLVES*

Introduction: A detailed analysis of *Julie of the Wolves*, by Jean Craighead George, is found in Chapter 4. In developing a novel study unit, the following preliminary activities are suggested. Read three or four short stories, picture books, or folktales that introduce some of the same types of themes, conflicts, and character types found in the novel. Discussion of these shorter works helps familiarize students with the kinds of reading they will be doing when they get to the novel. Because students at all elementary and junior high levels like to be read aloud to, the novel in its entirety should be read to the students before class sets are given out. This reading will give all students a familiarity with the plot of the entire book. Some teachers find it useful to have students make brief summaries at the end of each chapter, listing setting, time, and characters present, and giving a three- or four-sentence summary of the main events. The completed summaries give students quick access to all of the novel, helping them both to recall and, if necessary, to locate important events. *Julie of the Wolves* is not divided into chapters. However, within each of the novel's three large sections are several smaller units each divided from the other by blank spaces on the page.

Text: *Julie of the Wolves*, by Jean Craighead George (Harper and Row).

Objectives:
1. To discuss the ways in which Julie/Miyax is able to survive physically and psychologically in the wilderness and thus to be reunited with human beings.
2. To discuss how Julie learns to understand the natural environment in which she lives by remembering the lessons her father taught her.
3. To discuss how Julie comes to understand the value of the old Alaskan Eskimo ways of responding spiritually, as well as physically, to the environment.
4. To discuss Julie's attitudes toward her father, noticing how these are ironically destroyed when she meets him at the story's conclusion.
5. To examine the symbolic meaning of the wolves, seeing how they represent beings living in an harmonious relationship with nature, the old Alaskan Eskimo ways, and, until the end of the novel, Julie's father.
6. To trace thematic patterns that run through the novel: songs, references to airplanes, Julie's name changes, her memories of her father.
7. To relate the story, generally, to the situation of contemporary Native children living between two worlds and, specifically, to Alaskan Eskimo children.

Preliminary Reading: *The Green Man*, by Gail Haley (Scribner's), deals with how a young man's attitude to old traditions changes during the year he spends in the wilderness. *The Bear Who Wanted to Be a Bear*, by Jörg Steiner and Jörg Muller (Atheneum), is about the conflict between a life lived according to the rhythms of nature and one imprisoned in the clockwork rigidity of the modern industrial world. James Houston's *Tikta'Liktak* (Harcourt,

Brace) is a short Arctic survival story. After reading these stories, explain to students that several of the themes, conflicts, and character types will reappear in *Julie of the Wolves*. Ask them to look for these as they progress through a first reading (the read-aloud sessions).

Presentation Activities: Have the students carefully reread pages 5-25 ("Chapter 1"). They should list all the obvious and potential conflicts they notice and should make a list of any references to Julie's father, her name, airplanes, or songs. After a general discussion of these elements, students can be told they will be divided into four groups. Each group can be responsible for discussing the progress toward resolution of the conflicts or the introduction of new conflicts, as well as references to father, planes, names, and songs, in a specific number of pages in Part I (pages 25-37, 37-49, 49-61, 61-70). Each group can give a 15-minute presentation on the conflicts in its pages and can provide other students with four lists of the references.

The entire class can discuss Part II. Focus here can be on how the conflicts developed that led to Julie becoming lost on the tundra at the beginning of the novel. Students should notice the conflicts between traditional and modern ways and Julie's changing attitudes to these. Students should also notice the various settings in this section: seal camp, Barrow, Mekoryuk, and San Francisco (seen only in Julie's imagination and in Amy's letters). They can discuss what each of these places represents to Julie and should compare each with the tundra as it is described in Part I. They can explain why they think this account of Julie's earlier life is placed in the middle rather than at the beginning of the novel. Students should update their four lists.

The four groups can discuss and then report to the entire class about the conflicts and Julie's changing attitudes to the tundra and San Francisco in Part III, pages 108-122, 122-138, 138-147, 147-161. Each group can also update the lists for their pages and provide these to the other students. The entire group can study the final "chapter," pages 161-70. They should notice how the conflicts are resolved and how the resolutions are sadly ironic. What comment is Jean George making about the old ways and the natural environment? Julie has survived, but will the traditions and the tundra survive as well? How does Kangik relate to the other settings in the novel?

As follow-up activities, students should consider the significance of the references to names, her father, songs, and airplanes in the novel. How does Jean George use these to embody her themes and conflicts? They can discuss how the wolves are used by the author to symbolize the old ways, a linked world of human beings and animals, and Julie's father before he succumbed to the modern world. In writing activities, they can pretend they are Julie writing a letter to Amy the day after she has returned to her father's house. They can hypothesize how the heroine will relate to her father and compare their hypotheses to events in *Julie*, a sequel to *Julie of the Wolves* that Jean

George published in 1994 (HarperCollins). Finally, students can compare the plot and themes of this survival novel with Gary Paulsen's *Hatchet* (Bradbury Press), Armstrong Sperry's *Call It Courage* (Macmillan), and Scott O'Dell's *Island of the Blue Dolphins* (Houghton Mifflin). They can also compare the book with other novels by George, including *My Side of the Mountain* (Dutton), *The Talking Earth* (Harper and Row), and *Water Sky* (Harper and Row).

OTHER UNITS FOCUSING ON NATIVE TRADITIONS AND LEGENDS

This appendix has mentioned only a few of the possible ways that units of stories about Native peoples, their traditions, and their legends can be developed and used in elementary or junior high school classrooms. Other thematic units might be developed around such themes as the acquisition of fire, the coming of horses, the creation of the seasonal cycles, or the gift of corn. Author study units can be built on the works of Joseph Bruchac, Michael Kusugak, C.J. Taylor, and others. The works of a specific culture group could be examined using picture books, collections of adapted folktales, and novels. The possibilities are almost limitless. In the reading lists concluding Chapters 2, 3, and 4, there are many cross-references to other similar stories and many suggestions for presentation activities.

Whatever books teachers use, it is important that these be carefully examined to ensure that they are both accurate to and respectful of the cultures they depict. Finally, it is important that the stories also be related to non-Native stories dealing with similar themes and character types. Native literature should not be "ghettoized." Nor should it be limited to being presented extensively in only one or two years in the elementary and junior high school curriculums. Only by being introduced to new books from a variety of Native cultures over several years can students become more understanding of and respectful towards the first North American settlers, people who have a proud and grand history and heritage but who themselves are not historical artifacts or museum specimens. In celebrating their past in literature, it is also crucial to celebrate their present as it is reflected in many excellent books. Only then can teachers and librarians assist young readers of all cultures in creating a future in which all members of these cultures are honored.

AUTHOR, ILLUSTRATOR, TITLE INDEX

SUBJECT INDEX